DATE DUE

los republicanos

los republicanos

Why Hispanics and Republicans Need Each Other

Leslie Sanchez

LOS REPUBLICANOS
Copyright © Leslie Sanchez, 2007.

First published in 2007 by
PALGRAVE MACMILLAN™
175 Fifth Avenue, New York, N.Y. 10010 and
Houndmills, Basingstoke, Hampshire, England RG21 6XS
Companies and representatives throughout the world.

PALGRAVE MACMILLAN is the global academic imprint of the Palgrave Macmillan division of St. Martin's Press, LLC and of Palgrave Macmillan Ltd. Macmillan® is a registered trademark in the United States, United Kingdom and other countries. Palgrave is a registered trademark in the European Union and other countries.

ISBN-13: 978–1–4039–7802–8
ISBN-10: 1–4039–7802–6

Library of Congress Cataloging-in-Publication Data

Sanchez, Leslie.
    Los republicanos : why Hispanics and Republicans need each other / by Leslie Sanchez.
        p. cm.
    Includes bibliographical references and index.
    ISBN 1–4039–7802–6 (alk. paper)
    1. Republican Party (U.S. : 1854–) 2. Hispanic Americans—Politics and government. I. Title.

JK2356.S28 2007
324.2734089'68—dc22   2007003056

A catalogue record for this book is available from the British Library.

Design by Newgen Imaging Systems (P) Ltd., Chennai, India.

First edition: August 2007

10 9 8 7 6 5 4 3 2 1

Printed in the United States of America.

For mom
with love

Like most Americans, I live for the future. I hope you will let me talk about a country that is forever young.

—Ronald Reagan, excerpt from a speech at the 1992 Republican Convention, Aug. 17, 1992

contents

List of Figures and Tables   xi

Introduction   1

One   Someone Like Me   9

Two   A Changing America   23

Three   The Latino Moment   41

Four   The Emerging Latino Republican Majority   61

Five   Disconnect   85

Six   Our Solutions Work   107

Seven   The Whining City Upon a Hill   143

Eight   The Credit Card   161

Nine   Dis-Inviting the *Familia*   173

Ten   *"Reaganismo"*   199

Postscript   209

Notes   211

Index   225

Acknowledgments   235

list of figures and tables

figures

2.1	Hispanics as a Percentage of the U.S. Population	26
2.2	Projected Hispanic Population Growth	27
2.3	Hispanic Presidential Vote, 1972–2004	32
2.4	Hispanic Vote: Timeline of Key GOP Events (1970–2006); 1972 and 1974	37
3.1	"Hispanic Heart"	48
4.1	Hispanics Describe their Political Views	63
4.2	Hispanic Political Views (Female)	64
4.3	Hispanic Political Views (Male)	64
5.1	Hispanic Party ID	88
5.2	Hispanic Party ID (Female)	88
5.3	Hispanic Party ID (Male)	89
5.4	The Reality Today: How Parties Speak to Our Values	102
5.5	"Hispanic Heart": Creating the Ideal Model	105
6.1	Hispanic Business Owners' Views on Taxes	113
6.2	Educational Attainment by Hispanic Subgroup Aged 25 Years and Older	126
6.3	Education Costs Per Pupil	128
7.1	States Represented by Hispanic Members of Congress	148
7.2	Latino Vote by Income	152

7.3   Percent of Hispanic Dissatisfied with their Treatment Rises   157
7.4   Immigration Timeline   158

8.1   Hispanic Vote Breakdown by State, 2004   169

10.1 Hispanic GOP Elected Officials by Profession   204

tables

5.1   Whites, Minorities Differ in Views of Economic
      Opportunities in U.S.   87
5.2   Which Party is Best For . . . ?   90

8.1   The Republican vs. the Democratic Party   163

9.1   Districts lost by GOP with large Hispanic Population   188
9.2   Close GOP Saves in Districts with large Hispanic
      Population   189

los republicanos

introduction

This is a book about Hispanics in America. Who are we? We're not exactly a "race." We're more than just a "group"; and we are certainly not all the same. We and our families come from more than 20 different nations and cultures, each of which see and approach the world a little differently.

Each of our stories is unique based on where we live, how we grew up, our income, education and, ultimately, our ingrained ideology. Some of us share similar experiences, and many of us share a sense of "familia," but how can a book actually define us when we have different ideas of how we define ourselves?

Ask any number of us what we consider ourselves, and that's how many answers you'll get:

"I'm not Latino, I'm Cuban."
"We're Mexican American, not Latino."
"*Mami, yo soy Boricua.*"
"I'm not a hyphenated American."
"Dominican—Latino and black."
"*Somos Latinos.*"
"*Salvadoreños.*"
"I hate the word Latino."
"I hate the term 'Hispanic.' "
" 'Hispanic' is a made-up word."

Whatever we are, we're that strange new animal that everyone's talking about—testing, surveying, examining, analyzing.

We are now the largest minority group in America, but most Americans know almost nothing about where we came from. Beyond the bit about Christopher Columbus sailing "the ocean blue," American schoolchildren are taught almost nothing about our hemispheric neighbors.[1]

We started at the bottom rung of American society—many of us are just getting here and starting at the bottom now—but we are climbing fast. We are breaking the mold of what others think of us, and of what we think of ourselves. We are not just growing in population, we're also rising in income and creating wealth. We are starting new businesses in the United States at three times the rate of the general population.

When we're asked, we state that we care deeply about family in general and about *our* families in particular. We believe strongly in traditional marriage, and we put our money where our mouth is, marrying and keeping our families together at rates as high as any other group in the United States. We oppose abortion. On average, we attend Church more frequently than the general population, and we identify ourselves as Christians at a higher rate as well.

When Washington's political wonks and strategists hear about a group like us, one word comes to their collective minds: "Republican." Married, religious, up-and-coming economically: They have to be Republicans. But that's never been the case with Latinos. Granted, our vote is not a monolithic endorsement of either party, but we have had an unmistakable Democratic lean ever since the Nixon administration created the "Hispanic" box for the 1970 Census, and exit polls began singling us out to see whom we support in politics.

Some people don't buy the idea that, as Ronald Reagan said, we are Republicans but we just don't know it yet. They think Latinos are just another minority voting bloc, and they know what happens to *all* minority voting groups, because they've seen it happen before. We may be natural conservatives, they say, but we are destined to be a solid voting bloc that Democrats can take for granted.

This book is written on the belief that these people are wrong. We're in uncharted waters with the "Hispanic" or "Latino" vote, and none of the stereotypes or precedents apply.[2] This has never been clearer than it is now in 2007, given the results of the last two elections. We went out in 2004—a controversial, closely contested election year—and gave a Republican candidate 44 percent of our vote. The only Republican to do nearly as well with Hispanic voters was Ronald Reagan, 20 years before, and that was in his landslide reelection over the hopelessly liberal and out-of-touch Walter Mondale.

Then, despite our level of support for George W. Bush in 2004, we turned around in the 2006 election and did the opposite, giving Democratic candidates nearly 70 percent of our votes.

It would be easy for Republicans to say we are a lost cause, and some do. But that would be to look at the small waves atop the ocean, and to miss the powerful underlying current that defines who we are and what motivates us not just today, but in the long run.

Trying to get a clear intellectual grasp of the Latino vote is like trying to sculpt Jell-O; we defy explanation in so many ways. Even the best Hispanic advertising executives, whose profit motive drives them to spend millions of dollars to solve the puzzle of who we are, have had to turn traditional thinking on its head in order to get the real picture. The days of only understanding us in terms of Spanish language and our degree of acculturation are long gone.

Since Latinos are not easy to identify, it is fitting that we are the next genuine swing vote. We still have a center of gravity far to the left of our natural spot on the political spectrum, but our votes can and will move right over time. This book is not about how Republicans can immediately begin winning absolute majorities of the Hispanic vote. It will not make claims that a quick and easy appeal to Hispanics—such as a one-shot immigration policy, or any other gimmick—will turn us all into one party's loyal followers.

Rather, this book stipulates that it is worth Republicans' while to court us in the long term, because we are less interested in identity politics than we are in fresh ideas that will make America a better place. My experience in seeking out Hispanic voters for the Republican National Committee— and our success in the last two presidential elections—confirmed that Latinos will listen, as long as there's someone who wants to talk to us.

One thing is certain: We cannot be ignored. By our size, our growth, and our geography, Hispanics will determine who becomes the next president in 2008. And beyond that year, our influence will only grow. Look at some of the key battlegrounds in presidential politics: Florida, New Mexico, Nevada, Colorado, Arizona. Hispanics are there in large numbers, and a careful study of our voting habits in those states proves that no one owns us.

The big question after the 2006 election is whether the Republicans will write us off. Their crushing election defeat of November 2006 demonstrated that they cannot win solely by relying on the traditional base of whites. Republicans need to attract new blood. I believe they can do so because their ideas work—ideas on economics, education, defense, and culture that will benefit all Americans.

The Republican Party—my party—faces challenges that could determine whether it continues to exist as a viable political entity, or becomes a permanent minority. The party that wants to lead, to assemble a national majority, will have to seek out and embrace America's newest and fastest-growing voter bloc.

Regrettably, some of my Republican colleagues simply discount Latinos. They resent the increasing influence of Hispanic culture, which they see as the product of excessive immigration. To be certain, not all of their concerns in the immigration debate are unfounded. There is a legitimate debate to be had over border security, because there are serious reasons to worry about our porous border in an age of terrorism.

But is it not telling when a politician such as Tom Tancredo (R-Colo.), the famous immigration hawk, refers to Miami as a "Third World" city because of its heavy Hispanic population? That he should do so even though so many of the Spanish speakers there are naturalized refugees from Communism, or even native citizen Puerto Ricans?[3] To Tancredo, Miami is "Third World" because anything "Spanish" is by definition backward. His problem with Miami has nothing to do with national security, sovereignty or the rule of law. Rather *Latino culture itself* is the real problem. The logical implication to some avid supporters—rarely spelled out—is that Hispanics represent a threat because our inherently corrupt Third World culture is a pollutant to an idealized Anglo way of life.

Given the underlying ugliness of this view, it is no wonder that the immigration debate became so heated and then so destructive for Republicans in 2006. Hispanic voters found the debate and its tenor offensive—even the ones who worry about national security and *favor* a border fence, which is more than a few.[4] And white voters, the ones that all this tough rhetoric was supposed to impress, just failed to show up for the Republicans at the polls. The immigrant-bashing card proved to be a loser for the GOP. If the Republicans follow this disastrous path into 2008, they may never win another presidential election.

But a lot of Republicans—most, I believe—get it. They want to attract and welcome Hispanic support. The party faces a difficult challenge, since a very vocal minority seems happy to reject Hispanic voters altogether in favor of the "No Way, Jose!" approach of Pat Buchanan. Meanwhile, many left-wing advocates in the Spanish-language media deliberately attribute undue importance to the voices of the anti-immigrant faction, even though nearly all of its representatives are or have become minor figures on the national political stage.

As great a challenge as Republicans face in working to woo Hispanics, Latinos face an even greater challenge, and one that is really more important in the long run. The Republican Party might lose power, but it is just a political party. The Hispanic population is 42.7 million people, and our entire future is at stake. Do we want to base our vote on our principles, many of which are deeply ingrained in us by our cultural heritage? Or do we want to take on someone else's paradigm, and become a new victim class for the benefit of the American Left?

Today's Democratic Party, bearing its message of dependency, perceived injustice and victimhood, thrives from the near-unanimous support of African Americans. But what has this loyalty done for them? A wide variety of African American public figures from every part of the political spectrum—from Bill Cosby to Juan Williams to J. C. Watts—have identified the cultural, social, educational and economic ills that perennially plague black America—poverty, family breakdown and joblessness, to name a few. For all of this, their liberal elected leaders identify racism as the sole cause of every problem, and government as the sole solution. Unsurprisingly, these problems are never solved. In return for blacks' monolithic support, the Democratic Party offers nothing but the same old bromides and takes them completely for granted.

Latinos must ask themselves if they want a share in the empty promises that have so failed black America. Should we be satisfied with an America in which the only Hispanics elected to Congress come from impoverished, gerrymandered majority-minority districts? Will we be happy to be represented in the political arena only by the shrill purveyors of identity politics, who have almost no crossover appeal whatsoever in mainstream America?

There is an alternative. Although Republicans can be imperfect messengers, they offer solutions that can make life better for Hispanics, African Americans and every other immigrant or native-born American as well, if we give them a chance. It may even force the Democrats to come up with some genuine new ideas of their own, beyond the old "Latino Family Agenda" they dusted off in 2006—a document nearly identical to the one they had presented two years earlier.[5] Republicans will lose out if they write us off, but we will lose out if we write them off. The thesis of this book, therefore, is that Republicans and Latinos need one another in order to create a better America.

I am one of nearly two million Hispanic business owners. My strategic communications and market research firm seeks to forge connections, to deliver a message so that people don't just understand it but *believe* it. We look at lifestyles, gender and age differences and a host of other characteristics and cultural nuances that refine or *define* the wants and needs of our clients. It is just that kind of connection that Republicans and Hispanics need to make with one another.

My firm specializes in the women's and Hispanic markets, as well as for their small and medium-sized business sectors, and so I often get the call when Republican politicians are looking for ways to attract voters in those two groups. I call it "establishing connectivity."

What I discovered in both my work in politics and now at my firm is that my experience selling encyclopedias to pay for college was more than just a sales job. It helped me make real connections with people I didn't know—to understand their hopes and aspirations. What I had learned from talking to people in both garden apartments and million-dollar homes I now apply to my current role advising corporate and political titans.

The lesson is simple: Don't forget whom you are speaking to, because everyone has a story. The newlywed couple sitting on the living room floor, writing thank you notes for their wedding gifts; the single dad with three sons, trying to make sure they comb their hair and tuck in their shirt tails before they walk out the door; the Hispanic mother who worries her daughter may learn "*their* ways" and forget her family if she leaves home to pursue her education; these folks are always with me. I learn so much from every new focus group or interview I conduct that I am amazed how little I had known beforehand about what makes us all tick.

There is nothing more American than our entrepreneurial spirit, our ability to dream big dreams and take big risks. It is precisely this ideal—and the prosperity it has engendered in the United States—that has attracted millions of Latino immigrants in the last 30 years. This shared ideal should generate great hope for Republicans. People with such economic ambitions, who work on their own to succeed, seldom have any use for left-wing causes. No tax hike or wild-eyed feminist rant has ever helped a single immigrant family succeed in this country. Republicans can draw Hispanics in America away from the siren song of government dependency—if only they are smart enough to welcome their neighbors.

In each chapter, I have included a short memory from a prominent, politically active Hispanic leader that provides insight into the Latino experience. These personal stories—mostly from interviews that I conducted—connect to the values of Hispanic life and how, in many cases, they are truly identical to the values of the Republican Party. They represent the part of this book I enjoy most, seeing life through the eyes of others. My marketing and political research into the Hispanic population has taught me that Hispanics and Republicans share far more in common than either group may at first believe.

Ultimately, there is no such thing as a political party for white, black or brown people. There are just ideas that work and ideas that don't work. Focus on the ideas, and make an informed choice.

one

someone like me

U.S. Senator Mel Martinez, on the November morning after he was named Chairman of the Republican National Committee.

I came here as a child. I was nurtured by the compassion of American families as a foster child. When my parents came here [later, from Cuba], I relived the immigrant experience. Because my parents were in their late forties, they didn't know the language, they didn't know the customs or how to go from A to Z living in America. I was acculturated; I'd learned the language and understood what America was about so I became head of the household.

I helped my father get a job and find a home for us to live in. I was the one who was taking them around, showing them how to shop, showing them how to organize their lives.

I taught them how to make it in America, being responsible and having car insurance—since that's such a big deal in our households. They were making ends meet by paying rent, but just as soon as we could we wanted to own a home. We didn't think it was possible, but I helped give my dad the gumption, the idea that "yes, we can have a mortgage."

Years later, . . . my dad would say things like "*Tenemos casa propio.*" [We have our own home.] You know? "*En los Estados Unidos, una casa propio!*" It meant, we've arrived! It really was his way of saying "We're far away from home, but we're back to where we were."

I was a Democrat most of my adult life. I didn't leave my party, and we're not suggesting you leave yours. I am telling you that what I felt was that the leadership of the Democratic Party had left me and millions of patriotic

Democrats in this country who believed in freedom. Walk with us down that path of hope and opportunity, and together we can and we will lift America up to meet our greatest days.

—*Ronald Reagan, September 19, 1984*

Is it true what they say about Latinos? In a word, *Si*!

Hispanics are affectionate, hard working and loyal. We drink too many *cervezas*, eat *chicharones*, and wear tight, brightly colored Spandex so that we look thin. We never eat a meal without *queso*, we consider heavy cologne and layers of gold jewelry to be fashion essentials, and we bear the face of Jesus and *la Virgen* on our tattoos and bumper stickers.

We are all bilingual, never on time, watch Spanish *telenovelas* and drive lowriders. We are overly affectionate (did I mention that already?) and we value big families. We make the sign of the cross in desperate situations and we spend more money than we make.

Yes, everything you know about Hispanics is true—we are the *Omero Simpsones* of American culture.

That is, until you actually meet us.

I'm a fifth generation Mexican-American. I eat organic chicken, not *arroz con pollo*. I speak to my mother in English and she answers in Spanglish—a language best described by comic Bill Santiago as having "two vocabularies and half the grammar." Folks in my family are the last to find Iraq on a world map, but also the first to join the Army when our country is in danger. We pray religiously and perhaps curse a bit too religiously as well.

I don't have one identity but many: I am a conservative, a lover of chocolate and a practitioner of yoga. I am a Tejana, an assimilated small business owner, a political hack, a friend, a shopper and a Latina who always calls herself American first.

But that was all cast into doubt the day I moved to Washington.

It was a bitterly cold evening in January 1994 when I boarded a Continental flight to Washington, D.C., holding two personal checks and a rosary, and wearing jet black cowboy boots. In the Latino way of eternal optimism, I had failed to appreciate what it would mean to land in a blizzard. Catapulting sideways down an icy runway in pitch darkness with the screeching sounds of metal and ice beneath you, it's amazing the things you think of. I grabbed the hand of the woman beside me and held it tightly.

"If we go, at least we'll be together," I said, only half-kidding. It was the instant shake-and-bake way Latinos form relationships. I knew that if it was our time, at least we'd be going as *familia*.

Moments later, still thrilled to be alive, I followed a trail of weary passengers through the late-night silence of the airport terminal. I watched as the people ahead of me huddled together, then leaned forward to trigger the automatic doors. One, two, three . . . go! It looked like a Nordic ski jump competition as the frigid wind burst through.

Now let's not be dramatic, I thought. How bad could it be? The doors slid open and a blast of ice, wind and snow tossed me sideways onto another stranger. I'd walked into a life-sized snow globe!

Frantic at the bitterness of Washington's blustery winter, I flagged down one of the few cab drivers bold or delusional enough (I don't know which) to drive through the sea of white that had settled over the ground that night. As we made our way slowly through the slush, the driver tried to reassure me, "Good thing we have enough weight in the back to keep us steady."

Did he really say that? But I've been dieting!

Determined not to lose the euphoria of surviving my near death experience, I kept smiling. "Yep!"

Throughout the slow, dark ride to my final destination, I thought about my decision to come to Washington. I had just sold all I owned to get here, and I wasn't going back. There was nowhere else I wanted to be.

This step was my life's greatest undertaking yet, at the age of 24. My trip had a purpose beyond just finishing my education and landing a good job: I had to believe that someone like me could make it in Washington. People like me could become the advocates, the champions for a stronger, better America—something all of us could share.

My trip to Washington came after four years of selling P. F. Collier encyclopedias. It may sound odd, but my time as a salesperson had crystallized so many of my beliefs and so much of the optimism I had for our country's future. I had sold books to rich families and poor ones, newlyweds and families with children. Some lived in trailer parks and others in mansions. All told, I sold books in 23 states and more counties than I can remember.

It's not a glamorous job, and nothing you would do for the sake of stability (we were paid straight commission—you don't sell, you don't eat). You had to have a passion for it, though, because you can't sell what you don't love. Dogs would bite you, kids would kick you. It was all about the heat, the late-night truck-stop cuisine, the cheap hotels, the time away from home (about 20 days a month), the worn-out shoes and the constant need to perform.

Yet I really considered it an indoor job. I loved the families and their willingness to be open about their most private hopes, aspirations and perceived personal shortcomings. Talk of education built our bonds. Regardless of race, financial circumstance or geography, we shared the value of what a quality education provided—a better life for ourselves and for our families. I felt I was selling hope, so that these families could dream bigger dreams for their children.

When I stopped selling books and jumped into politics I found the same calling. Selling candidates is much like selling books, only the payoff is different.

After working for two dozen Republican political campaigns in Texas, I learned about an internship program in Washington with a conservative think tank that trained young leaders. I applied and was accepted. This was my break. I also scrambled to apply to The George Washington University, to finish my education. "G-Dub," as it is known locally, was close to my internship and accessible by public transportation. With 26 community college credit hours on my transcript, I sent in my application, sold all my belongings, set a small savings account aside for my mother and grandmother and boarded a plane to Washington. I did not even know if I would be accepted to the university, but I knew I was not returning home.

And there I was, sliding about in the back of a cab in Northern Virginia. After what seemed an ice-covered eternity, the cab driver took all of my worldly possessions, which I had packed into two over-stuffed suit-cases, and dropped them at the front door of my new home, an intern house in northern Virginia. As I attempted to traverse the treacherous ice toward the door in my cowboy boots, it occurred to me that my idea to arrive as a confident Texas woman could backfire.

I managed to get out of the car and cling precariously to the icy fence post, struggling to keep my balance and kicking up ice and snow with my boots as I did so. Standing at the front door, with a look that could only be construed as bewilderment, were my new house parents, an impatient cab driver and a growing crowd of fellow interns.

Seconds before I finally crawled on my hands to the front door, I yelled, "Hi! Nice to meet you! This isn't quite what I expected."

From the looks on their faces, I could tell that they thought the same. In South Texas, we expect floods or hurricanes, but not ice storms—and I'm not talking about the weather.

* * *

I was the first of two children born to Mexican American parents at the tail end of the 1960s. We lived in Corpus Christi, Texas, a town translated from Latin to mean the "Body of Christ," which is considered the gateway to the Texas Rio Grande Valley. My father worked in maintenance, my mother as a store cashier.

It was an age of cultural liberation. Seventy million children from the post-war baby-boom generation had moved away from the conservative 1950s to witness growth in the NASA space program, the start of the modern gay-rights movement with the Stonewall riots in New York, Woodstock, and the first military draft lottery in the United States since World War II.

Isolated from the main cultural centers north of our city boundaries, we lived like other Mexican American families throughout the southwest. With little to distract us, education became our top priority. Our mothers would walk us to one-story elementary schools where we would speak in English but learn words like *pájaro* (bird) and *árbol* (tree) in Spanish class one hour a day.

Like many Tejanos, our parents dreamt in brown and white, with their economic reality intertwined with their aspirations. On Saturday afternoons, Mom would pack our family into our canary-yellow Toyota Celica to drive along the winding coastline on Ocean Drive, where the "rich" people lived. We'd gaze at their spacious art-deco homes.

"Here's where the doctors live," my mother would say, as if no other profession were worthy. We would sit in silence, wondering what it was like inside.

I think of the work and jobs that defined us. One of my father's seven siblings, Uncle Julian, owned a carpet store and drove a red Lincoln Town Car. Our *compradres*—godparents—owned a used car lot and lived in a large brick home, which was in itself a sign of success. Uncle Robert, my father's twin, worked at the naval air station. Every man in the family was a military veteran.

In the early 1980s, Robert did what was unthinkable to us and divorced his first wife. Later he wed a young, voluptuous, conservative-minded Latina named Blanca, who was one of the hardest working women I would come to know. The fair-skinned beauty was funny, with bright eyes, a broad smile and wore no fewer than half a dozen gold crucifixes around her neck. A devout Catholic (except, ahem, for the Catholic rules on divorce), Blanca kept a mammoth glow-in-the-dark Rosary with beads the size of billiard balls hanging in a closet near the bedrooms. At the age of 12, I stayed the night at their house. Late that night, groping through the dark for the bathroom, I opened the wrong door, only to be startled by an enormous, glowing crucified Jesus. For just a moment I was sure that the Second Coming was upon us!

Blanca balanced two jobs to make enough money so their two boys could attend Catholic school, the first staple of Latino economic success. Raised poor, she had eventually become the primary breadwinner for her family. Years later, she confessed that as a young teenager she used to care and clean for wealthy, older white women in their homes.

"It was work you never want to do," she would tell me, and then she would look me dead in the eye: "Finish high school."

I remember feeling that Blanca did not fit in with the family. She was a renaissance Latina, bold and opinionated. Other women whispered about her clothes and makeup when she walked by. She did not care, and that alone may have sparked more curious gossip. But Blanca was committed to her family, and pressed me particularly to push ahead, despite the machismo of the culture we lived in.

Mexican machismo—you can't escape it. It's the thump-your-chest, testosterone-driven male chauvinism of which Spanish-language *telenovelas* (soap operas) are made. To some men of Mexican descent, it's a badge of honor to be called *machista*. It's not the kind of thing young Hispanic girls talk about, but it's woven into our society.

Years later, I had the privilege of attending a luncheon in Washington with Marta Sahagún de Fox, the former first lady of Mexico, and I asked her, with all of her successes in promoting early childhood education, what were her biggest challenges. Her answer? To get families who live in the rural parts of Mexico, particularly the fathers, to buy notebooks and pencils for their daughters and send them to school. For boys, school was a priority. For girls, it was not. Removed by hundreds of miles and five generations from Mexico, old ways died hard.

Our mothers and aunts, with limited education, traditionally worked as teachers' assistants, cafeteria managers and bank loan officers, or sometimes at the late and weekend shifts at the HEB grocery. I think of the countless times I would be checking out of the line only to see a face I knew.

My mother, a 25-year employee at JCPenney's, was asked one day to give the store-closing announcement, which required repeated warnings to customers to head for the check-out. The sales associates could not stop grinning at her thick accent—every five minutes she kept saying, "Thank you for *ch*opping at JCPenney's."

When it came to politics, our family was decidedly Democratic. My second grade class was once asked to compile a collection of sentimental pictures and bring them to class for a special craft project. Mom cut out a large picture of the Carter family—Jimmy and Roselyn, smiling with a young, red-haired girl sitting on their laps. It had likely come straight from the pages of the holiday issue of *Good Housekeeping*.

"Here, *mija*, look . . . for your class!" She said. "See, her name is Amy. She's just like you!"

"But Mom," I objected. "Our house doesn't look like *that*!" (Come to think of it, this may have been one of the early traumatic experiences that made me a Republican.)

Two days later I came home with my creation: a padded seat made of two brown grocery bags glued together, stuffed with newspaper and decorated with the pictures we collected. We covered the seat in thick plastic and then stitched the seams with thick brown string. On one side were the photo clippings I had collected: Raggedy Ann, a large cutout of *Sesame Street*'s Mr. Snuffleupagus, a family photo from my birthday party and an image of Benji, our new golden-haired puppy. On the other side was the photo my mother had given me, the smiling Jimmy Carter and his family. Out of respect for Mom, but still having no idea what I shared in common with these people, I decided that's the side I'd sit on.

We were a Democratic family, and so it was only natural that I would rebel and announce at the age of 16 that I was a Republican—at least that's the way my father saw it. The day I announced to him my chosen political affiliation, he had one of those looks of disbelief: "She's either gone mad or she just needs a swift kick in the pants."

My friends and acquaintances did not respond much better. *"You were cool. I thought I liked you."*

But, for me, being Republican came naturally. The face of the Democratic Party I knew was Gov. Ann Richards, the loud, abrasive white-haired lady with a sharp tongue. It was rare to see her and not think she was picking a fight with someone. Democrats, I'd come to believe, were sour pusses.

The other active Democrats I knew of always overwhelmed me with their sense of entitlement. I have early memories of Democratic events in Texas, at which a group of Hispanics or "Chicanos" would sit together on one side of the room commiserating about how bad life had come to be. " *'They'* need to be doing more for us." My mom would use that term often: "*Mija*, that's what '*They*' are wearing." But who was this mysterious "They," and why were we depending on "Them"?

To be sure, my family probably could have used a little help from "Them," or anyone else. As a teenager, I lived the American dream in reverse. I went from middle class to working poor in the blink of an eye when, after 23 years of marriage, my parents divorced. Dad got the house; mom got a one-bedroom apartment. Having seen my father leave my mother, I was not about to do the same. I asked him if I could live with her until she was established, and he responded by packing all of my belongings into Hefty trash bags and leaving them on the driveway.

Just like that, I had been cast out of a middle-class existence and into poverty. We were so poor that I came to know many of the local repo men personally. (That came in handy the day "Big John" let me finish my cereal before he hauled away the kitchen table.) And the worst part was that, in the Latino tradition of denial, Mom would never let us know this was going to happen, so as not to upset us until the latest moment possible. So every three months or so, movers would show up at the door in matching t-shirts that barely covered their beer bellies and demand their merchandise.

We had our own way of paying for things, termed "Latino" financing. The electricity was disconnected almost monthly, our car repossessed with alarming frequency. In my stubborn persistence not to switch from the good school to the inferior one, the drive back and forth from the rich neighborhood (where my school was) to the poor neighborhood was a constant reminder of how hard life had become.

"We still have each other," Mom would say. "*Don't worry, mija, take a ch-ower, you'll feel better.*" Or there was also my favorite un-carb-conscious phrase of comfort, "*Eat a tortilla.*" That I could do, just not at a table.

While most of my classmates thought about football rallies and the prom, I had to worry about whether or not we could eat and put gas in the car. And where my next kitchen table was coming from.

But never during that time did we look to welfare or state assistance for help. We were both able to work, so why would we take it? It was there for people who needed it and we weren't them. It's a staple of who we were: independent, driven by faith and aspiring for more through education. I may not have known it then, but this too helped form my self-identity as a Republican.

My mother was certainly not immune to the pattern of ridiculous comfort buying that is so integral to Latino economics. I remember how I once failed to talk her out of buying a small 2'x3' red floral rug for our living room. "Mom, it's too small. It looks like a placemat on the floor." She liked it. It was comical, even if somewhat appalling, to see her bring home a nacho cheese colored *quesadilla*-maker that imprints tortillas with a cactus, sun, guitar and *jalapeño*, when we were struggling to pay for food, electricity and gasoline. By the time I was working to provide for both my mother and grandmother, I could still expect Mom to come home with a set of pink shag slippers from JCPenney. "They were marked down to 99 cents," she said. "And with my discount—I got them for a dime!"

Mom did a lot of other things that made little financial sense but are common among Latinos. When I left Texas, I urged her in the strongest terms *not* to cancel her health insurance policy at work just to save a few dollars a month on premiums. No sooner had I walked out the door than she did just that. The bill was too expensive, she said, not realizing it would be tremendously difficult to enroll in a new plan.

My family's poor economic situation was not about to lead me into the clutches of Ma Richards (may she rest in peace) or any other Democrat. Their approach of throwing money at poverty had never helped anyone. The Republicans I knew offered a sharp and refreshing contrast to all of the Democratic hand-wringing. It is true that where I grew up, in the suburbs of Houston, Republicans were not like me. They were mostly white, and many of the women looked like the sort of blue-haired old ladies and you'd see at a Daughters of the American Revolution reunion or a bingo match. But none of that mattered so much to me as the fact that they were optimistic and eager about the future. In a way, they were a lot like my very Democratic mother, who may have been in tough shape financially, but nonetheless dreamed and aspired to own her own home.

The Republicans I knew were similarly optimistic. They spoke about family, faith, honor, love of country, and hard work. They bore a sense of national purpose. They inspired my hopes about creating opportunities for everyone in education, in jobs, in small businesses—for everyone, regardless of our circumstances. By standing firm and by taking personal responsibility, we could achieve so much more—together.

*   *   *

As I stood outside the intern house in my weather-inappropriate boots, barely managing to stand on the icy sidewalk, I experienced the first hint that I was different. Things would get worse during my first stay in Washington.

In Texas, strangers are always looking out for each other. This isn't just something you see in the Westerns—it's true. But when it came to my fellow interns, let's just say that we didn't exactly hit it off. I guess I never realized I was Hispanic until I moved to Washington. Up until then I had always thought of myself as a Texan and an American, and I was proud of both. But my fellow interns saw me as a Mexican, even though in most cases my family had been in this country longer than theirs.

I was a Republican all right, just like they were, and shared many conservative values with my fellow interns. But these narrow-minded folks just weren't interested in warming up to someone so different. I was Catholic, they were Christian—and oh no, they're not the same thing. They were white, and to them I was brown. I had had a career and supported myself, and these students, all of them younger than me, had for the most part never been outside the bubble of home and school. We just weren't on the same planet.

The staff was kind enough, but my fellow interns and I just didn't click. When they left in their cars each morning to drive the eight miles to work, they wouldn't give me a ride even when there was room in the car—I took the bus. They ridiculed the way I expressed my faith. They derided me for reading the liberal *Washington Post* as opposed to the conservative *Washington Times*, and seemed to constantly question my commitment to our shared values. These definitely weren't the Republicans that I'd grown to know in Texas.

My time as an intern made me feel that I really was not equal. We may all be equal in Texas, but these kids were much more interested in how different rather than how similar we were.

Those were bleak months for me. By spring, as the ice began to thaw, my drive and spirit had also evaporated. Discouraged and alone, I was not sure where to turn. No permanent home, job, car or prospects. Mom even sensed my uncertainly on the phone. "*Mija*, come home," she said. A thought came to me: Focus on what is familiar, on what you know. I set my sights on Representative Henry Bonilla.

Bonilla, then a young, charismatic force, had been elected in 1992 to the House of Representatives, making him the first Hispanic Republican from Texas and the only Mexican American Republican in Congress. He was an inspiration—a rare archetype for conservative Latinos and a reminder of the ideals that had brought me to Washington.

I went to his office and knocked on the door. Naively, I waited at the door for someone to answer, missing the sign that said, "Please come in."

"I want to tell the Congressman that he's my hero!" I blurted out to Bonilla's staff secretary. "He's the reason I'm here and he represents everything I believe in." You could see the startled look on her face and almost imagine her thinking "Security!" I launched into my brief background in politics. "Hold on a minute," she said. Uh-oh, I thought; my doubts surfaced. Maybe this wasn't such a great idea after all; I sound like a nut. Minutes later my reservations faded when I met Steve Ruhlen, Bonilla's chief of staff. He was warm, professional and took me seriously. (Plus he had an uncanny resemblance to Jim Carrey—he must be friendly!)

After we talked for a few minutes, he said, "Oh, Henry has to meet you." Henry Bonilla was everything I imagined him to be—kind, intelligent, compassionate and dedicated to the true ideals of the Republican Party. However, the warm reception wasn't enough to counter the doubts I had been harboring ever since I arrived in Washington. What Reagan had described as a "shining city on a hill" wasn't shining so brightly for me.

Once my term at my internship was up, I did not follow my fellow interns into a job in a congressional office or political campaign. Six months with these closed-minded kids made me loathe the thought of devoting my life to their ideals. Instead, I enrolled in journalism school at The George Washington University, dropped out of politics entirely and got a job selling wedding dresses to support myself.

But for some reason, even though I quit politics, it never quite quit me. Bonilla kept reaching out to me, and eventually I reached back. I became one of about 150 self-identified Hispanic staffers—out of thousands—on Capitol Hill, and one of just 22 Hispanic Republicans.

During my time on the Hill, I had dinner at the home of a Hispanic Democratic staffer who had become a good friend. As he complained that Latinos were always taken for granted in his party, I asked him how he could handle it. "You always get relegated to the sideline," I said, after listening to him talk about his work.

"Well, I agree with you," he said. "One thing you have in the Republican Party is opportunity." It was true—there were people at the top of the Republican Party who really wanted to learn more about Hispanics and involve us in the process. The result was that we had a better chance for advancement—not just in the narrow sense of my own career, but in the broader sense that despite our small numbers, we could collectively accomplish something real on Capitol Hill, in Washington, and in politics in general.

What I learned is that there was a place for me here in Washington. Long before, I had seen and believed in what the ideals of the Republican Party had to offer me, my family, and my country. Then I came to Washington, and I felt personally excluded by the people who were supposedly champions of these ideals. Suddenly the political world no longer seemed like such a great place for me. But finally, someone had given me a place in it all, and since then I have never wanted to leave. But how many people like me simply feel shut out and never come back?

Every time I see a young mother asking her daughter to translate at the sales counter, or the downward glance of a young Latino who is embarrassed by his limited English vocabulary, I think back to the years I spent trying to correct my mother's accent: No, mom, not "*ch*opping," *shhhh*-opping.

"*Shhhh*-chopping," she would reply.

I think of the words my mother has always struggled to pronounce—*chhoes, chower, chaving, chopping*. Everyone is just trying to get it right. Everyone is just trying to fit in. Politics is all about including people, not leaving them out.

Republicans should never frighten away their own allies—people like me—just because we look different or come from a different background. Look at Latinos and see a helpful brother with both assets and needs. Connect with us, let us be part of it all. Earn our respect, and you can win our gratitude and loyalty as well.

two

a changing america

Anna Escobedo Cabral is a quiet giant in the world of commerce. Confirmed in November 2004 to be U.S. treasurer, she holds an office that is older than the Department of Treasury itself.

I'm from a fourth generation farm-worker family. In the early 1900s my great grandparents came to the United States in search of opportunity. They crossed the Rio Grande by foot, and ended up making their way to the Santa Clara valley, where the only work they could find was to work in the fields. And they picked crops, everything you could imagine. And soon their children, my grandparents' generation, joined them in the fields. Later, my father's generation joined them in the fields. And, for little while, our generation worked in the fields. . . .

When my father decided to start his own family, he had a goal: to move out of the field and find other kinds of work. He took pretty much any job that he could. He would move from place to place. He would be offered a job here, and he'd go do that. And he'd be offered a job there, and he'd do that. He worked in a mental institution, in the laundry facility. He worked as a garbage man. He worked eventually as a busboy, and then taught himself to be a fry-cook, and then a chef. Each of those jobs required that we be on the go constantly. I once tried to count the times I changed elementary schools and quit at twenty. I thought that really wasn't that big of a deal: it was fun, we got to meet people.

But it was tough. I had to work to make sure we had enough to eat . . . so I worked after school in a federally funded after-school program job, and on weekends cleaning houses. My father borrowed a hundred dollars and bought a tiny pickup truck, and started picking up people's trash on the curb. Metal trash—old washing machines, aluminum cans, dryers, car parts, whatever it was.

My after-school jobs and my father's junking business kept us afloat, we were able to keep it together, but I was thinking I should probably go out and get a real job. I had done well in school, really loved it, and I was ready to graduate early at age sixteen. A high school teacher heard that I was going off to get full time work, called me into his office. He said, "You know, you might think instead about going and applying to college. Maybe this is a better opportunity for you and your family in the long term."

And I said, "Mr. Lamb, that isn't possible. My family really needs me to get a job, and I have to do that."

He said, "Well, here's the application. You and I are going to fill it out together. I'll come visit your father this evening, and I'll tell him why this is a better plan."

He did just as he promised, came to visit my father, a very strict, very traditional Mexican American male. Spent a couple hours with him, and my father agreed that if Mr. Lamb could find the scholarship dollars, I could go off to college several hundred miles away. So before you knew it, my father was sending off his sixteen year old daughter to University of California Santa Cruz.

. . . When my father used to come to visit me when I worked for the United States Senate, his favorite place to go was the Bureau of Engraving and Printing. He was fascinated by the money, and his prize possession was one of those 32 piece uncut sheets of dollar bills. He promptly hung it up in his home, and every time I'd go visit, I'd notice that the sheet got a little smaller. I'd say, "Dad, what happened to that sheet?" And he'd say, "I ran out of money so I needed this row." Before I knew it he had one dollar left. Even though he is no longer with us, it's nice to give my mom a replacement sheet of thirty-two singles with my name, and his name, on it.[1]

> The Hispanic-Latino community in the United States of America appreciates freedom, free enterprise and entrepreneurship. They are pro-family, they're pro-education. They represent the best of the values of our Judeo-Christian system. So my hope is that the Republican Party will welcome immigrants, and recognize people don't come to America for welfare, they come for their future.
>
> —*Jack Kemp, Jr., a former professional football quarterback who went on to serve as a Member of Congress and cabinet secretary*

When the immigration issue comes up for congressional debate, Republican Rep. Tom Cole of Oklahoma likes to remind his colleagues that he is the only Native American serving in Congress. "I'm an enrolled member of the Chickasaw Nation," he says. "And as far as I'm concerned, you're all illegal!" Of course, everyone knows it is too late for Native

Americans to assert their dominion over North America. But the myth dies hard that there is some race that can.

Crazy as it may sound, some conservatives actually believe and propagate the myth that Mexicans are coming here as part of a massive plot to retake the American Southwest, lost by Mexico piece by piece during the nineteenth Century. Glenn Spencer, president of the California-based group Voices of Citizens Together, voiced this view in an interview with a widely-read conservative Internet magazine in 2002. "Unless this [immigration] is shut down within two years, I believe that it will be irreversible, and that it will most certainly lead to a breakup of the United States," he said. "I don't think there is any doubt about it."[2]

Of course, the big secession still has not happened four years later, nor does it appear to be in the works.

But it doesn't matter how you feel about immigration, amnesty, guestworkers or border security. Hispanics are here—native-born citizens and immigrants, legal and illegal—and their numbers are growing so rapidly that they will be the voters who decide future elections. The political warriors of both parties share the same reality: They do not have the option of stopping this demographic train as it hurtles down the mountain.

At the same time, Republicans are wrong to fear that demography will bury them, making them a permanent minority. Not only is the Latino vote winnable for the GOP, but the party has shown demonstrable progress with Hispanics in the last decade, even if they lost ground in 2006. In any case, the Latino vote is not a vote that Republicans can afford to write off.

by the numbers

By now, Americans are familiar with the Hispanic population explosion. According to U.S. Census estimates, Hispanics represent America's largest minority group, with nearly 43 million who comprise 14 percent of the U.S. population. And the trend toward a more Latino America shows no signs of letting up.

In 2004, the latest year for which statistics are available, approximately 4.1 million Americans were born. Of those, 900,000, or 22 percent, were Hispanic.[3] Unlike the 43 million Hispanics in the U.S. population at large—of whom 8 million or more are estimated to be here illegally—these 2006 babies are *all* U.S. citizens who will be eligible to vote in the 2024 U.S. presidential election.

To put it into perspective: Even if Congress halts all immigration today by building a 20-foot barrier that stops every single unauthorized border-crosser, Hispanics will *still* continue to increase their share of the U.S. population, this year and in every year for decades to come.

And because no such impenetrable wall will be built, the Hispanic-American baby boom comes over and above this year's expected Hispanic immigration, both legal and illegal. Over time, this will also make the Hispanic native-born share of the population even greater than it is now.

The trend toward a more Hispanic America is not simply a question of immigration, or even of outstanding Hispanic fertility. Even as Hispanics in the U.S. continue to multiply, the rest of America is shrinking because Americans on the whole simply are not reproducing fast enough.[4]

By 2050, the Census Bureau estimates that the Hispanic population will have increased by 188 percent—that is, it will have almost tripled—while the white, non-Hispanic majority will have increased by a mere

Figure 2.1   Hispanics as a Percentage of the U.S. Population

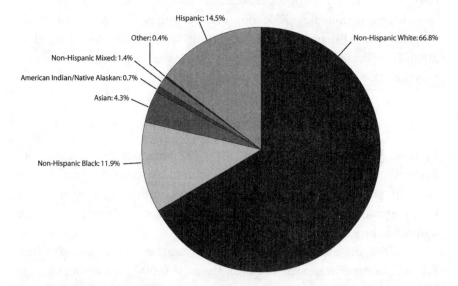

Source: U.S. Census Bureau, 2005 American Community Survey

Figure 2.2 Projected Hispanic Population Growth

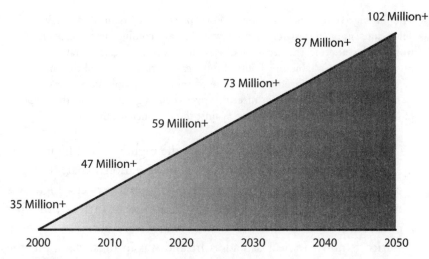

Source: U.S. Census Bureau, projected population of the United States, by race and Hispanic Origin: 2000 to 2050

7.4 percent.[5] That means 67 million more Hispanics, and 14.5 million more non-Hispanic whites. Based on current trends, the Census Bureau predicts that between 2040 and 2050, the number of whites in America will actually *fall* by 48,000.

In that same decade, there will be almost *one billion people* living south of the U.S.-Mexico border. The hope is that at some point, most Latin American countries can follow the lead of the United States, Canada and Chile by improving their economic situations so that mass migration is no longer necessary. But either way, there will be no shortage of Latino immigrants between now and then—we are here, and not only are we not going anywhere, but we're going to keep coming.

Our presence is felt so keenly that the business community is taking notice. The business of advertising to Hispanic consumers in the United States is now valued at nearly $5 billion per year,[6] and U.S. Latinos controlled more than $798 billion in purchasing power in 2006.[7]

Some people don't like this. Even in North America, which has absorbed more immigrants over the centuries than any other region on earth, fear and mistrust of immigrants has always persisted. Consider the writings of one political leader on immigration to his country:

> The immigration which is now taking place is a frightful scourge. . . . Thousands upon thousands of poor wretches are coming here incapable of work, and scattering the seeds of disease and death. . . . Considerable panic exists among the inhabitants. Political motives contribute to swell the amount of dissatisfaction produced by this state of things. The opposition make the want of adequate provision to meet this overwhelming calamity, in the shape of hospitals, etc., a matter of charge against the Provincial Administration.[8]

The above quotation from Lord James, the Eighth Earl of Elgin, must ring a few bells for those following the immigration debate today—particularly the complaints about hospitals and public services. Elgin was writing about Irish immigrants who arrived in Quebec in 1845, the first year of the nationwide potato famine that emptied Ireland.

Mexico is nowhere near as bad as Ireland was in those days, but the situation is similar: Corrupt governments in Mexico City and in state capitals limit economic opportunity. According to the CIA factbook, within Mexico, 40 percent of the population lives below the poverty line, and 25 percent of Mexicans in Mexico are underemployed.[9]

Because we enjoy the benefits of the rule of law in the United States, it is hard to explain to an American how difficult it really is to succeed in Mexico and other countries of Latin America. Although many nativists argue that Mexicans and other immigrants will bring corruption into the United States, in fact they are usually coming here precisely to escape that corruption.

The United States, on the other hand, with the economic freedoms we enjoy, represents a stark contrast to the world they know. Our nation's unemployment rate stood at just 4.5 percent in February 2007—full employment by any economist's measure—at just the time when many Americans complained that immigrants were "taking away our jobs." The average wage for an American non-supervisory worker is about $17 per hour, several times higher than that of Mexico. There are jobs available in the United States, and big money to be made.

Meanwhile, as Americans get older and more go on Social Security and Medicare, there is a dire need for salaried workers to continue filling the programs' coffers. This is one of the reasons why President Bush and other Republicans view a "seal-the-border" approach as futile in the long run.

From its very founding, America has suffered from labor shortages, beginning with the original settlements and continuing with the establishment of the 13 colonies. The ubiquity of indentured servitude in early America—and sadly, the proliferation of race-based slavery—provide historical testimony to this fact. Lord Baltimore, the founder of the Maryland colony, did not adopt a policy of religious toleration in his colony just because he was an enlightened man. He did so also because he thought he could attract more workers if Catholics and Puritans were allowed to take refuge in his colony.[10] Those who came from Britain and other parts of Europe found a tight labor market that offered much better terms to workers willing to make the ocean voyage to America.

Economic incentives are as meaningful and powerful now as they were 400 years ago. As America's majority population continues to slow its growth and enter its decline, it is no surprise that someone is willing to fill the vacuum. Economic incentives continue to direct a one-way traffic of workers, mostly Hispanics, into the United States.

nixon's "hispanic strategy"

So many Latinos—what are we to do? That's the reaction of some Republicans who believe that we are hopelessly predestined to follow African American voters into becoming thoroughly and irretrievably Democratic.

But they're wrong. They have failed to note our economic and social progress in this country—something I'll discuss more in the next chapter. They have failed to keep an open mind about who we are and what motivates us.

Let's just scratch the surface for a moment. A survey taken in October 2006, at the worst time for Republicans in at least eight years, finds that 34 percent of us self-identify as "conservative," a number similar to the white population. The same survey finds that Latinos in America are very pro-life—54 to 36 percent, more conservative than the population at large—and that we strongly support traditional marriage, with 59 percent saying they are "less likely" to back a candidate who supports same-sex marriage. When given choices and asked, "What do you think is the best strategy to begin growing the economy again?" 56 percent of Hispanics said "cut taxes."[11]

We are also the most optimistic voting bloc in the United States. After the 2006 election, a *Wall Street Journal* poll showed that even though Latino voters were more negative on President Bush than the overall sample (63 percent to 59 percent), we were also ten points less likely (30 percent to 40 percent) to say that we "believe life will be worse for the next generation."[12] And even though we are still poor, Latinos reject the class warfare paradigm of "two Americas" by a wider margin than non-Hispanic whites.[13]

At first glance, there appear to be at least the beginnings of a beautiful friendship between Hispanics and Republicans. Fortunately, for every one that fears us, there are many more forward-thinking Republicans who have approached us as friends and managed to form an alliance with Latinos. Richard Nixon was out courting Latinos way before it was cool.

Nixon had already become the first president to count Hispanics in the Census—which was a major controversy at the time. Lance Tarrance, now a prominent Republican pollster, was serving as Nixon's special assistant to the director of the Census from 1970 to 1973 when the change took place. As a former senator from California, Nixon took great interest in the Hispanic population, and he demanded that a question about Hispanic origin be included in the Census questionnaire that year. "That question was inserted into the survey at the last minute under orders from Nixon himself," said Tarrance. "I was there and the Census bureau pushed back and said 'it's too late, we're not going to change it.' That meant we would have gone another 10 years without knowing much about the Hispanic community in this country." The Census Bureau had already sent its nationwide survey to press in January 1970, but Nixon insisted that the presses be stopped and the question be added to the longer survey that went to 1 in 20 households.[14]

From 1940 up to that time, the Census had only counted two races— "white" and "non-white." As for Hispanics, the survey looked only at the surnames of first and second-generation Mexican Americans in five states. If your family had recently arrived in California, Arizona, Colorado, Texas, or New Mexico, and your name was one of 400 Spanish surnames on a list at the Census Bureau, then congratulations, you were a "Mexican!" This method totally left out the longest-standing Mexican American families, who had found themselves in the United States in 1848 after the borders changed,[15] not to mention non-Mexican Hispanics in every other part of the country. A decade had already passed since Fidel Castro began destroying Cuba, sending political refugees to Florida by the boatload, and yet the Census simply assumed there were no Hispanics there.

The 1970 Census became a milestone for Latinos. Suddenly, we had a real idea of how many of us there were. "That's very important in terms of mobilizing a group to show their significance and draw attention, the same way African Americans did in the 1950s," said Tarrance. "Politically, it pushed us [the Nixon White House] to do some hard thinking beyond just the South."

Nixon created the President's Cabinet Committee on Opportunities for Spanish-Speaking People—a significant cabinet-level position. In 1971, when it still appeared that Nixon might have a serious reelection challenge on his hands, he visited South Texas. Historian Tony Castro described his greeting by a massive crowd of 36,000 cheering Mexican Americans.[16]

> Grandmothers in mantillas. Chicano majorettes. Farmers in denims. They packed the narrow city streets and stood six deep cheering "Hola Nixon" and "Bienvenido," as Mr. Nixon, for the first time in thirty-two years, returned to the place where he and Mrs. Nixon spent their honeymoon.
>
> An hour later, courtesy of the presidential helicopters, the President was in dusty Rio Grande City, where he met 1,300 high school students, almost all of them Mexican-American. . . . "The American tradition," he said, "is that we help ourselves when we can. . . . That's what made this country great."
>
> The President urged the largely Mexican-American student body to take pride in themselves and in the nation's diversity. In an oblique reference to the traditional Democratic voting patterns of Mexican-Americans, he urged them to "let your minds become as open as they can" to all facets of the political process. "I am not going to talk about whether you become Democrats or Republicans," he said. "The future of the country is more important than any party label. . . .
>
> Be for your school, be for your team, but above all, be for your country, for America."

"The Nixon effort to woo Hispanics in 1972 was the first time in history a non-Democratic party tried to make headway, recognizing that Latinos were not married at the hip to the Democratic Party," Castro told me. "At that time, Mexican Americans were such an afterthought. It was like being 'Ugly Dora,' where a little attention went a long way. When the Democratic candidates came in to the state to campaign, it was token politics—mostly beer buses and taco giveaways. Looking back, it was very degrading, but that's what it wound up being."

Unfortunately, and for obvious reasons, Nixon is remembered for other things besides his pioneering "Hispanic Strategy," a counterpoint to his "Southern Strategy" that would seize the South from the Democrats. But his outreach to Latinos was ahead of its time. It was also undertaken with some risk, as there was much more racial tension then between whites and Hispanics than there is now. Nixon's outreach could have upset some white voters, just as the Democrats' outreach to African Americans had cost them the white vote in the two previous elections.

Figure 2.3   Hispanic Presidential Vote, 1972–2004

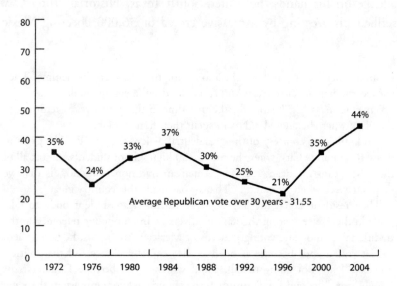

1972		1976		1980		1984		1988	
Nixon	35	Ford	24	Reagan	33	Reagan	37	Bush	30
McGovern	63	Carter	76	Carter	59	Mondale	62	Dukakis	69
				Anderson	6				

1992		1996		2000		2004	
Clinton	61	Clinton	72	Bush	35	Bush	44
Bush	25	Dole	21	Gore	62	Kerry	53
Perot	14	Perot	6				

Source: Voter News Service Exit Polls

As it turned out, Nixon had nothing to worry about in 1972—he was reelected in a landslide, only to fall in the Watergate scandal afterward. But whatever his other failings, his outreach to Hispanics was groundbreaking in a time when words like "diversity" and "outreach" did not roll as lightly off of tongues everywhere as they do today.

Nixon was actually continuing a tradition that had begun with a pioneering Republican politician little known or appreciated by most people outside of Texas. In his first reelection campaign of 1966, Senator John Tower courted the Hispanic vote like no Republican before him. Tower had risen in the ranks as a Republican organizer and a delegate to the Republican National Convention of 1956. After losing an election to Sen. Lyndon Johnson (D), who was running for reelection to his Senate seat and the vice presidency at the same time, Tower won a special election for the vacant seat and became the first Texas Republican senator since 1870.

Tower was just one man challenging one-party rule in Texas. He was fighting a Democratic Party that took Mexican American voters for granted and still consisted largely of the same Dixiecrats who had ruled the South for a century. He helped in the foundation of the group Mexican American Republicans of Texas, which would remain influential until Tower's untimely death in a plane crash.

Robert A. Estrada, who eventually served as state director for Tower, remembers him from his freshman year in high school as a total stranger who did his family a good turn. Tower appointed Estrada's older brother to the Air Force Academy—a small but meaningful gesture that created a long-lasting relationship. "He had never heard of my brother, never crossed paths with either of my parents," says Estrada. "There was no political relationship at all, other than his staff person he had going through the files, looking at his qualifications and thinking this sounded like a great young man to nominate. So my brother ended up living his dream and going to the Air Force Academy as John Tower's appointee in 1962, and he graduated in 1966. From the day he left to go be a cadet, in our family John Tower walked on water. . . . Suddenly, Republicans could be great guys, and that opened the door for me."

Estrada's fondness for Tower, combined with his interest in politics, eventually led to his taking a job working as an advance man in South Texas for the losing 1970 Senate campaign of George Herbert Walker

Bush—a job that brought him into contact with a young George W. Bush. Later, Estrada would work for Tower himself.

In appealing to Hispanics, Tower was seeking out a natural ally whom he could help by bringing defense contracts to their parts of the state. Tower would take 30 percent of the Mexican American vote in 1966— no other statewide Republican candidate had ever received more than 8 percent.[17]

Tower had also been the first Republican to speak at the convention of the League of United Latin American Citizens (LULAC). He saw to it that Celso Moreno was hired in 1965 by the Texas Republican Party to institute a Hispanic outreach effort for his 1966 campaign.

By 1978, Tower had solidified his ties to the Hispanic community. During that race, he commissioned Lance Tarrance to conduct a statewide study of Hispanics for the Republican Party—it was probably the first such poll ever conducted.

"The specialization of political polling was becoming a revolution in political science," said Tarrance. "This kind of specialized public opinion polling had just started, and Tower was the only one interested in looking at the Hispanic vote."

Tower would win that, his last election, by less than a percentage point, and he always believed that his 37 percent showing among Hispanics put him over the top. He achieved this success with the help of an ad strategy by political operative Lionel Sosa—now considered the guru of Hispanic Republican advertisers.

Tower was known for campaigning on the back of a flatbed pickup truck, driving from town to town in the heavily Mexican areas of South Texas. He would stop at the ice houses to drink *cervezas* with the Mexican American workers there. It was something no other Republican had tried, and it was symbolic of the strong effort Tower put into reaching out to Latino voters. In 1984, he made the trek through South Texas with Ronald Reagan and Phil Gramm, who was running for Senate. "Tower really believed that he had to get down and visit the people," said Jose Martinez, a former senior aide to Tower. "And I'm telling you, when we were there, you had the whole community talking. . . . We spent the whole day in the valley. He would stand in the back of the truck in Laredo to deliver Reagan, Bush, and Phil Gramm, and that's something nobody else has done."

Although Reagan gets credit for beginning a strong Hispanic outreach program in California, he was standing on Tower's shoulders when he did so. Reagan hired Sosa for his 1980 run at the White House, and brought in 33 percent of the Hispanic vote nationwide. In 1984, he would improve that number to 37 percent. In Texas, Reagan carried many of the state's most heavily Hispanic counties in South and West Texas—particularly Cameron and El Paso counties. In California, his home state, Reagan opened nine Hispanic field offices after his campaign produced poll numbers showing him leading Mondale with Hispanics.[18] He was going to win California either way, but he was looking to the future, to the opportunity to bring more Latinos into the fold.

"Reagan really energized a lot of Latinos and Hispanics that just were not part of the process before and felt this surge of enthusiasm to get on the Reagan bandwagon," says Estrada. "It was almost more of a personal following . . . the people he brought into the Republican fold were not saying, I woke up this morning and I saw the light and I believe in all the Republican philosophy in every issue. On the Hispanic side, it was much more of a personal connection to Reagan than one of party loyalty. There was some spillover, some continued to support Bush when he ran for President."

Tower's Hispanic strategy became a model for other Republicans, especially in the Southwest. Sen. John McCain of Arizona cruised to reelection in 2004, and as he did so he reeled in 74 percent of the Hispanic votes. "Tower counseled [McCain] early on, telling him don't write off the Hispanic vote. In fact that can be your margin of victory—as Tower always felt it was in close elections," says Estrada.

In neighboring New Mexico, Pete Domenici was elected to the U.S. Senate in 1972 and has gone on to be one of the classic examples of a social-conservative senator who aggressively reaches out to Hispanics and wins their votes. As liberal pundit Al Hunt noted in 2000, "no Anglo politician in America has done better with Hispanic voters than Pete Domenici."[19]

Today, Domenici is a grandfatherly figure beloved among Hispanics and most other people in the state. But that trust wasn't built overnight. His long-standing commitment to recruiting and funding Hispanic Republican candidates has gone beyond the call of duty—and it is also common sense, since New Mexico has the highest percentage of Hispanics of any state. When Republicans wanted to pressure Democrats to give Miguel Estrada a confirmation vote for a judicial appointment in 2002, they sent Domenici out as one of their spokesman.

Tower's Latino Strategy has culminated with George W. Bush. Dubya, who likes to tell Latino audiences, "*Mi corazon es Hispana*" ("My heart is Hispanic"), would be the first Texas governor to break the Democrats' lock on the Texas Hispanic vote. "Bush changed the way the Latino vote was going to be perceived forever," says Democratic pollster Sergio Bendixen. "Bush broke the mold."[20]

There was a lot more to it than the fact that Bush spoke pretty decent (if sometimes badly accented) Spanish, although that did help. Bush, who unlike his father had grown up in Texas, went out of his way to show his concern for the Latino community.

Immediately after his election in 1994, the Texas governor rejected attempts by some Republicans to extend anti-immigration measures such as California's Proposition 187 into his state. That landmark proposition had cut off funding for education, non-emergency healthcare, and other state services for illegal immigrants until it was struck down by a federal judge. Its campaign had caused a massive alienation of California Hispanics from the Republican Party that has never been healed.

Bush took his state party in a different direction. After the 1994 election, the new governor quickly called a press conference to announce that he was not interested in such measures. A recent article in the *Los Angeles Times* documents a 1994 post-election confrontation between Bush and California Gov. Pete Wilson over Proposition 187. Wilson had just successfully used the anti-immigration measure to help his own flagging reelection campaign.

> Rather than applaud Wilson's support of Proposition 187 as a deft move, Bush told Wilson to his face—and in front of other governors—that it was a disaster. "He really minced no words," recalled former Michigan Gov. John Engler, who witnessed the exchange. "He told Wilson, 'You're wrong,' and that it was . . . a catastrophic position. He was very clear. He felt that Wilson had made the issue one where it had become an anti-Hispanic issue rather than a solution to illegal immigration."[21]

Meanwhile, Bush cut taxes and implemented a tough welfare reform measure that required recipients to work. As he would later on the federal

Figure 2.4 Hispanic Vote: Timeline of Key GOP Events (1970–2006)

1970 Manuel Lujan, Jr., first Hispanic Republican from New Mexico wins second term
For first time, U.S. Census includes self-identification questions on Hispanic origin
Nixon transforms Inter-Agency Committee on Mexican American Affairs into the Cabinet Committee on Opportunities for Spanish-Speaking People

1972 *Latino vote*: Nixon 35% vs. McGovern 63%
Nixon introduces "Hispanic Strategy" to woo Hispanic voters

1974 RNC chairman George H.W. Bush forms Republican National Hispanic Assembly

1976 *Latino vote*: Ford 24% vs. Carter 76%

1980 *Latino vote*: Reagan 33% vs. Carter 59% vs. Anderson 6%
Reagan's optimistic message of hope and conservatism appeals to Hispanics

1984 *Latino vote*: Reagan 37% vs. Mondale 62%
Reagan wins with strong Hispanic support

1986 The Immigration Reform and Control Act supported by Reagan allowed blanket amnesty for 2.7 million illegal aliens
Bob Martinez of Florida becomes first American governor of Cuban descent

1987 Proposition 187 in California passes with over 50% of vote; cuts funding for education, non-emergency health care, and other state services for illegal immigrants; backfires politically

1988 Reagan nominates Lauro Cavazos to be first Hispanic U.S. cabinet official
Latino vote: Bush 30% vs. Dukakis 69%
George H.W. Bush wins in continuation of Reagan legacy; however start of 12-year trend in decline of Hispanic support for GOP presidential candidates

1989 Ileana Ros-Lehtinen becomes first Hispanic female member of Congress

1992 *Latino vote*: Bush 25% vs. Clinton 61% vs. Perot 14%
Henry Bonilla becomes first Hispanic Republican congressman from Texas

1994 GOP takeover of Congress promises conservative agenda, but GOP still has only three Hispanic Members of Congress
Robert J. Dole is GOP nominee; 1950s-type campaign unappealing to Hispanics

1996 *Latino vote*: Dole 21% vs. Clinton 72% vs. Perot 6%
GOP Congress approves federal charter for American GI Forum

1999 Candidate George W. Bush introduces pro-Hispanic platform

**1999
2000** First major Hispanic surveys undertaken by the RNC

2000 *Latino vote*: George W. Bush 35% vs. Gore 62%
Largest RNC & Bush campaign investment in Hispanic vote ($5 million); Bush percentage of Hispanic vote highest recorded

**2000–
2004** Bush makes series of Hispanic appointments to high level cabinet posts

2003 Hispanics eclipse African Americans as largest minority group

2004 *Latino vote*: George W. Bush 44% vs. Kerry 53%

2006 Harsh anti-immigration rhetoric contributes to Democratic takeover of Congress
Florida Senator Mel Martinez named first Hispanic chairman of Republican Party

level, he increased state public education spending and money for bilingual programs, but he also worked to enact a school choice program that would give students in the lowest performing schools—most of them African Americans and Hispanics—a way out.

Bush won reelection easily in 1998, and he earned an impressive 49 percent of the Latino vote. This is the highest number yet for Texas Republicans, and the highest number Bush has achieved to date among Hispanics. Still, Bush's later performance with Hispanics as a presidential candidate would be even more impressive, because in both of his nationwide elections, he did well among Hispanics even as he was winning by narrow margins overall.

Bush's father created the Republican National Hispanic Assembly when he chaired the RNC in 1974, but it was his sons George and Jeb who would finally bring Hispanic Republicanism to its high point.

*   *   *

Republican scoffers should not underestimate Hispanics, but if they do then I hope that what they see in this book will cause them to reconsider. Just 30 years ago, the South was overwhelmingly Democratic, but a realignment has turned it into the Republican Party's most solid base constituency. Such realignments do take place over time. And already, we have seen evidence that Republicans can win Hispanic votes—something we will discuss later in more detail with a closer look at Bush's 2000 and 2004 victories.

In their 2002 book *The Emerging Democratic Majority*, John Judis and Ruy Texeira argued that Latinos, women and professionals would be the groups that delivered Democrats an unbreakable long-term majority like the one they enjoyed after the Great Depression. But the presidential election results above already show a chink in the Democrats' Latino armor, as do the stories of growing success by GOP candidates among Hispanics in various states.

"They assume that because you're Hispanic, and Hispanics are lower income, they'll all vote Democrat," says Lance Tarrance, referring to Texeira and Judis. "It's an arrogant viewpoint that all you have to do is give

Hispanics a little money and some social programs and they'll all vote for Democrats."

After that book was written, a Republican White House won a strong 44 percent of Latinos by appealing to us as *individuals* who have similar characteristics, rather than as a single group that can be bought with goodies. Given that women and "professionals" are not becoming demonstrably more Democratic over the long run, the emerging Democratic majority lives or dies with the Hispanic vote. Unless Latinos let them have that majority, that majority does not exist.

three

the latino moment

Carlos M. Gutierrez, Secretary of the U.S. Department of Commerce, on his rise from truck driver to CEO of Kellogg Company, and the Latino identity

I had a general idea that I wanted to go into business. My father was in the food industry so I thought food would be a good business. I decided to start from wherever I could get in, which was the bottom, and then work as hard as I could with the objective of doing the best job possible at whatever job I had. I didn't start shooting for the top from the very first day, but I did try to do my very best. . . .

I think that there is a practicality that is very much part of the Latino experience. Perhaps this is a historical practice or something that just happens because of how their countries are, and how they get things done. But I do find that there is a very practical philosophy and a practical approach to things that serve Latinos very well. . . .

I believe the bilingual and bicultural opportunities of Latinos will be very important in a world where speaking more than one language is important. The first thing one has to do is speak English. As the President has said before, it then becomes English plus. And that's a huge advantage Latinos have, because businesses are more and more global.

I believe because Latinos grow up in two cultures essentially, that when they deal with foreign executives or with foreign governments, they are more capable of recognizing cultural differences and understanding that the world is not made up of one culture. I think Latinos have from the very start: hard work, the hunger to get ahead, a certain loyalty to a cause, and a certain level of moral values, a commitment to family, a commitment to stability, a commitment to tradition.

When I came to the U.S. I did not speak English. So it was a bell hop [who taught me] at a hotel in Miami Beach called the Richmond Hotel. I remember he was a middle-aged man, and he used to take time to teach us English words, and we practiced with him . . . one time he took a rubber band out of his pocket and he said, "Rubber band. Repeat after me." That was one word, I don't know why I remember that.

I believe that the values of the Republican Party are very consistent with what Hispanics seek. I believe there is the desire to conserve certain practices, certain traditions, and so I think by nature we are conservative. I also believe because of the experience many of us have had in other countries, we tend to be suspicious of big government and suspicious of solutions that come from big government, therefore we embrace the ideas of lower taxes and smaller government, which allow us to be individuals and allow us to pursue our individual freedom through individual responsibility. I also believe that because of our entrepreneurial nature that there is a tendency toward small businesses, so we have something to pass on to our children. The Republican Party wants to create an environment where businesses can flourish and do well. We do not want to punish those, whether it's through death taxes or regulation, who have accomplished the American dream.

> Our cultures are ingrained in us because they have to be. It's a belief that if we don't preserve our culture it's going to get lost. I think the first generations feel the pressure most. You may not like the way your mom dresses, but you owe it to the mother country. She did teach you the culture of a country that was left behind because they came here and made sacrifices. They want you to remember this country that taught you traditions and taught you values. Maybe it's mom propaganda. You're not just breaking your mama's heart, you're letting down an entire country if you don't remember how to make a tortilla.
>
> —*Cathy Areu, author and founder of* Catalina *magazine*

Not only are Latinos thriving in this country, but we've actually become *avant-garde*—we're "where it's at!" Everyone else wants to be like us. How else could salsa have become the new ketchup? Why else would folks in Kentucky celebrate *Cinco de Mayo*?

Not only is everyone eating our food, they're learning our parents' language, they're listening to our music, they're dancing our dances. Take a trip to Adams Morgan, a trendy Washington, D.C. neighborhood, and you can get ten-dollar salsa lessons from an excellent instructor—who happens to be Persian! The new *salseros* are people who don't have so much as a Latin twig anywhere in their family trees.

Gone are the days when Hispanic actors like Ramon Estevez (now known as Martin Sheen) changed their names to fit into the American mainstream. Americans are eagerly watching and reading about famous Hispanics, whether it's the glamorous J-Lo in the *New York Post's* Page Six, the accomplished A-Rod in the sports section, the powerful Carlos Gutierrez in the business section, or Attorney General Alberto Gonzales on page one.

The country's largest Hispanic food company, Goya Foods, has introduced 400 new products in the last two years because they find themselves suddenly catering to people of 23 different Hispanic nationalities in the United States. Eighty billion tortillas are sold each year in the United States. In Lexington, Nebraska, the Hy-Vee grocery store sells more *pan dulce* than it does bread, eggs or milk.

One could describe today's America as being in a "season of self-identity." We have gone through generations of integration between various waves of immigrants from numerous countries, so that race and heritage matter less than they ever have before. Yet everyone is suddenly returning to their roots—proud to be Irish! *Viva Italia*!

Sure, this sometimes has absurd results and encourages a misguided "multiculturalist" curriculum in schools. But it also brings back many legitimate ethnic traditions that had fallen off over the years. The effect of this is amplified among Latinos, because we are the only group in America that is being constantly and massively replenished by new arrivals of still-unassimilated immigrants. America never shared a territorial land border with the homelands of previous waves of immigrants, nor did there exist the technological ability to communicate instantly with the old country. Now that's all changed. As much as we assimilate—to two and three and five generations—our culture refuses to fade away.

Now America is embracing our cultural heritage, and likewise *fully assimilated* Hispanics are becoming interested in learning Spanish again, in recovering what is unique about Latin American culture. Call us the "born-again Hispanics."

We are not, as Pat Buchanan suggests, "dissimilating," "balkanizing," or refusing to become Americans. Nor are we, as Univision commentator Jorge Ramos wishes, losing the various identities of our families' nations of origin—Mexicans, Cubans, Salvadorans—so as to become "a united front"[1] of generic "Hispanics" or "Latinos" that work together as a racial group to maximize our political power as a whole.

The studies actually show that Hispanic voters are assimilating, and especially learning English.[2] In 1999, our Hispanic strategy group at the Republican National Committee conducted a study in which we found that even though just 60 percent of Hispanic voters say they were born in the United States, *80 percent of them prefer English* to Spanish in their political communities.[3] We also found that although 56 percent of Hispanic voters speak to their parents only in Spanish, just 28 percent say the same of their conversations with their children—a sign of generational acculturation.[4] And overall, Latinos are intermarrying seamlessly: Between one-fourth and one-third marry non-Hispanics today.[5]

The phenomenon we see with Latinos reaching back to their roots is something totally different from dissimilation. These are educated people who speak perfect English and are proud to be American, but their cultural heritage keeps reasserting itself in their daily lives. Other groups came from a snapshot in time—as the Irish fled the potato famine, the Jews fled the czar and later Hitler. Latinos, on the other hand, just keep coming, not as in a snapshot, but as in a *telenovela*. And we are not the peasant army that Tom Tancredo sees descending on the Rio Grande, with the aim of seizing the American Southwest and returning it to Mexico. Rather, as the numbers and trends show, we are the vanguard of America's economic growth and an emerging force in her middle class, a growing population that cannot be controlled either by Mexico City or Washington, D.C.

Karen Fourquet is not Hispanic but is married to one. A former CIA operative and now a stay-at-home mom, she sees a very different picture of America's transformation: "Some who do not have much interaction with the Latin culture are afraid that no one is going to be able to communicate with them. They don't realize that most of these businessmen also speak English. They're choosing Spanish because if it's a common language, it's comfortable. This goes back to raising the children to be bilingual. I have a relative who said, 'Just make sure I can always talk with your kids.' She was worried about them learning Spanish, which is ridiculous. Of course they will speak both languages perfectly."

As Latinos, we are living in reverse. Or rather, we are moving forward in a way no other ethnic immigrant group before us has done. As America becomes more like us, we are straddling two cultures, finding a way to become both more American *and* more Latino at the same time. We don't get the high-powered job and then forget where we came from—we get the job, and then we still lapse into Spanglish when we're just among friends.

Cid Wilson, a top Wall Street analyst and president of the Dominican American National Roundtable, says that his experience in the financial world has never made him forget his black-Hispanic background. "It really wasn't until college that I started to study it more and learned that it was okay to embrace both your Latino and African heritage," he says. "I may be in a surrounding that is truly color blind, but you're always going to be conscious that you always need to be excellent or outstanding at what you do." Before rising to become *Forbes*'s top-rated retail analyst, Wilson got his start in the mailroom of Paine Webber. "It has allowed me not to take my success for granted . . . and when others are coming up, it has made me a little more likely to help out that other minority, Latino or African American, who may be trying to get an internship."

what makes us tick

Given our demographic ascendancy in America, it's no surprise that marketers have jumped all over us, trying to figure out how to make a buck selling to us. As our numbers grew in the 1990s, the idea of defining a "Hispanic identity" became profitable. Companies saw a market that was growing fast, and wanted to find out how to service it.

The marketers were at first frustrated by our diversity, because we were so difficult to define. We come from so many different cultures and geographical locations that even the terms "Hispanic" and "Latino" can at times seem a bit misleading.

"Latino identity is as complex and, perhaps, as fragmented as the general market," Hispanic marketer Carl Kravetz told a convention of Latino marketers in Miami last September. "One would not define all American consumers across the nation with a one or two dimensional segmentation model, so why should it be acceptable to do so for Latino consumers?"[6]

Still, there are important commonalities. Or more accurately, as the marketers put it, there are key things that make Hispanics *different* from the rest of the U.S. population. The Association of Hispanic Advertising Agencies (AHAA), Kravetz's group, had commissioned a massive study on Latino identity, and came up with some very insightful conclusions.

The study, called the Latino Identity Project, dissected and described Hispanic cultural attitudes in a number of ways. Most importantly, it said the time was right to move away from just considering the use of Spanish and the process of acculturation as the primary ways to define what it is to be Latino. *Finally*.

Far beyond these incidental qualities of Hispanics, Kravetz contends that we are wired differently from other groups. I would emphasize the study's attempt to describe us in terms of our strong commitments to our families and our faith, and the strong, collective sense of community we share. This all rings true when I think back to my childhood, of growing up in South Texas in a community that held faith and family so dear. The marketers may have been driven by a desire for higher profits, but this forced them to devote serious resources to finding a core set of values that is particularly acute among Hispanics as a group, regardless of our nationality or origin.

The study is fascinating, and many of the conclusions make me laugh and nod in agreement. Kravetz, offering a summary, noted that Latinos tend to:

- Consider time commitments as more of a goal than real commitments.
- Change plans often and easily.
- Care about close friends and relatives more than privacy.
- Are more involved with each other, interact frequently.
- Casually touch each other with ease.

So, do you know any Latinos who fit this description?

To return to the big ideas, the study identifies *familismo*, faith, and collectivism as key parts of our identity. It also notes that it is not just the presence of these qualities that gives us our uniqueness—it is their simultaneous presence in the same person. As they put it: "While there are qualities of Latino cultural identity that may be familiar to us . . . things like collectivism, *familismo*, or *simpatia*, it's the interconnectedness, and not the simple presence, of these attributes that challenges our conventional view of what makes a Latino Latino."

It is impossible to describe an entire people in a paragraph, a chapter, or even a book. But the conclusions of this study ring true for me, and I believe they will ring a bell for anyone who knows some of us well.

The study is seminal because it moves beyond the simple ideas of acculturation and language as identifiers of who is a Latino. But as we try to apply this description to Hispanics in the political arena, we also must include one other characteristic that some fail to recognize in us: As a group, we are tremendously entrepreneurial. Like other ethnic groups that preceded us, arriving in the United States in large numbers, we are making our way economically, and doing it with great speed and success.

* * *

Political scientists like to talk about what motivates people to vote, and to vote one way or the other. Some people and groups vote differently depending on their income, or the amount they have invested in the financial markets. Voters tend to be different depending on their level of education and frequency of attendance at their churches, synagogues and mosques. We also divide voters according to their religion, their race or ethnicity, and their membership in various social and business communities.

Sometimes we say that people vote according to their "self-interest," but this short-changes the American voter. The wealthy often vote against their self-interest, for example, out of concern for their neighbors who are less fortunate. Many people who don't own guns still support the NRA's candidates because they believe in the Second Amendment. Many poor people rarely support Democrats just because of their stance on abortion. Many rich suburbanites rarely support Republicans for the opposite reason.

The element at the heart of it all is not mere self-interest. People vote their *lifestyles*. What I hope to do here is describe the Latino lifestyle as well as I can in just a few short pages. The AHAA study partly describes the Latino lifestyle as a heart with four chambers. Their version is slightly different, but for political purposes the diagram looks like Figure 3.1.

Of course, none of these attributes are unique to Hispanics in and of themselves. One would expect (or at least hope) that everyone cares about their families, has some community sense, and is entrepreneurial to some

Figure 3.1 "Hispanic Heart"

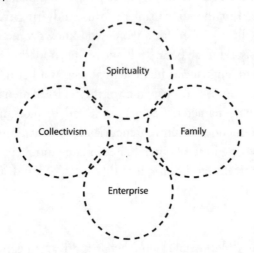

degree. Rather, like the marketers, I am arguing that these lifestyle-features are more *interconnected*, and in some cases also more acute in the lifestyle we attribute to Hispanics as a group. Again, one can make only so much of generalizations about a large group of people, but since we are studying the Hispanic vote, we must draw some conclusions from them.

Let us take a look at each chamber of this "Hispanic Heart."

spirituality

"Religion and spirituality influence nearly every aspect of U.S. Latino life, and they affect how Latinos see the world," Kravetz told his audience of advertising execs in Miami. "From Catholicism we acquire Fatalism and External Attribution. . . . And rituals and celebrations are as much a part of a young Latina's dreams for her *quinceañera* ["sweet 15" birthday celebration] as they are about *abuela*'s [grandmother's] annual pilgrimage to visit *Nuestra Señora de la Divina Providencia*."

The phrase "*lo que Dios quiere*" (it's in God's hands) goes back centuries, and is still a common utterance in the Spanish-speaking world. The Arab-influenced Spanish word "*ojalá*,"—usually translated as "hopefully"—has a similar origin: "may God will it." Even our language suggests that God is a central part of Latinos' lives.

There is no question about the importance of faith among American Hispanics, who attend church very frequently—66 percent of us attend church at least once a month, compared to 54 percent of Americans overall.[7]

Christianity has a long and rich history in Latin America. It was first brought by Spanish conquerors, and many Indian conversions to Catholicism came early. But the *Santa Fe* (holy faith) really began to spread after 1531, when a middle-aged Indian Christian peasant, St. Juan Diego, received an apparition of the Virgin Mary in modern-day Mexico City. After promising him a sign, *la Virgen* sent him to the top of Tepeyac hill to pick roses—which should not have been growing there in the middle of December—and bring them to the local bishop. Juan Diego folded the roses into his *tilma*, an external peasant cloak, and carried them back to the city. But when he unfurled the cloak before the bishop, letting the roses fall to the ground, he got a much greater miracle than he'd bargained for. The Virgin Mary had emblazoned her now-famous image on his *tilma*, incorporating various Aztec colors and symbols.

Millions converted to Catholicism after the historic event, and Our Lady of Guadalupe still holds a place of incredible importance throughout Latin America.[8] The poor peasant garment remains well preserved after nearly 500 years and an attempt by anti-Catholic extremists to destroy it with a bomb in 1921. *La Virgen* is still on display at Mexico City's basilica, but it has meaning far outside of Mexico. For Latinos, her image has become the symbol of an entire continent. Even Hispanics who become Protestants often continue to keep their images of *La Virgen* on display—many of their Protestant *churches* display her image.

In the centuries following the apparition, the common religion of the Spanish and the Indians acted as a soothing influence, allowing for a much more harmonious interrelationship than the English had with the North American natives they conquered and eventually sequestered on reservations. Various Spanish missionaries, such as Bishop Vasco de Quiroga, raised hell in order to prevent at least some of the abuses they saw and protect Indians' rights under Spanish rule. With a common faith, intermarriage also came fairly easily between Spaniards and Indians, so that a vast *mestizo* population arose.

After independence from Spain, various governments—particularly the socialist government that seized power in Mexico in the early twentieth century—tried to stifle religious expression by persecuting believers. Graham Greene's famous novel, *The Power and the Glory*, tells the story of the ruthless Mexican governor of Tabasco, who offered every Catholic priest just three choices: marry, leave, or die. Without priests, he hoped, the Christians would give up and become believers in "reason" and "science." But as often happens, the faith of believers was strengthened under persecution. Eventually, after the strong-arm tactics backfired and the regime was threatened with possible collapse by the armed *Cristero* resistance movement, the Mexican government backed away from enforcing its anti-Catholic statutes and returned to its usual practice of corruption and plunder. In subsequent decades, revolutionaries in Latin America—even the Marxist ones—would carefully avoid falling afoul of the Catholic Church.

Today, this innately conservative religious influence lives on, although in various forms. In the United States, surveys suggest that 70 percent of Latinos are Catholic, translating into 29 million Latino Catholics (compared to 22 million white mainline Protestants).[9]

A new manifestation of the Latino faith experience comes in the form of charismatic Catholics, which constitute 22 percent of U.S. Latino Catholics, and Hispanic Evangelicals. That is not a misprint: an estimated 37 percent (14.2 million) of all Latino Protestants *and Catholics* say they have been "born again" or are "Evangelical."[10] The lines are often blurred: It is not uncommon for Latino families to attend Protestant Church on Sunday morning and then to show up in the evening for Catholic mass.

Unlike the African American community, which has been historically mobilized vertically by an array of great Baptist and Pentecostal preachers and civil rights activists, the Hispanic community is interconnected horizontally along ethnic and geographic lines. The Catholic Church's lack of political grassroots activism is part of the reason for that difference. It has made it difficult to bring disparate ethnic groups to act upon a single set of ideas. But this is slowly changing as Hispanic churches become more involved in calling their members to action.

This movement is young, earning its genesis with the release of the 2000 Census data indicating for the first time that Hispanics were on the verge of becoming America's largest minority. The combination of a demonstrated market among Latinos, increased capital for faith-based institutions, and a new generation of Hispanics with the training and credentials for such a task, formed the first crop of Hispanic American preachers who combine a Pentecostal flavor with social concerns in their daily evangelism. The result is potent and viral; and more importantly, a connection can be made in people's lives between faith and practicality.

Additionally, both the Catholic Church and Latino evangelical churches are active in outreach to gang members and in providing faith-based social action programs. It is another sign of the unique importance of faith for Latinos that even the worst among us—the bloodthirsty MS-13 gang-bangers—will let members leave the gang if they experience a religious conversion. The other way out of the gang is death—the *only* way out of most gangs.

collectivism

As a child in south Texas, I thought I was related to everyone. At the market: "That's your *Tio* Chalito." At the movies, "See your cousins Gracie and Inez?" Driving down the street, "That car used to belong to your Aunt Maria. It's probably her; let's catch up and see!" It was life through the lens of community, and—though I was very young—I had a holistic sense that we thought as a group rather than as individuals. One person's success was considered everyone's: if someone went to college, we had *all* made it in, too.

We laughed when my friend Maria Perez Brown, a native of Puerto Rico and creator of Nickelodeon's hit show *Taina*, said her mother proudly announced to her entire neighborhood her daughter's major accomplishment. "My daughter is going to jail! She's into jail!" After a few minutes of confusion, Maria stepped in to clarify her mother's thick Spanglish accent, "Yale, *mami*, Yale!"

We would celebrate every occasion—birthdays (piñata in tow), births, baptisms, weddings, graduations—together with this endless sea of friends, extended family, cousins and godparents (*compradres*) who were the fabric of life in a predominately Mexican coastal town. We met at Sunday afternoon backyard barbecues (often called "*panchangas*") or held potluck dinners in any public park we could find with an outdoor grill. The mothers conversed in Spanglish and opened plastic containers of *arroz con pollo*, refried beans and loaves of Wonderbread. The men stood by the coolers of beer, and above them the air was awash in the thick, sweet smell of their heavily applied cologne.

We were proud of our heritage, and of the contributions of our great Mexican or Indian ancestors past who carved this new America. Late at night (after a few *cervezas*) the men would proudly narrate what could only be described as Tejano folklore, each trying to add to the mosaic.

"You know, our family had one of the original land grants in Texas," one would say. "We lost it in a poker match."

"Well, my father was a ranch hand on the King Ranch, mending fence posts," says another.

"Well we're part Indian and we were here before any of you!" quips yet another.

A friend of mine once went to drop off his business associate at the San Antonio airport. The man walked in and saw a massive crowd near the security check and said, "I'll never make it."

"Relax," said the Texas native. "That's one guy leaving and 20 cousins here to say goodbye."

Our strong collective sensibility also shows up in the attitude of established Hispanics in the United States toward the new Latino immigrants. Often, we are the ones hurt the most by mass immigration in economic terms. More often than not, at least in Texas, the impoverished *colonias* of the newcomers spring up near our more established Hispanic neighborhoods and bring down our property values. There's all kinds of grumbling, to be sure—even immigrant-bashing among Latinos who have been here longer and found a way to fit in. But most of the same Latinos who put down the newcomers become livid if they hear a non-Hispanic person saying exactly the same things!

The marketers, with lots of money on the line, came up with the bullet points I mentioned earlier, including our famous disregard of personal space. "Think about the first time you tried to kiss an Anglo client hello!" Kravetz quipped in his Miami presentation.

Kravetz broadly contrasted our collective sense with the values that other groups tend to live by:

> Compare this to one of the key non-Latino American core values: individualism, in which equality, self-development, and self-expression take precedence over key values for Latinos such as cooperation and cooperative approaches; and familial needs vs. individual needs. Ours is a collectivist culture in which the goals and interests of the group are emphasized over those of individual members.

In politics, this plays out in a number of ways. When I conduct studies on Latino voters, I try to talk to them about why they believe one way or another, and about how people view the political parties. I have found that rather than developing into a policy discussion about lower taxes or the environment, this question often triggers a personal, emotional reaction. It often becomes a question of how inclusive, how welcoming or how friendly a party is, even more than a conversation about the ideas the parties espouse. As the activists would say, it's an issue of how they treat the *community*.

la familia

When President Bush made a nine-point gain among Hispanics in 2004, Sen. Pete Domenici described it in terms of family issues: "Values, values, values—that's what happened. And I mean—by values, I mean the things I've been talking about: marriage, family."

This is the sort of thing we usually discuss in American politics when we talk about the family, and it is worth mentioning with regard to Latinos in terms of statistics and poll numbers—even if it is just a small part of the picture. One of the major social ills in the Hispanic community today is the high rate of out-of-wedlock births among young Latinas. To some degree, we share with the black community this indicator of familial breakdown that was dramatically identified by the famous Moynihan Report of 1965.[11] Yet, Latinas are also the group most likely to marry their baby's father. According to a recent Gallup survey, 57 percent of Hispanics are married, compared to 65 percent of whites and 41 percent of blacks.[12] In fact, the percentage of married Hispanics is actually lowered by the high number of single migrant laborers from Latin America.

Hispanics are also far more likely than whites to believe that it is important that unwed parents legally marry—only 45 percent of whites believe that, compared to 58 percent of Hispanics.[13] Latinos also tend to hold the opinion that a man and a woman should marry if they intend to live together—64 percent of Hispanics hold this view, compared to just 51 percent of whites.[14]

But there is so much more to the deep-seated Latino concept of the family than just the "family values issues" we commonly discuss in American politics. This isn't just about Latino support for the traditional institution of the family and a rejection of alternatives to it.

The bond of *familia* is strong. What else could motivate some of these Mexican men to live ten to an apartment, so that they can afford to send a larger portion of their wages as day laborers back home to their wives and children via Western Union? Mexicans alone sent $20 *billion* home in 2005!

The bond of *familia* is lasting. According to the U.S. Census, 65 percent of minor Hispanic children live with both parents, compared to a national average of 67 percent—a clear sign that the Latino family is as healthy as that of any other group in America. Latinos in the United States are also less likely to be divorced (my own parents' experience notwithstanding). Only 6 percent of American Latino men are divorced, according to the U.S. Census, compared to 9.2 percent of non-Hispanic white men and 9.5 percent of black men. A similar difference exists among women.[15] Hispanics are also more likely to want their children to live with the family until they marry. In most Spanish-speaking countries, that's the way it's still done!

The bond of *familia* is warm. I think of my mother's effortless ability to make all of us feel included. At Christmas dinner, Mom finds it essential to prepare *everyone's* favorites. The small dinner table is crowded with all traditional foods: turkey, cornbread stuffing, cranberry sauce (from a can), and everything else she knows how to make: four types of spicy tamales, enchiladas, a ham, coconut cream pie and the ubiquitous fruit salad. This combination leaves us all with that special feeling inside: indigestion.

The bond of *familia* is also protective—sometimes overprotective, like a coddling mother who never wants her children to suffer. This also reminds me of my mother, of the times she would avoid telling us that our furniture was about to be repossessed. This side of the family can at times be dark, triggering our defense mechanisms—instilling in us the fear that there is someone out there trying to hurt our family.

enterprise

We've all seen the stereotype of the lazy Mexican on television, lounging in the desert sun with his sombrero covering his face. But one place you probably haven't seen that stereotypical figure is in real life. Walk out your door in any major U.S. city and you'll see plenty of Mexicans, but they are sombrero-free, and they're less likely to be lying about than laying bricks, loading trucks, hanging drywall, welding, washing windows or selling drinks.

Walk into a few shops and you'll probably see Hispanics running them, perhaps with our families—owning many of them and reaping their profits. And it's not just the *taquerias* any more, we run every kind of business in every part of the country, from David C. Lizárraga's TELACU, a Community Development Corporation (CDC) in Los Angeles (named the forty-fourth largest Hispanic business in the United States) to Jose's Lawn Care in Tacoma, Washington, to my firm, Impacto Group in Washington, D.C. We own furniture stores, sporting goods stores, construction firms, law and consulting practices, banks and tech companies. Increasingly, you've even probably seen some of us on television—not just Univision and Telemundo, but network and cable news, sitcoms, reality shows and even touting financial news on CNBC.

We're not just losing the sombreros, we're exploding all of the stereotypes. As we grow in population, we are also building serious wealth—buying homes, opening bank accounts and small businesses, investing. We are surging into America's middle class.

In 2002, there were 1.6 million Hispanic-owned businesses in the United States, providing work for more than 1.5 million employees on payroll and 1.3 million more go-it-alone business owners (not to mention their family members).[16] Between 1997 and 2002, new Hispanic-owned businesses cropped up at a rate of 31 percent, more than three times the rate of businesses nationwide. In 2002, nearly 30,000 Hispanic businesses had annual receipts of $1 million or more, and 1,510 employed more than

100 people. Hispanic-owned businesses generated $222 billion in revenue in 2002, according the U.S. Census Bureau—nearly one-third of Mexico's gross domestic product for 2005.

Many Hispanics who are not building wealth in businesses are instead building wealth through homeownership. At 49.7 percent, the Hispanic homeownership rate stood near its all-time high in the third quarter of 2006.

Even though the newest arrivals drag down the numbers, we are making money and building wealth. We have also grown in our understanding of financial and economic issues affecting our lives. According to the Hispanic Business Roundtable survey of 2000.[17] Among Hispanics surveyed

- 43 percent reported having a 401(k) or an IRA.
- 69 percent favored an IRA-type Social Security Reform program with personal accounts.
- 56 percent said that taxes are too high.
- 53 percent said that reducing taxes is "very important" in deciding whom to vote for this year.

In his new book, *One Nation, One Standard* (2006), former Rep. Herman Badillo argues that Hispanics are failing in the United States—an honest impression surely colored by his experiences in the Bronx, one of the toughest places in America to raise a family. A leader in New York's Puerto Rican community, he makes a compelling case about the sorry state of education in our community. Hispanics suffer many social ills, including a proclivity toward births out of wedlock and an increasing number of Latino high-school dropouts.[18] But our situation is not even impossible there—40 to 50 percent of U.S.-born Mexican Americans are now attending at least one year of college, by some estimates.[19] And in economic terms, the Latino future is very bright indeed.

Hispanic unemployment last spring stood at an astoundingly low 4.9 percent, down from 7 percent in 2004, with Latinos comprising 40 percent of all newly employed workers.[20] At $433 per week in median wages, Hispanics are still at the bottom of the pile, but we've come up a long way. Our low unemployment level and low median age (27 years, as opposed to 31 for Blacks and 36 overall) partly explain our lower average wages. That average is also reduced sharply by the new arrivals, who make on average just $389 per week. In 2006, native-born Hispanics tied blacks in wages with $487.[21]

"I think anyone willing to walk 40 miles through blazing Arizona desert to get to a job interview is the kind of highly motivated employee you want to find," writes one blogger, weighing in on the immigration issue.[22] This applies regardless of one's view on immigration. Even if we'd rather not see Juan break the law to get here, his ambition and willingness to take a risk at least make him the *right kind of guy* for America.

Most of us have never made that crossing, but the death-defying border crossers embody Latinos' cultural optimism and our sense of enterprise. What is it but enterprising to take the bold step of leaving a bleak situation, at great personal risk, just to improve one's life? In that light, it's no surprise that Mexican citizens living in the United States cast their absentee ballots overwhelmingly for the free-market conservative candidate, Felipe Calderon, in the 2006 Mexican presidential elections. Nor is it odd that new immigrant Latinos make up one-third of self-identified Latino Republicans (34 percent) but only one-quarter of self-identified Latino Democrats (26 percent).[23] By comparison, the largest percentage of Latinos who consider themselves Independents (77 percent) are native born.

We get some of the most driven and entrepreneurial people our neighbors to the South have to offer. Millions of eager workers are fleeing the heavily regulated economic systems of their homelands, where bureaucracy and corruption have excluded them from the world's economic life. They are fleeing a failing barren successor economy to the failed Spanish feudal system, in which peasants tended the lands of their patrons in exchange for their housing, food, and everything they needed to survive.

"If you're poor, there's no work," explains Miguel Prado, a naturalized U.S. citizen from Peru who now runs La Asociacion Nacional de Inmigrantes. "You can't own a car because there's no credit, and you can't get title to your land because they won't give it to you."

Prado, whose nonprofit group works with the Catholic Church to offer legal help and sell medicines and educational materials at cost to the poorest new immigrants, says that the backward economic systems in many Latin American countries stifle the economic opportunities of a people that is in fact very enterprising. The result is a black-market, cash-based economy that fails to reward (and therefore to encourage) economic risk-taking. With the bureaucratic strictures and the corruption in some countries, it can take months or even years to start a business legally, so that millions are left behind in subsistence agriculture and have no way out.

Peruvian economist Hernando de Soto describes the phenomenon in a similar way for Latin America and the world:

> Two thirds of the world population, four billion people, are locked out of the capitalist system. They want to participate, but they can't, because participating means being able to make safe contracts with everybody, being able to get credit, having an identity that will be recognized on a broad scale throughout the world, and the possibility to organize production so that they can enter foreign markets.[24]

Even in this area, Republicans have so much to offer the more recently arrived Hispanic Americans who care about their families' country of origin. By opening our markets to Latin America—particularly our closed agricultural markets—we could improve our neighbors' situation and partly obviate the need for mass immigration to the United States. We would also be creating a huge job market for bilingual U.S. Hispanics, whose cultural and linguistic understanding helps them build bridges in international trade.

But these are reforms that the Democrats have decided in recent years to oppose *en bloc* for purely political reasons, under the pretext of labor or environmental concerns. In fact they are catering to their unionist supporters and well-moneyed special agricultural interest groups, at the expense of Latin American economic development.

As much as the immigration hawks disagree, new Latinos do not come here just to get something—to have it handed to them. Even the ones that do get something for free are not getting that much—certainly not enough for them to survive, as nearly all of it comes in the form of medical services. In 2001, fewer than one percent of illegal immigrant-headed households received Temporary Aid for Needy Families—what we properly refer to as "welfare"—and fewer than five percent got food stamps, with the two adding up to an average payment per year of $116 for each family that received them. The real money the immigrants receive is in Medicaid for their eligible U.S. citizen children—it's used by 20.4 percent of illegal immigrant households for an average of $888 per year *within that pool.*[25] This in-kind service doesn't cover the rent, or feed a family, nor can it be sent back home in the form of remittances. It does represent a cost to the United States and state governments, but it is not, in itself, enough incentive to emigrate.

Latino immigrants, for the most part, aren't coming here to sponge off the taxpayer, to "get goodies." They're coming here to work their fingers to the bone, and this typifies the culture they share with U.S. citizen Latinos.

*   *   *

No one can completely define a whole group of people by four, ten, or even a hundred shared characteristics—people are just too complicated for that. But in the business of marketing, we try to get a broad feel for what appeals to a group, and this is what I have tried to do here. I have identified four key values that Latinos share in common, in an interconnected way that makes us unique. Keep these in mind as you move to the next chapter, which examines the conservatism of Latino opinion and identifies three trends that are slowly opening Latinos' minds to the Republican message.

four

the emerging latino republican majority

George P. Bush, son of former Florida Governor Jeb Bush, is a Mexican American who helped lead the charge campaigning for his uncle in Spanish-speaking communities in 2000 and 2004.

A lot of elderly folks within the Hispanic community view the civil rights movement as their overarching issue. I think for my generation, the new focus is economic empowerment, creating wealth within our respective communities, and finding educational opportunities. There's less party affiliation. That's the case in the Anglo community as well. My generation, typically, is more willing to look at both sides, and sometimes even at candidates like Kinky Friedman—they tend to think outside the box. And so the Republican party has an opportunity there, but the party in the past has overlooked us, and has assumed that the Hispanic bloc always goes Democrat.

The weakness of focusing on the civil rights messages of the past is that they are then viewed as being divisive. I know that the National Council of *La Raza* and other civil rights groups that represent the Hispanic community have been criticized in the past for not doing enough to connect the barrio with Wall Street. And only now has NCLR [National Council of *La Raza*] responded. For example, their new president comes from a business background. It means we've got to stop thinking about the issues from the 60s; we need to start thinking about how we're going to create wealth and opportunity for younger Latinos that define economic decisions. And, with that, political opportunities will follow.

> It was an eye opener to see Hispanic women with no political experience willing to run for office as independents or from one party or another. Reason being, home is home. You always go back to where you came from. Latinas are tied to the grassroots and they realize that to change big ticket items like the economy and health care, they have to become the decision makers.
>
> —*Marisa Rivera-Albert, president of the National Hispana Leadership Institute,*
> *an organization dedicated to developing Latina leaders*

Political parties profile voters based on their lifestyles, to see whom they are most likely to vote for. They look far beyond party registration to other minutiae—magazine subscriptions, purchases, church memberships, and countless other small details of a voter's life—to see if their constituents are more likely to vote for them or for their opponent.

Are you married? Married people gave Bush 57 percent of their votes in 2004. So if you see a ring, you're looking at a Bush voter six times out of ten. Another classic tell, cited on many occasions by former RNC chairman Ken Mehlman, is what kind of car a voter drives. If you drive a Volvo, you're probably a Democrat. If you drive a sportscar, you're probably a Republican.

Right now, the partisans look at Hispanics and say they must be Democrats. But when you profile us as a group, without looking at our surnames, you would get a very different impression.

Cast aside your preconceptions, and take a look how we live and what we believe, instead of our heritage. We attend church at higher rates, we form more businesses and at a faster rate than the general population. We marry at a high rate and we raise our children in intact families at about the national average. We support tax cuts, we are pro-life, we oppose same-sex marriage. Ask your local political scientist: These descriptions could all apply just as easily to Republicans as they do to Hispanics.

President Bush and other Republicans seeking liberalized immigration laws often argue that Latino immigrants have "shared values" with Americans in general, and with Republicans in particular. To many ordinary Americans, this sounds like a bad political cliché, and some Republicans consider it an excuse for a preordained immigration policy. But these "shared values" are real. Consider the studies we conducted at the RNC on Hispanic voters before and after the 2000 election that indicated strong conservative sensibilities, and countless other surveys confirm this fact.

White Evangelical Christians and traditional Catholics—the Irish and Italians who were Democrats less than 40 years ago—share many of the same values espoused by Hispanics. These groups have already migrated to the Republican Party as the Democratic Party and its leaders have become increasingly wedded to easy abortion, the elimination of sexual mores, and at times hostility toward people of faith.[1]

As Latinos become faith-based voters and activists, achieve greater economic success, and absorb more of the political culture around us in our expanding geographical surroundings, we should become more Republican. (This rise in Hispanic conservatism is evident below in a Gallup poll conducted over a three-year period.[2]) The percentage of self-proclaimed liberals also declined considerably from 2005 to 2006.

Opinion polls repeatedly show how conservative Latinos are on the issues. They show that we possess a strong work ethic and a healthy distrust of government that leads us to express disdain for the idea of government dependency. All of this should result in our voting Republican someday. We don't vote Republican yet, but many of us are willing to consider it.

The 2006 Mexican elections provide just one confirmation of this fact. Even as he was collecting 36 percent on his way to a narrow plurality

Figure 4.1   Hispanics Describe their Political Views

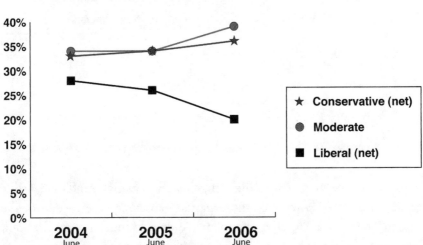

Source: Gallup Poll Social Series: Minority Rights & Relations/Black-White Social Audit 2004–2006

Figure 4.2   Hispanic Political Views (Female)

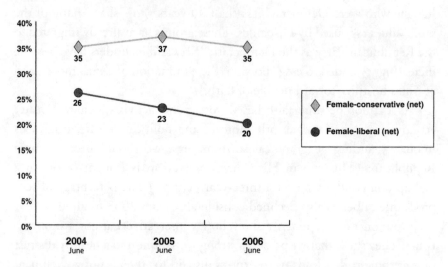

Source: Gallup Poll Social Series: Minority Rights & Relations/Black-White Social Audit 2004–2006

Figure 4.3   Hispanic Political Views (Male)

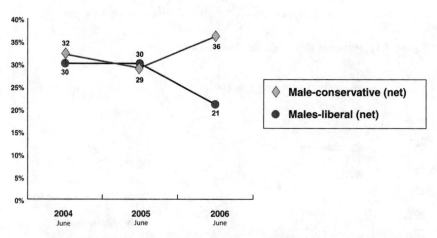

Source: Gallup Poll Social Series: Minority Rights & Relations/Black-White Social Audit 2004–2006

victory, the free-market, pro-life, religious conservative candidate Felipe Calderon took *57 percent* of the expatriate absentee vote cast from the United States. His socialist opponent, Andres Manuel Lopez Obrador, took only 34 percent of the American ex-pat vote. The tiny remainder went to the fading left-wing party that ruled Mexico for most of the twentieth century and is responsible for much of the nation's poverty and lack of economic opportunity—the government whose ill effects many Mexicans came to the United States to escape.

Of course, Mexican politics are not the same as ours, and only a relatively small number of Mexicans in the United States took time to vote in the Old Country's elections. But it is significant that the Mexicans in the United States who did vote overwhelmingly backed a very fiscally and socially conservative candidate.

These basic conservative sensibilities are not limited to Mexicans (who make up 60 percent of the Hispanics in the United States) but extend to Hispanics from other national backgrounds as well.

The Republican National Committee agreed to release previously undisclosed findings from our surveys of Hispanics leading up to the 2000 election.[3] We found that:

- Three to one, Hispanic voters said that government should be based on "personal responsibility" rather than "group guarantees" or "bureaucratic paternalism."
- Hispanics view welfare, four to one, as a "safety net" rather than a permanent source of income. Also four to one, and unlike liberals of all races, they believe that the American dream is real for them—that "opportunity related to the work ethic will make them successful."
- Eighty percent of Hispanic male voters and 75 percent of Hispanic female voters report being part of the labor force, a sign of a strong cultural work ethic, and a flat contradiction of the myth that Hispanic illegal aliens come to the United States to go on welfare.
- Among the Hispanic voters we surveyed, about 53 percent are both married and own their own homes. This fits the demographic for Republicans in most racial groups.

To be sure, much of the Hispanic leadership is way out of touch with this cultural conservatism, often reaching to the farthest left extreme of the American political spectrum. But it's not as though this tension goes unnoticed. Brooklyn Congresswoman Nydia Velazquez (D) is among the most liberal of them all. She was one of just three House members who abstained from the unanimous vote in 2002 condemning the Ninth Circuit Court ruling that struck "under God" from the Pledge of Allegiance. When she returned to New York after the vote, Velazquez was excoriated by her Democratic Hispanic backers. "[S]he was met on the steps of City Hall by 50 Latino clerics protesting her action. Bronx Pentecostal minister Ruben Diaz, who also happens to be a City Council member, summed up their complaint: We're a very conservative community . . . and we were offended."[4]

Ask Hispanic voters what they think about immigration, and you'll hear mixed attitudes. When asked what to do about the illegal immigration problem, with an open-ended answer, Hispanic voters' top five responses were:

1. "They should be sent back." (10 percent)
2. "They should play by the rules, period." (9 percent)
3. "Make Green Cards easier for illegal workers." (9 percent)
4. "Add more border police." (8 percent)
5. "Governments should attack the primary cause, poverty and famine." (8 percent)[5]

In 2006, our firm conducted a survey on the issue of whether to build a border fence, and found that among the more than half of Hispanics who named terrorism and national security as their top issue, 70 percent favor a physical security barrier.[6] Among Hispanics most concerned about immigration as a drain on social services, 48 percent favor a physical barrier.

Education consistently ranks at the top of Hispanic voters' concerns, no matter who is doing the polling. But during my time at the RNC, we had access to outside polling that showed their concerns about education have a distinctly conservative flavor to them. Asked in an open-ended question what the biggest problem is with public schools, Hispanic respondents gave these top answers:

• Students are being taught nontraditional values and are not learning discipline (27 percent).
• Students are not getting the knowledge and skills they need (24 percent).
• Students are being exposed to violence and illegal drugs in school (23 percent).[7]

You don't see anything here about raising taxes or spending more money. All of these Hispanic concerns represent natural Republican territory on education. The same is true of the results gleaned from Hispanics by Univision's survey on economic issues. Although 53 percent said that the government should spend on social programs where necessary, a striking 40 percent agreed with the statement that "the government should stay out of the economy altogether so private forces can compete and create jobs." This may be a minority, but it is a large minority to take such a hardline economic libertarian position.

Eighty percent, meanwhile, agreed with the statement that welfare "must be replaced with an employment system so that welfare recipients develop an attachment to the workforce and can become independent." If that's not a conservative attitude, what is?

Clearly, Latinos are conservative in their views. This fact, combined with three emerging trends of Latino economic success, political mobilization through our churches, and our geographical expansion to new parts of the country, will contribute to a new paradigm that will shape the Hispanic vote in future elections. This new Latino political paradigm will bring more and more Hispanics to the GOP, resolving the obvious tension between Latinos' beliefs and an incompatible Democratic platform.

the youngbloods

I first saw them as a sea of smiling faces staring back at my podium—a group of well-educated Latino accountants and investment bankers in New York. As their keynote speaker, I smiled and wondered, what would these folks think of our old family joke that it takes five relatives to buy a car? One has the credit, one holds the title, one makes the payments, one drives the car, and another guy is just along for the ride?

Are these the "un-Latinos" who break the Hispanic cultural norms? You could say that. These folks are far more sophisticated than those of us whose families always overspent, and whose financial plan consisted of "taking our money back to Mexico." Many of them are second- and third-generation Latinos. In New York, many are of Puerto Rican or Dominican descent—they live in a colorblind, merit-based environment that ignores ethnicity, race and national origin. They are the up-and-coming class of Latino professionals that form the Association of Latino Professionals in Finance and Accounting (ALPFA).

"Our goal is to expand Latino leadership in the global workforce," says Manny Espinoza, former senior partner at PricewaterhouseCoopers and ALPFA's CEO. "This is the first time we've been able to combine professionalism with our culture—and it's fun!"

And these guys (and gals) are good at both. We looked in the last chapter at the broader economic success of Latinos in America—the large number of small businesses we form, our growing rate of home ownership, and our formation of family wealth. These professionals at ALPFA represent the tip of the spear in the world of big business—the vanguard of Latinos making it in corporate America. Their success will in turn breed more Latino success at all levels of the business world.

ALPFA is actually a part of a much larger phenomenon that I call the "Hispanic Youngbloods." These young (under 40), well-educated and business-minded Latinos are growing in numbers, as are the groups that serve them. Over the past three years, ALPFA's membership alone has grown from 1,200 to over 7,000, with chapters in 26 cities. Initially established in 1972 as the American Association of Hispanic Certified Public Accountants, ALPFA hit its stride when Espinoza expanded its membership into the finance sector. The group's officers make up a star-studded corporate cast—partners, managers and directors from the big accounting and consulting firms.

Major companies notice this. They see for themselves a vested interest in helping these organizations grow, and they are investing their political capital. In 2005, Walt Disney Company decided to invest $1 million in ALPFA, signing a multi-year contract to do market research among the group's chapters and enhance ALPFA's professional development programs. It was an offer not extended to any other minority group, and the first such investment in Disney's history. Surely their goal was more than just ensuring that a few upwardly mobile Latino families would resonate with the message, "I'm going to Disneyland!" Mercedes-Benz called to offer ALPFA one of the three cars they give away annually, so that ALPFA could raffle it off at their annual convention.

Demand for the ALPFA professionals' time and interest is quickly rising, and major corporations are extending their presence to ensure that ALPFA and similar organizations succeed.

At a time when most civil rights and ethnic organizations are searching for causes that relive the 1960s "we shall overcome" spirit, ALPFA and organizations like it represent the rise in professional Hispanics who are for the first time flexing their political and financial muscles in the economic arena. "Now we have COOs and CFOs of McDonald's and other major corporations," says Espinoza. And unlike members of other Hispanic advocacy groups, these folks do not necessarily consider themselves Democrats—and that includes the New Yorkers. They are conservative independents who feel no strong ties to either party as they make their own impact on the American electorate.

"You can really influence these young professionals with great ideas," Espinoza continued. "They're just looking for something. Our profession of accounting and finance lends itself to the Republican viewpoints, but our organization does not support candidates. We're not like La Raza that just stands behind issues. If issues come up that are focused on finance and accounting, we do work them, but we're not huge in terms of that."

What is unique about these Hispanic Youngbloods is their attempt to create a cross-section of business and culture for both professional comraderie and cultural relevance. These leaders are the engine behind the accelerated growth of Hispanic affinity groups in every major corporation in America, from Cisco Systems' Conexion to AT&T's Hispanic Association of AT&T Employees (HISPA) to Bank of America's Hispanic/Latino Association for Leadership and Advancement (HOLA) or Deloitte's Hispanic Business Resource Group.

It was a vice president at Prudential Financial—Edgar Morales—who had asked me to speak at ALPFA's event as part of a litany of seminars and CEO roundtables they hold annually. Each has its own purpose, offering advice on such business topics as raising capital, best practices to bolster corporate return on investment, and how to gain support for the group's networking initiatives. The day concludes with a staple of all Latino events—an evening of salsa dancing! Don't think of small disc jockeys in black tuxes spinning LPs—try mariachis from Michoacan. These elaborate productions rival the Latin Grammy's. To connect with the culture some Fortune 500 chief diversity officers are "taking salsa lessons and supporting our salsa contests," adds Espinoza. I'm convinced that the television show *Dancing with the Stars* was created by some television executive who accidentally wandered into a *Hispanic Business* awards gala at the Millennium Biltmore in Los Angeles.

Leadership groups like ALFPA will shape the national political dialogue in ways that did not exist before. Consider the Latino Coalition, a pro-business, pro-growth thinktank that focuses on the economic empowerment of Latinos. This group brought newly elected Mexican President Felipe Calderon to a luncheon shortly after the November midterm elections. Another noteworthy organization is Hispanic Alliance for Progress Institute, which yielded a most impressive "who's who" to speak on trade, financial security and education reform, not to mention Dominican American National Roundtable, the National Hispana Leadership Institute, and the National Society of Hispanic MBAs (NSHMBA), which serves 29 chapters and 7,000 members in the United States.

This phenomenon is not limited to the top echelons of the corporate world, either. Ali Curi, a Texas native born to a Syrian father and a Mexican mother, has founded the four-year-old Hispanic Professionals Networking Group (HPNG) to serve Latino middle managers. He told me that he founded his organization because he saw nothing out there offering a professionally vigorous interaction with other Latino professionals at that level. "Hispanics in *Hispanic Business* magazine already know each other," he said. "We're motivated to develop professionals in the mid-sector." Curi began HPNG with 15 members in 2003, and the group has since grown to nearly 3,000. He has plans to expand nationally.

Numerous other such groups exist to serve Hispanics in various professional sectors and sub-sectors. For Latino computer professionals, there is Latinos in Information Sciences and Technology Association (LISTA), founded by former Fortune 500 IT professional Jose Marquez. The group now boasts eight chapters nationwide, with a dues-paying membership of 3,000 and a monthly newsletter that goes to 35,000 Latino professionals.

Marquez said his group's members tend not to identify with one political party, but are a genuine swing constituency, more so than average Hispanic voters. "The new professionals, this 'Generation ñ,' have no political affiliation," says Marquez, who worked with several Republicans on the telecommunications legislation in the 109th Congress. "We're not Democrats and we're not Republicans. We vote for someone who has integrity. My members are tired of the *bodega* politics," he adds, referring to the street-corner activism that was once integral to Latino politics.

"They want serious people to step out and do the right thing for the community."

The business influence spreads into government economic policy discussions as well. In Washington, a group of Democratic-leaning Hispanic groups opposed George W. Bush's nominee to the U.S. Court of Appeals for the District of Columbia, Honduran-born Miguel Estrada, because he was not "authentically" Hispanic enough.[8] The four Hispanic Republican Members of the House and Rep. Devin Nunes (R-Calif.)—of Portuguese descent—organized their own separate Hispanic caucus called the Congressional Hispanic Conference (CHC). Within eight months, Rep. Lincoln Diaz-Balart (R-Fla.) founded CHC's nonprofit arm, the Congressional Hispanic Leadership Institute (CHLI, pronounced *chili*), to build alliances with the private sector. "We needed an organization that provided an alternative voice because the community is diverse—and we have diversity of thought," Diaz-Balart tells me. "We also feel that a voice that supports the common market in the Western Hemisphere is important. A free-trade bloc among all the Hemisphere's democracies is going to be good for the entire Hemisphere, and very much so for U.S. Hispanics. If there's anybody that can benefit from trade among all of the democracies of this Hemisphere, it's U.S. Latinos, because we can serve as a bridge between North and South."

Latino professionals are clearly being underserved by the Hispanic organizations that focus mainly on immigration and perceived discrimination. The Hispanic Youngblood phenomenon, moving from urban centers on the East Coast to include Latino professionals in the West, offers a mirror image to the 1960s Chicano civil rights movements, whose influence began in California and moved eastward. These professionals are Hispanics who don't automatically vote Democrat. They are nonpartisan professionals who may support Democrats at times, but are also open-minded and understand that the Democratic Party has it all wrong on many issues that affect them, including free trade and an investor-friendly tax policy.

"I happen to lean a little Democratic," says Cid Wilson of Dominicans on Wall Street. "But I'm very proud of the relationships I have with both parties. I have a very strong relationship with many Republican members of Congress. And if a Dominican is running for elective office as a

Republican, I'll give him the same exact advice I would give if he was running as a Democrat."

As their numbers and influence swell, the Hispanic Youngbloods will have a dramatic impact on politics as community leaders. Even if they do not become rabid Republicans, they will at least shed an unthinking and obsolete historical allegiance to the Democratic Party.

faith seekers

Not only do we have the polls to show how conservative Latinos are, but we also have real signs that a conservative awakening is happening in our faith communities.

The Lakewood Church in Houston is best known for its famous pastor, Joel Osteen, whose television ministry reaches seven million viewers and whose book *Your Best Life Now: 7 Steps to Living at Your Full Potential*, sold over four million copies and remained on top of the *New York Times* bestseller list for over two years.

But unlike many megachurches in the South and Southwest, Lakewood's congregation reflects almost perfectly the ethnic and socio-economic diversity of the community that surrounds it. And one reason a lot of the folks are there Sunday after Sunday is Marcus Witt, one of today's growing crop of Latino pastors.

I had learned about Lakewood a year earlier when Marcus came to the White House to perform at the Hispanic Heritage Month ceremony. He sang with such clarity and intense emotion that the audience sat mesmerized, staring as if a fog had cleared long enough for us to see, for one small moment, life through this man's eyes. The president thanked Marcus for his prayers. "Tell everybody at home hello. That would be Houston, is where he lives. And Laura and I are Tejanos."[9]

Who is this preacher, I wondered, and why don't we know him?

A year later, on a visit to Sugar Land, Texas, I told friends about my interest in visiting Lakewood. "You'll love it. Leave early . . . the crowds are massive."

First we saw Joel Osteen preach—*TIME* magazine once described his sermons as "a nonstop declaration of God's love and his intent to show it in the here and now, sometimes verging on the language of an annual report."[10] We sang and laughed. Afterward, hundreds flocked to the bookstore, where eight rows of cash registers hummed amid a frenzy of buying excitement. Down the massive hallway, folks were waiting an hour in queue to meet Joel. Single dads lined up with their sons and daughters to take a picture.

Meanwhile, new crowds of Hispanic faces began to amass, preparing for Marcus Witt, and for the hyper indulgence of music and prayer to begin again . . . in Spanish.

Witt represents what to contemporary America is very much a counterculture. One religious leader said Marcus is to preaching what Celia Cruz was to salsa. He represents a bridge between contemporary Evangelical America and its rapidly growing Latino cohort.

Conservative, Christian, charismatic and, most importantly, credible, Witt offers a soulful blend of optimism and inspiration to Houston's Spanish-speaking legions, who arrive more than an hour before services begin. The attendees, who have swelled from 500 to 6,000 people in less than five years, mix, mingle and talk in a way only Hispanics seem to. For most traditional Evangelical churches, it's the period after church that is used for socializing. For Hispanics, whose faith experience is central to their identity as a community, this period of time beforehand allows the church to become the equivalent of an indoor central plaza, the familiar Latin American convergence of prayer, family and, now more commonly, politics.

The United States is home to some 9.5 million Latino Protestants— there are more of them than American Jews, Muslims, Presbyterians and Episcopalians combined.[11] They are a big part of this new dynamic within the Hispanic body politic—mobilization in the name of social compassion, and often for causes we would consider "conservative."

Aside from a soccer match, I had never seen such openly expressive Hispanic men as the ones at Witt's service. One in particular, a dark-skinned man in the 100-person choir, resembled a Mexican American man I grew up with in Corpus. But he was different. Not stoic and thoughtful, but overly enthusiastic, with raised arms—almost like he was having an intense and public conversation with God. At the end of Osteen's televised broadcast, when he made an impassioned altar call for those who had grown distant from God to rise up, other men echoed his fervor. Over a thousand people stood, mostly Hispanic men. Many had come alone, some with cowboy hats in hand—the macho image temporarily forsaken to expose their humanness and vulnerability. A movement was growing.

Generally, much is made about the impact of the evangelical turnout in elections. According to a Pew Research study, 23 percent of Republicans are white evangelical Protestants, 78 percent of whom voted for Bush in 2004. Yet few ponder the impact of Hispanic evangelicals within this segment. Are they like-minded? Do they have the same motivations? Are they willing to take action and vote?

"Hispanics, we have a very existential society," Witt tells me. "We live for today. When you look at Hispanic culture as a whole, we don't have a culture of savings, we don't have a culture of thinking about what our kids are going to have to deal with 10 or 20 or 30 years from now, much less 50 years from now. . . . And I think that's one of the reflectors as to why they're going to vote according to what their problem is today. So if the Democrats come up and say, we're going to get immigration reform if you vote for me, they'll vote for it. They won't stop and ask, you know, what does he stand for, what are his morals, what are his values, how is this going to affect my family ten years down the road . . . they don't think about that, they're thinking about, we need immigration reform today.

"I know Hispanics who will vote for extremely liberal, pro-gay marriage, pro-abortion legislators just because they said, we'll give you immigration reform," says Witt. "And they're Christian Hispanics. I think we still have a ways to go in that."

David Contreras is among those who want to take up this task. He is Texas director for the Council on Faith in Action (CONFIA), a non-profit organization that focuses on educating Hispanics on civic issues.

"Republicans have neglected the Hispanic Evangelical community in the mistaken belief that the pastors and churches cannot mobilize congregations to turn out the vote," says Contreras. "CONFIA is changing this by educating Hispanic pastors about their God-given right and Biblical responsibility to vote." Contreras helped mobilize thousands of Hispanic voters during a 2005 referendum in Texas in favor of a constitutional amendment to preserve the traditional definition of marriage.

Another leader in this area is the Rev. Luis Cortés, Jr., chairman and CEO of *Nueva Esperanza* in Philadelphia, who was named one of the "25 Most Influential Evangelicals in America" by *Time* magazine. "Part of integrating is understanding power," says Cortés. "Our people have power but they have never used it."[12] In recent years Cortés has worked hard to test the scope of this influence. In 2002 he created the National Hispanic Prayer Breakfast, which the president has addressed annually and which boasts an attendance of 700 Hispanic pastors. The president only canceled his appearance once, he claims, and that was to meet the pope.

Cortés attributes the Latino evangelical success to aggressive outreach and establishment of the connection at home. "Most Latinos have three areas to congregate: bars, bodegas and nail salons. None has a group like this to welcome them and say 'you are all right. I'm all right. We're going to get through this together.' We're home to these families. All of our clergy are Latinos who use tradition. We want to be familiar, like home. We offer help for struggling parents, alcoholics, victims of domestic violence; we help them with filing their taxes, we call on each other. We say 'God speaks Spanish too.'

"Latino Pentecostal churches dot the landscape of Los Angeles and serve as beacons of hope against the gang culture," adds Cortés. These churches are particularly active in reaching out to the deadly MS-13 gang. Many members of MS-13 are former child soldiers from the civil war in El Salvador in the 1980s.

Mexican Americans in California may be Democrats, but they have also mobilized through their churches in the recent past for conservative political causes. In 2000, when a law to protect the traditional definition of marriage was brought to the ballot in the form of Proposition 22, Catholic and Evangelical leaders worked aggressively to bring out the Latino vote. The measure passed with 61 percent of the vote, with 62 percent of Latinos in support, according to exit polls.

"Some politicians are really cunning in knowing how to cater to the Hispanic vote and they use that knowing that Hispanics aren't going to dig deeper to know what they actually stand for," Witt says. "I really hope the Christian Hispanic movement in the United States can help turn that around. I see the potential that we have because Hispanic evangelicals are very serious about their faith, very serious about their family. I think there's a trend toward Hispanic Christians being able to swing those votes."

The American Catholic Church, almost silent for decades now on political questions, also shows signs that the tide is turning. For the first time in many years, bishops such as John Myers of Newark and Charles Chaput of Denver have begun taking on Catholic politicians who espouse extremely un-Catholic values. Chaput took the risk in 2004 of tangling with Ken Salazar, another Catholic Democrat who was running for the Senate on a pro-choice abortion platform. If the bishops continue to educate their flocks at election time, then faith can become a powerful force in better informing Latino votes so that they are cast with more of a long-term view of our values and our families.

This change has been very slow in coming—Washington's archbishop was much faster to condemn attempts to restore the Second Amendment for citizens of the District of Columbia than he was to admonish a Catholic presidential candidate who voted repeatedly for partial-birth abortion. But as new, zealous leaders are installed throughout the country, the Catholic Church appears to be moving in a more political direction both in the United States and internationally. This phenomenon will eventually make its effect felt in larger ways.

Mexican Americans, and increasingly immigrants from Central and South America, mobilized by the power of faith, are fighting crime and gangs in our communities, and mobilizing to preserve the institution of the family and prevent its decay. Upon "socializing" ourselves through churches and other civic groups, the natural next step is for us to "politicize" and "mobilize"—to take our concern for the community with us to the ballot box on behalf of candidates who stand up for our values.

southern newbies

We have seen the conservatism of Latino opinion, and the fact that Latinos are becoming more active in their churches. We have also seen the level of economic success Latinos have achieved as a group in a relatively short time, and the way our increasingly active faith communities are beginning to make us take stock in what values we vote for.

Another factor in transforming the Latino vote into a Republican majority will be our expanding footprint within the United States. Just 15 years ago, no one would have expected Hispanic communities to take root in such states as Tennessee, Georgia, Arkansas and South Carolina, but today they have. And wherever we go, we tend to absorb the political culture around us. It's not because we are losing something about our identity—it is because the needs and concerns of Latinos in one part of the country are different from those in other parts, plain and simple.

The idea of a party having a permanent electoral lock on a state or district is always short-sighted, a fact that long-term veterans of politics know because they have often learned it the hard way. Every 10 to 20 years, states change demographically, politically, culturally—and it always happens quickly. GOP demographer John Morgan once told Michael Barone, "Wherever you see a McDonald's and a Pizza Hut coming, the Republicans aren't far behind." Twenty years later, he's changed that to: "You can safely say now that the Latinos are not far behind."

Today, 75 percent of Latinos live in just five states—California, Texas, New York, Illinois and Florida. Together, these account for 180 Electoral College votes. But only five states with proportionally large Hispanic populations are usually in play: Arizona, Nevada, Colorado, Florida and New Mexico, accounting for 56 electoral college votes.

These states are clearly important in any close election, and so obviously the Latino vote is critical there. But look beyond 2008 at the political impact of our growth in nontraditional areas: Lexington, Neb.; West Des Moines, Iowa; and Dalton, Ga. New waves of Mexican, Central and South American immigrants and transplanted Mexican Americans and Puerto Ricans—from states like California, New York and Texas—are converging in small cities, especially throughout the Southeast, where jobs are plentiful, housing is cheap, and the entry barriers to starting a business are minimal.

As it happens, these are places where folks vote Republican. Seven of the fastest growing Hispanic populations since the 2000 Census are in places like the Carolinas, Georgia, Tennessee, Alabama, Kentucky and Arkansas. These growing communities will play a major role in Hispanics' political future. Their geographical location represents an opportunity for Republicans who are willing to reach out to them.

Luis Fortuño, the Republican congressional delegate from Puerto Rico, tries to keep track of Puerto Rican voters among the diaspora who have moved to the mainland. "Historically, Puerto Ricans in the Northeast have voted Democrat, while Puerto Ricans in the Southeast have voted Republican," he said. "I believe they are just resembling their environment, to a great degree."

"We would have given anything to know 20 years ago about the pattern of Puerto Rican New Yorkers heading south to the I-4 corridor in central Florida," says Republican pollster Lance Tarrance. Today, countless sociologists and historians chronicle the replacement of whites—almost two-for-one—in these central Florida counties. This was the topic of many conversations at the RNC when we laid out our 2000 Hispanic voter strategy. At that time, led by John Morgan, we pointed to the rise in Puerto Rican voters and the need to address them. We made a hard pitch to them, because even though some believed they would stick to their Democratic roots—following the path of Jewish New Yorkers who first started coming to Florida 40 years ago—we hoped that their economic independence might leave them more open to the GOP.

We were right. Demography had given the Democrats hope, since they believed Latinos' natural progression is to vote Democratic. Again, they saw the waves but misinterpreted the current. The stereotypes that pre-define Hispanic voters have already begun to change. Florida's increase in Puerto Ricans and Central and South Americans led Democratic operatives to theorize about an unbreakable Democratic majority there. What they did not expect was that these voters would become ticket splitters, giving a substantial percentage of their votes to Republicans like Mel Martinez and Jeb and George W. Bush.

"There is a misperception that Hispanic voters are monolithic," says Ed Gillespie, the former chairman of the Republican National Committee. Gillespie offered the Catholic vote as a more appropriate comparison, an example of a heterogeneous voter block. "There's little understanding of the many distinctions amongst Catholic voters—Irish Catholic from the Northeast, Italian Catholics and Polish Catholics from the industrial Midwest, they are both different from Cuban Catholics in Florida or Mexican Catholics in Texas, or Mexican Catholics in California.

There are German Catholics in Illinois, and they don't vote the same. The same is true of the Hispanic vote."

To see the difference between various Hispanic nationalities, one need only compare the poor refugees from countries such as Mexico and Honduras to the wealthy professionals who have fled countries such as Cuba and Venezuela to take up their homes in Miami and southern Florida. One group comes here seeking economic freedom, whereas the other seeks political freedom. And that only accounts for the current situation in their respective countries—it says nothing of the long-standing cultural differences between them.

Not only do Latinos vote differently based on our families' nation of origin, we also vote differently according to the cultures of the places we live in now. We already see vast differences between Mexican Hispanics in California and in Texas, between Puerto Ricans in Florida and in New York. But as our communities take root in more and more unlikely parts of the United States, completely new and even more diverse interests will arise. We will also absorb more of what we see around us.

"Hispanics tend to vote a lot like the people around them except maybe 10 to 15 points more Democratic," says Michael Barone, senior writer for *U.S. News & World Report* and coauthor of *The Almanac of American Politics*. "You go to Central LA, they're all Democrats . . . in Orange County they voted for Bush. In west Texas, those counties that have 30 percent Hispanic are voting 75 percent for Bush. Maybe the Hispanics aren't voting there yet, but if they are, they aren't voting heavily Democratic or you wouldn't see those 75 percent numbers."

Over the next 10 to 15 years, that structural 10- to 15-point Democratic edge will erode as Latino values and economic success begin to affect our voting behavior.

Geography may sound like a superficial, accidental factor in political participation, but it isn't. Think back to how formative and important your place of upbringing was for forming your worldview. Where we live shapes who we are as much as or even more than our family's ethnic backgrounds. We're all hyphenated Americans, but we're also Texans, Hoosiers, New Yorkers, Yankees and Southerners. It's a testament to how we live and adopt the culture around us.

I love to see the changes in America; I love to watch how new communities come together. I remember my days selling encyclopedias in new suburban housing developments like Rio Rancho, New Mexico, where children rode fluorescent-colored bicycles with plastic streamers on the handle bars. These young, predominantly Hispanic children would follow me down the street, telling me which families had children and which ones didn't. Today, Rio Rancho has evolved into the third-largest city in New Mexico, with over 75,000 residents. Didn't it start as subdivision?

Later, in my work for Impacto Group, I would drive down the newly paved highways in Nashville and Atlanta to see the city sprawl and meet the people driving the transformation. America is changing, and in many places we are seeing more Hispanic faces.

One such place is Greenville, South Carolina, a community in the midst of a major transition. The tree-lined streets of Greenville-Spartanburg are teeming with new Latino residents. According to the U.S. Census Bureau, South Carolina's Hispanic population increased from 30,551 in 1990 to 130,432 in 2004, more than half of Mexican origin. Greenville is home to the state's largest Hispanic population, with about 18,000 Latinos. A technologically modern industrial city, it is a model for the New South.

Founded on land formerly inhabited by Cherokee Indians,[13] the city is centrally located between Atlanta and Charlotte. Like any city with growing pains, Greenville is situated in a whirlwind of economic and social cross-pressures that will cause it either to succumb to the weight and needs of a growing immigrant population, or else to prosper and become one of America's best small cities. My belief is that the latter will prevail.

You only have to meet the leaders to see why. In 2005, Greenville's city fathers put out a sign that says Greenville is open for business, and the Hispanics came running. From 2000 to 2004, an additional 7,000 Hispanic newcomers showed up.[14] One was Javier Garcia, a military veteran who moved there from the small upstate New York town of Sterling.

"I was standing on the roof of my house, shoveling snow, and my brother called," says Javier. "He spoke to my son, Gabriel. My son comes out and throws the phone up, and all I hear is this laughter. He says, 'you've got to be crazy, to subject yourself year after year to that environment, it's just terrible up there.' And I said 'you know what, you're right.' One thing led to another, we had more conversations and we decided to start a corporation in Greenville. On *Cinco de Mayo* of '05, I flew down from New York with paperwork and started our corporation."

The city's economic development office "welcomed me with open arms and said this is what Greenville has got to offer," he says. "We pride ourselves in Greenville because it is green, it is beautiful . . . the air is very crisp and clean. I fell in love with the area and I knew I'd really like to be a part of it long term."

Not all is rosy, however. The city has several unique challenges related to education, housing and health care, part of them due to the influx of newcomers. But it is a prosperous place, characterized by its heavy Republican tilt—Greenville County gave 66 percent of its vote to President Bush in both 2000 and 2004. It is Carroll Campbell country, the home of the much-loved Republican governor who passed away in December 2005.

In *The Right Nation* (2004), Adrian Wooldridge and John Micklethwaite suggest that Latinos appear to be headed more in the direction of Italian Americans than of blacks when it comes to political participation.[15] Part of the historical trend for immigrants, they argue, is that they "move to the suburbs, losing touch with the Democratic Party's great urban political machines. They start their own businesses, making them more receptive to the Republican Party's antiregulation message." These things seem to be happening throughout the New South, but the biggest roadblock may be an unwelcoming attitude in the Republican Party.

Rep. Bob Inglis (R-S.C.), who represents Greenville, is a Bush Republican and one of the best friends Latino immigrants have in Congress. He has connected with the Latino community in his district thanks to the hard work of Marvin Rogers—an African American conservative who spent six years as a missionary in Latin America. Rogers, who speaks perfect Spanish, says that his outreach to Hispanic business owners has been a hard sell, but the harder sell has been to Republican leaders.

"When I go out and I talk with Hispanic business owners on the streets of Greenville and I say Republican, they think 'Tom DeLay,' " he says. "This is a lot of the challenge. I talk to them about why Hispanics should vote Republican, and how it's very much aligned with what they come to America for in the first place. But when I go to the party leaders to talk about the things we can do to push that message—home ownership, small business ownership, I don't get passion, I don't get hardly anything here.

I've tried to do so many things, small business forums . . . a lot of the local Republicans are not really plugged into that."

Republicans are so dominant in Greenville that a lot of party leaders are not far-sighted enough to take interest in reaching out to the newcomers as they should. Inglis is an exception. In the many town hall meetings he holds in the district, he discusses the reluctance he finds among many white Republicans to embrace the newcomers. "I was in Congress from '93 to '98, then gone six years and back in '04," he tells me. "In the two years I've been back, immigration has become an issue, and it's become the issue with the most heat and the least light. A whole lot of misinformation, a whole lot of distrust."

Inglis tells the story of one constituent who launched into a racist tirade at a town hall meeting. "He says to me, 'This is a country for white people.' Everybody's white there except Marvin, who's sitting across the table from me. He says, 'Who needs the Asians, who needs the Hispanics? Can you imagine if your daughter goes to school and comes home with some black guy, Asian guy?' I'm thinking, I cannot believe this guy is saying these things. After a few more hateful words, the man stormed out, shouting, 'I'm not voting for you!'

"Later, Marvin was very insightful," says Inglis. "This is Tancredo and Buchanan in their fullness," Marvin had explained, referring to the anti-immigration congressman and the erstwhile presidential candidate. "They established a rhetorical position out there, and their followers go beyond that. This guy is in the wave ahead of Tancredo and Buchanan."

*   *   *

Inglis may receive a primary challenge in 2008 from the anti-immigration Right, but he said he finds that he can reason with most of his constituents on the issue. When holding town hall meetings, Inglis says, "I try to get buy-in from the audience. I say, now would you agree with me that Hispanics are hard-working people? And what I found very interesting is that nobody in the crowd has disagreed with that assertion. I was in my law firm for those six years, and I watched two buildings being built on opposite corners from the building my law firm building occupied. I found it very interesting that I would see the Hispanic laborers literally running on the job site and I said, 'You know, have you had that experience?' Usually the audience will give me a nod.

"This wave of immigrants is renewing American culture by reminding us of the work ethic and by reminding us of the importance of family," he goes on. "And so I go on to say, in addition to working hard, you notice folks line up on Friday afternoons to send money back home . . . supporting their families? Isn't this the family value proposition we're about as Republicans? I don't want to romanticize the situation, but they're working hard and sending the money home to their families, and they're connected physically to their church, so they have a faith underpinning, these are Republicans."

Political considerations obviously come into play as well. South Carolina may currently be among the most Republican states in the country, but there is no reason to believe it will stay that way forever. African Americans cast up 30 percent of the state's votes in 2004, and 85 percent of them backed John Kerry. The state remains Republican for now, but that could change if Democratic leaders such as Rep. James Clyburn do as Sen. Barack Obama did in Chicago and win the hearts of South Carolina Hispanics. The local Spanish-language media is already intensely hostile toward Republicans, including Inglis—the media was part of an effort to organize immigration marches in Greenville last year. It is not impossible that in 10 to 15 years, southern newbies could transform South Carolina from solid red to purple.

It isn't going to change soon, Inglis notes, but he keeps an eye to the long-term future. "It's not about current politics," he says. "If you look at South Carolina's 4th district, the number of Hispanic voters is less than 1 percent of the electorate, or less. So I'm obviously not doing this in order to curry favor with a voting bloc in order to get reelected in '06, '08, '10. This is what I believe, this is a matter of civic faith. If it's right for America, it will work out politically because good politics follows good policy.

"If we're real good at it," says Inglis, "we can make sure to drive the Hispanics off just like we drove the Blacks off. We really have an opportunity to snatch defeat from the jaws of victory . . . We were predisposed to work with [Blacks] because of Lincoln, and we blew it. The reality is that Hispanic immigrants are hard-working, family-oriented people who align very nicely with Republican thought. We can drive them off, and we will be forever more the minority party. But if we want to learn from our mistakes in dealing with Black South Carolinians, we've got to figure out how to welcome Hispanics into the Republican Party and build a majority with them."

The new Latino South offers a different picture of the Hispanic vote than we have seen anywhere else before. Will the emerging Latino communities there become solid blue as in California, or more purple, as in Texas? Or better yet, will they become more conservative, multiethnic and internationally focused, as in they are in Florida today? Part of that depends on whether these new Latino colonies are welcomed or rejected. Will places like Greenville be welcoming or divisive? Some argue that our ability to accommodate each other in our new multiethnic suburbs will determine how well our nation can survive in a diverse, global economy.[16]

five

disconnect

Three generations of Latinas under one roof and Myrka Dellanos makes it work. An author, Emmy-Award winning journalist and star of the Spanish-language network Univision, Myrka's independence as a mom (and a voter) offers a fresh perspective to young Latinas. Her recent decision to homeschool her daughter raised eyebrows, and she explains why she made that choice.

People see me and they're like, "oh my goodness, you're homeschooling. So how is she?" Like she doesn't see her friends at school. Yet, for me it's working very well. I have support and I am blessed in a sense that my mom lives with us now and she helps me. She's a retired teacher. So many things in math that I forget, my mom remembers. It's not something everyone can do. It's very difficult.

My hope is that my daughter can learn something beyond trigonometry, geography and reading, which obviously she needs to learn. I sit with her and talk about current events and we'll watch the news in the morning. If something's happening, she may not be interested in it politically, but we'll talk about it. What's going in Iraq? What's going on in the war? They touch on this in school but everyone doesn't participate. Reading the newspaper is very, very important to be knowledgeable. It's the way society is taking shape. Part of being successful is not just success in trigonometry, it's actually knowing the way things work. Why it is important that you vote. How she should teach her children the same values. This type of education is a global education, which I think in the United States is not being taught unless you are in a gifted program or with self-motivated students.

My parents were both immigrants. My mother was a professor, but when she came to this country, at one point she had to work in a blood bank because she couldn't get an [academic] job. She had to learn English; she had to study again.

She went to Vanderbilt University, got her masters and then she became an educator—again. You have to do what you have to do and it is hard. It must be difficult to do so with children and not knowing a language, and feeling humiliated, like a second-class citizen because you do get treated like a second class citizen. To this day, my mother's been here 45 years and we could be somewhere, even in Miami, and you could meet someone who is not having a good day. They say "Oh, I don't understand you." It bothers me. I can speak the language, and I can stand up for myself but there are a lot of people who can't.[1]

> The stereotype is that we all start off as Democrats and liberals. Once we start making money, we start voting Republican. Reason is we want to keep more of our money. We want to support the party that supports tax cuts. A lot of it is bull—. A lot of it is put out by Democrats because they do a horrible job of trying to keep Latinos in the fold. . . . They are never going to say, 'We had Leslie and Ruben and we lost them.' They are going to say, 'We never had them anyway because they only care about tax cuts.'
>
> —*Ruben Navarrette Jr., syndicated columnist and editorial board member*
> *of the* San Diego Union-Tribune

There's an old folk tale of about a woman who always cut off the end of her Christmas ham before she cooked it. One Christmas Day her sister helped her do the cooking, and saw this unusual ritual. "Why are you doing it that way?"

"It makes it come out juicier," she replied. "Or at least, I think so. That's the way Mom always did it."

That unsatisfying answer led both women to find their mother, who was in the other room with the grandchildren. "It makes it taste better," the mother said. "Or at least, that's why I think my mother always did it that way."

And so they called Grandma, and asked, "Why did you always cut off the end of the ham?"

"Well, dear, our oven was so small that that's the only way it would fit!"

Sometimes, we find ourselves caught up in old ways for reasons even we can't even remember. That is where the Latino vote is today. There is clearly a disconnect between our values and those of the Democrats. Yet despite some successes, Republicans have not yet managed to connect in a serious way, to win the majorities that conservative Latino opinion would suggest are already out there.

Table 5.1 *Q. Some people think of American Society as divided into two groups: the "haves," and the "have-nots"—while others think it's incorrect to think of America that way. Do you, yourself, think of America as divided into "haves" and "have-nots," or don't you think of America that way?*

	Yes	No
Whites	42	57
Blacks	67	31
Hispanics	31	64

Source: Joseph Carroll, "Whites, Minorities Differ in Views of Economic Opportunities in U.S.," *Gallup News Service*, Jul. 10, 2006.

Some conservative writers treat such future dreams like those of Linus, waiting in the Pumpkin Patch for *la Gran Calabaza*! Again, they are wrong. The next time you hear presidential candidate John Edwards talk about there being "Two Americas," consider the question in Table 5.1, asked in a Gallup Poll from the summer of 2006.

Hispanics are forward-thinking and optimistic people. When we don't have a way, we create one ourselves. How else could anyone be possessed to make the trip on foot across the Arizona desert, or to try the 90-mile voyage in a tiny boat across the open ocean to Miami?

Yet our enterprising, practical spirit has not yet shaped the way we vote. Instead of finding our own way, we go back to an old way of thinking that never belonged to us. We may be the kind of people who will take three buses and wait an hour in the sun just to get to work, but when it comes to the one thing that can have the greatest impact in our lives— political participation—we revert to our grandparents' way of thinking.

Why is that? Why can't we shake the political label others have given us? If we're such natural Republicans, why hasn't the connection ever been made?

Despite the similarity in values between Hispanics and Republicans, there is obviously a major disconnect—most Hispanics vote Democrat. The "generic ballot" results from our seminal 1999 RNC survey found that by 52 to 32 percent, Hispanics preferred an unnamed Democratic candidate for Congress to an unnamed Republican. Such numbers persist to this day.

Figure 5.1   Hispanic Party ID

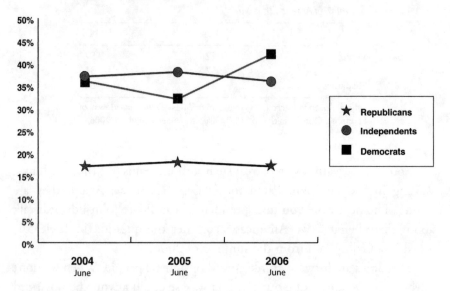

Q. In politics, as of today, do you consider yourself a Republican, a Democrat, or an Independent ["other" and "dk/refused" information not included]

Source: Gallup Poll Social Series: Minority Rights & Relations/Black-White Social Audit 2004–2006

Figure 5.2   Hispanic Party ID (Female)

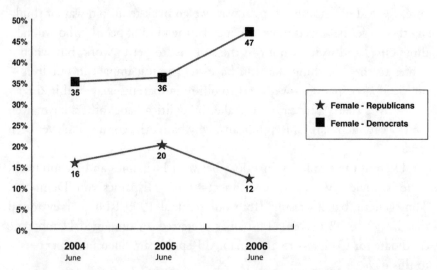

Source: Gallup Poll Social Series: Minority Rights & Relations/Black-White Social Audit 2004–2006

Figure 5.3   Hispanic Party ID (Male)

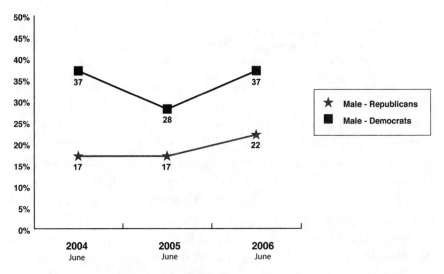

Source: Gallup Poll Social Series: Minority Rights & Relations/Black-White Social Audit 2004–2006

Many in the GOP recognize that Hispanics hold many of the same virtues and values as Republicans, but they continue to feel alienated by what they characterize as closed-mindedness on the part of Republicans. Hispanics are strong believers in family, church, and hard work. These are some of the same ideals embodied by the Republican Party. The challenge facing Republicans is to find a way to "connect" with Hispanics on these values without changing what the GOP stands for and without being adversarial in the process (as in the debate over immigration). These Republicans recognize that building this bridge with the Hispanic community will take several years—if not a generation—to complete.

One key indication that there is simply a disconnect—and not a real opposition between Latinos and Republicans—is the fact that Hispanics are not nearly as likely as the rest of the population to recognize what most other voters recognize as key Republican strengths.

The idea that Democrats should lead Republicans in being tough on crime, and run even on "moral values," is clearly a deviation from opinions among the U.S. population as a whole. Table 5.2 shows that

Table 5.2 *Which Party Is Best For...?*[2]

	Dem	Rep
Improving public education	56	28
Fighting crime and drugs	42	38
Focusing on the decline in moral values/family	39	41
Maintaining a strong national defense	32	53

Univision's 1998 survey actually gave Democrats a 44–33 percent advantage on the issues of crime and drugs![3] From the pessimist's perspective, this is a problem, but the optimist sees how great the upside could be if Hispanic voters and Republicans were speaking the same language.

There are big obstacles to this ever happening, and we must address them before looking at how Republicans can overcome them. First, there are mutual biases between Hispanics and Republicans—not necessarily in the sense of racial discrimination, but in the sense of prejudgements by one side against the other. Second, there is the Spanish-language media, for whom "left-wing bias" is a less apt phrase than "left-wing advocacy."

Still, Republicans should take heart. They have the right message; it's just a question of whether they are willing to apply it and work to earn Latinos' trust.

prejudice

It's always a mistake to neglect to visit new neighbors quickly after they move in. If you don't, shared moments later on the street or in the hallway will be awkward. If the awkwardness somehow escalates to suspicion—perhaps your garbage can mysteriously disappears, for example—there is no recourse. Suddenly, because there has been no connection, no prior relationship or friendship, the smallest misunderstanding becomes a major issue.

Hispanics and Republicans are suffering through the same kind of relationship problem that such dysfunctional neighbors have. Someone took the trash can. The biases that Republicans and Latinos have toward each other are in many cases amusing, but in most cases disappointing. Each side should reexamine the other with an open mind.

Often when our firm conducts focus groups for issue campaigns, we will ask participants to tell us what they think of the political parties or of certain candidates. The following exchange is a typical example. The woman speaking in the focus group, "Jessica," is an American citizen whose parents came from Mexico. She obviously came into the focus group with strongly negative prejudices against President Bush and Republicans, based on nothing substantial that she had seen or heard. But the terms she uses to describe him and where she got her opinion from, are indicative of pre-mindset:

MODERATOR: What's the negative about President Bush?

JESSICA: I think he's a racist.

MODERATOR: Why do you say that?

JESSICA: That's my opinion. I have no way to back it up, but I just feel like he's against the lower class 'cause he's up here and he sees us as down here. That's how I feel . . . I don't know, 'cause that's how his father was, so therefore like father like son, you know?

MODERATOR: Where do you get your information?

JESSICA: My parents. That's what they told me. I don't know . . . just from watching the news what I see, that's how I feel, that's how he is toward us, like he didn't care about us. He cares about him and the Republicans.

MODERATOR: Let me ask you, when you're saying that's how he feels about *us*, who's *us*—who are you talking about?

JESSICA: I mean the majority of the multiculture, like the African Americans, the Mexicans, the. . . . He doesn't care. I mean he doesn't care about us. He cares about these people like who's with him, the Republicans . . . the white people that have money, 'cause we have no money to do with nothing. We have no weight, you know?

There's probably nothing President Bush could do to make this woman think better of him. She doesn't really seem to know where her opinion came from, but it's hers and the intensity is strong. The stereotype of the bigwig Republican politician who only cares about and works on behalf of wealthy, white fat cats may seem like an anachronism to real Republicans, but a lot of people actually do see things that way.

These prejudices go both ways. Juan Guillermo Tornoe, a Guatemalan advertising executive who has been a permanent legal U.S. resident for four years, tells a story about the time his wife and two young children were leaving their local post office in Austin, Texas.

"We make it a point to talk to the kids in Spanish all the time so they maintain their language," he says. "So they were walking out of the post office, and my wife says, in Spanish, 'Hey guys don't run, be careful with the cars.' This old gentlemen, typical WASP, turns around and faces my kids, and tells them, 'You know kids, you live in America, you have to learn the English language to be successful.' A six-year-old and a two-year-old. My wife turns around and tells him, "Excuse me sir, my kids are fully bilingual." And the guy doesn't even acknowledge her, he just keeps on walking.

"Many of my friends root for Republicans," says Tornoe. "We were brought up in Guatemala to believe that a Republican in office in the U.S. was better for Latin America. But this man—I have no idea what his political agenda was, but unfortunately, from my experience, I would bet that he's a Republican."

This man on the street was talking down to the family of a successful corporate executive—young children who probably spoke more languages than he does—presumably because he saw Spanish-speakers as people to whom he could teach a lesson. It is no surprise that suspicions and prejudices develop when Republicans treat Hispanics not as brothers, but as the illegitimate children of America.

These mutual prejudices can be even more illustrative in cases where both sides—Latinos and Republicans—are more sympathetic toward one another to begin with.

I always think of the story of my friend Benito Montañez, a 30-year-old government professional who is by no means a typical Hispanic Texan. His family has been American, Protestant and Republican for several generations. On his father's side, Benny's family has been in Texas at least since Mexico's last European ruler, Emperor Maximiliano Hapsburg, was executed in Queretaro in 1867. His mother's family has more recent roots in Nicaragua—his grandmother's sour memories of the left-wing Sandinista government helped form his conservative politics as a boy.

Benny remembers that in 1988, he was one of a handful of students in his fourth-grade class at the predominantly Hispanic Westwood Terrace Elementary to vote for George Bush in his class's mock presidential election.

"Of course, Dukakis wiped the floor in my school," he says with a grin.

Benny is very typical in other ways. Although he speaks perfect English, he still lapses into Spanglish when he chats with his pals and his family back home on the heavily Hispanic west side of San Antonio. "As white as I get, I'm still brown on the inside," he likes to say.

Despite his long-held conservative leanings, Benny's experience in coming to the party was anything but easy. In fact it isn't hard to imagine that other, less Republican Hispanics would not have persevered. Benny still remembers the woman's voice on the other end of the line when, as a 17-year-old, he called the Bexar County GOP to sign up and get involved.

"What's your last name again?"

"Montañez."

"What's that?"

"*Montañez.*"

After three attempts, he had to settle for being called "Martinez."

"Oh," the woman on the line remarked. "We've got a guy who does Hispanic stuff."

Hispanic stuff. It didn't sound very appealing. "I don't want to be in a special uniform that says, 'Hispanic,' " Benny says. But he was soon contacted by the "Hispanic stuff" guy. "Good, we need Hispanics!" the man said. "Right now I'm the only one!" Terrific.

The first meeting Benny attended gave him a dose of culture shock, although he was not discouraged. "He told me the address, and it was the whitest area and the richest part of town," he tells me. "I'd never been there in my life. I mean I had just *never* been there. It was a 45-minute drive. And when I show up at the restaurant, it's all these guys in cowboy hats, buckles and boots." He laughs: "I'm an Emilio guy, not a Randy Travis guy!"

Benny cringes as he recalls pitiful attempts by the GOP to run token Hispanic candidates in San Antonio—one such candidate was Cuban, which is odd considering that all the voters were Mexicans. "His whole campaign was, 'Hey, I'm Hispanic like you!' " He grins as he shakes his head, "It was just wrong." Another Republican prejudice about Hispanics: *they're all the same.* (In the same vein, I once had to explain to a non-Hispanic Republican Party organizer why she couldn't hold a Republican *Cinco de Mayo* celebration in a Cuban restaurant, and she was genuinely stunned to hear it.)

Benny stuck to it anyway, and eventually he found himself the only Hispanic among 50 or so members of the College Republicans at St. Mary's College in San Antonio. But he went on to change that. One day, while suffering through a liberal feminist professor's tirade, Benny looked over at two Latino classmates nearby. "Can you believe that?" he asked. They smiled. It was the beginning of a new friendship.

"No one had ever talked to them before," says Benny. "No one told them they can be *la raza* and a Republican. So many of them have the wrong idea: If I become a Republican, I marry a white chick, I move to the North Side, my name changes from *Barrera* to 'Bear-air-a.'"

Benny's story had a happy ending. Despite Republicans who just didn't understand, and despite the patronizing idea of doing *Hispanic stuff* for the local party, Benny found his way into the GOP and, through politics, to a new career he loves. At the 2000 GOP convention, he received applause from Republican bystanders who heard him deliver a fantastic interview to a Latino radio host on radio row. His trip to Philadelphia eventually led to a White House internship, and then to his current successful career. Just as John Tower won over Robert Estrada by appointing his brother to the Air Force Academy—just as Henry Bonilla won me over by reaching out—someone gave Benny an opportunity to be a part of it all, and he saw clearly beyond the prejudices on both sides.

"The internship is the lock—that's how you get these people in," he says. "It's something the Democrats have figured out, and they recruit students and send activists back into the community. By the time they go back home, they have links to the Democrats."

Republicans can do the same in order to erode some of the old prejudices Latinos hold against them. They can do much more if they offer opportunities not just to Latinos that approach them like Benny, but also to people farther off the radar screen, like Robert Estrada.

Unfortunately, there can be a much darker side to the prejudices that alienate Hispanics from Republicans. The perception that our country is being "invaded" or "overrun" by hordes of Hispanics coming here illegally has at times caused the rhetoric concerning immigration to take on a distinctly racist tone. As George W. Bush once said to former California Governor Pete Wilson, many view the question of immigration—especially illegal immigration—less as a policy issue and more as an opportunity to launch into a diatribe against Hispanics.

In unguarded moments, some Republicans employ Hispanics as scapegoats for Americans' cultural and economic problems. They are a minority, but a large and loud enough minority that they must be addressed. This has traditionally been a cynical way for some to rev up the conservative base vote. In the election of 2006, which we will examine more closely in a later chapter, this ploy failed even as it resulted in the pointless alienation of many potential Republican voters.

The anti-immigration movement has many faces. In the West, a group of concerned citizens formed the Minuteman patrols in 2002 to troll the southern border for illegal immigrants. Many of these are honest, hard-working Americans—even if misguided—fearful of what the demographic trend of Hispanicization means for them. Others in the anti-immigration movement are openly racist.

"I'm a mother of two children—at this rate, they're not going to have a future in this country," shouts a frantic, hysterical California anti-immigration activist caught on a YouTube video. The woman, Chelene Nightengale, works for the group Save Our State, the original champions of Proposition 187. "I grew up in a safe, patriotic environment, but that environment is changing. We're becoming a nation of lawlessness and immorality. . . . I want them to have their rights, but I want them in their own country. Because this is my right and my country, and I'm losing my right." Nightengale goes on to tearfully blame illegal aliens for all of America's problems. "Our poverty is rising, our unemployment rate is increasing. Our students cannot get an education."

The heated chatter over immigration is not limited to a few activists on the fringes. In Congress, the Immigration Reform Caucus of Rep. Tom Tancredo (R-Colo.)—who has called for a moratorium on *legal* immigration—has grown from just 11 members in 2001 to 68 today.

Tancredo is known for his over-the-top comments on immigrants. After the midterm election, he got his name in the headlines when he declared that Hispanic immigration had turned Miami into a "Third World Country."

"Look at what has happened to Miami," Tancredo told WorldNetDaily, a conservative web magazine. "It has become a Third World country. You just pick it up and take it and move it someplace. You would never know you're in the United States of America. You would certainly say you're in a Third World country."

In a later statement defending his comments from critics, Tancredo added: "Moreover, the sheer size and number of ethnic enclaves devoid of any English and dominated by foreign cultures is widespread. Frankly, many of these areas could have been located in another country. And until America gets serious about demanding assimilation, this problem will continue to spread."[4] Of course, it is lost on Tancredo that so many Spanish-speakers in Miami are Puerto Rican American citizens, or legal refugees from the murderous regime of Fidel Castro. The main point is that people who speak Spanish are backward Third-Worlders, even if they live in a modern place like Miami. Tancredo is famous for producing the most strident anti-immigration rhetoric on the Hill, but even his more moderate colleagues have reacted to the demographic trend with perplexity, fear, and political opportunism.

Former Rep. J. D. Hayworth (R-Ariz.), once a proponent of increased immigration and a guest-worker program, totally reversed himself after the 2004 election. He began delivering bombastic floor speeches against immigration and even penned *Whatever It Takes: Illegal Immigration, Border Security, and the War on Terror* (Regnery), a book on the need for a nationwide crackdown.

A group of 17 Republicans co-sponsored a bill in February 2005 that would end "birthright citizenship"—that is, the guarantee that anyone born in the U.S. is a legal citizen. Given that many Hispanic Americans became citizens in just that way, it is not a formula for making friends.

Congressman Steve King, whose district is all of 3.6 percent Hispanic, compared illegal aliens to cattle when he suggested in July the need for an electrified border fence that would "provide a disincentive for people to climb over the top." Speaking from the House floor, he stated, "We could also electrify this wire with the kind of current that would not kill somebody, but it would be a discouragement for them to be fooling around with it. We do that with livestock all the time."

This spring, talk radio host Michael Savage managed to belittle both Hispanic immigrants and Roman Catholics, as he blamed the world's millennially conservative institution for America's problems:

> Make no bones about it, it's the greedy Catholic Church that was behind it, because the people of America walked away from the molesters' dens, and they need to bring in people from the Third World who are still gullible enough to sit there and listen to the molesters. . . . The Roman Catholic Church flooded the streets because they cannot get parishioners anymore amongst educated white people who have caught onto the racket and instead they need to import dummies to sit in the church pews.[5]

As egregious and as racist as Savage's comments were, he has his radio show because people listen to it—and they still do. He is speaking to some Americans' real fears and prejudices. Many Hispanics have the wrong idea about Republicans, it is certainly also true Republicans need to learn a bit more about Hispanics. Most importantly, that the changing cultural landscape is not a threat to this nation's survival.

meet the spanish press

Republicans generally think they get a raw deal from the media. But if you think the English media is bad, try the Spanish-language media on for size. As Republicans seek to bridge the disconnect between themselves and Latinos, the Spanish-speaking media serves as an obstacle at almost every turn, pitting the two groups against each other.

Moreover, they enjoy an impunity that would never apply to their English counterparts, since most Americans can't read or understand them well enough to realize how insidious or how blatant their biases can be. Even the Federal Communications Commission—the government's broadcast watchdog—has only one Spanish speaker on staff.[6]

"You've got a lot of things happening, because the language barrier isolates them from the normal pressures," says Dr. Robert M. Entman, head of the school of media and public affairs at The George Washington University.[7]

Chris Allen and Leslie Jackson Turner of the University of Nebraska compared 53 stories that appeared on the front pages of the *Los Angeles Times* and *La Opinion*—the preeminent Latino daily newspaper in Los Angeles—in the first three days after the election of 1996. At that time, President Clinton was already under fire for accepting illegal campaign contributions, and several questions had been raised in the mainstream media about his character. The Democratic Party had just been forced to return a $325,000 gift. These things were all reported by the *Times*—hardly a friendly paper toward the GOP—but not by *La Opinion*.

The results showed that "*La Opinion* concentrated on the election only as it related to challenges facing the president in the next 4 years and anticipated changes in the cabinet, with no mention of fund-raising, the president's character, or international issues." Compared to the *Times*, the Spanish-language daily's coverage of Clinton was fawning. "The common thread of the *Los Angeles Times* articles was not that Clinton was reelected but that the reelected president had a flawed character. In contrast, the articles in *La Opinion* simply identified that Clinton was reelected and that he faced many challenges during the next 4 years in office."[8]

When it comes to Spanish-language media bias, *La Opinion*'s fluff treatment of President Clinton is only the tip of the iceberg. Last year's debate on immigration reform produced some incredible examples of an unfair and broad use of the "anti-immigrant" label—they applied it last year to almost any Republican who supported tighter border security measures or opposed illegal immigration—even to those who *supported* a guest-worker program.

Rather than treating immigration as the complex issue it is, several leading news anchors and columnists mislead by painting the world in black and white—anyone who supports more border enforcement or opposes illegal immigration is automatically the equivalent of Tom Tancredo. Meanwhile, figures like Tancredo are frequently given undue importance, as though they represented the whole of the Republican Party. Outreach efforts by Republicans in any form are minimized, ignored, or even blatantly lied about.

In June 2006 the Associated Press published a story on Rep. James Sensenbrenner, sponsor of the REAL ID act—which tightened state standards for tamper-proof identification documents—and the House's border security bill. In English, the title was simply, "Sensenbrenner Declines Invitation to Hispanic Group's Yearly Convention," and the story talked about a convention in Milwaukee. Simple enough. But the Spanish translators at the Associated Press were less interested in an even-handed story. They headlined it, "*Legislador Antiinmigrante No Asiste A Convención Hispana,*" or "Anti-immigrant Legislator Won't Attend Hispanic Convention."

Sensenbrenner, as the floor manager for the more controversial House border security bill, had tried to highlight the bill's provisions to combat human smugglers, punish employers who hire illegal workers, and curb the influence of illegal immigrant gang members. But Democrats and Hispanic organizations, with the help of countless Spanish-language media outlets, noted only that it treated illegal entry into the country as a felony. Some leading Univision anchors continue to mention this every time they refer back to the bill, but they never mention that it does so only because Democrats voted almost unanimously to keep that provision in the bill. It was a political move to embarrass the Republicans who promised to remove the provision from the final version of the bill. The Spanish-language media were willing to go along and conceal the Democrats' involvement.[9]

The most absurd example of Spanish-language media bias came when Rep. Mark Foley's inappropriate behavior toward congressional pages was exposed last year. The *Washington Hispanic* reported the news in a rather unconventional way with the October 6 headline: "*Escándalo sexual involucra a republicano antiinmigrante,*" which translates to "Anti-immigrant Republican involved in sex scandal."[10] It's as though the papers had covered the assassination of JFK with the headline, "Tax-Cutting President Shot Dead in Dallas!"

What's more, Foley actually had a 0 percent rating with the anti-immigration group FAIR. Before he resigned from Congress in disgrace, Foley had voted against several truly anti-immigrant measures, including one that would have required hospitals to report illegal immigrants who sought out medical care.[11] He had even opposed a measure forbidding the U.S. government from discussing with the Mexican government the activities of the Minutemen on the border.[12] He wasn't exactly a fire-eating Tancredo-ite. No matter: He was "*antiinmigrante*" to the Spanish media because he was a Republican and he supported some border security measures.

I believe, as I think most Americans do, that a serious discussion is possible between people of good faith about how to reform immigration and keep America safe. Some believe that border security must first be tightened, and then we can proceed to a reform including some kind of program that will give legal status to some immigrant workers. But the Spanish-language media never brook the possibility that there is more than one view. Throughout the immigration debate, they tarred every Republican who supported border security as anti-immigrant—often using exactly that term—and went out of their way to do so even when reporting on unrelated matters.

Sometimes, Republicans found they were damned no matter what they did. That was the case for Rep. Bob Inglis, who supported a guest-worker program and was *still* labeled as anti-immigrant. The December 19, 2005, edition of *El Periodico Latino* in Greenville, South Carolina, sported this headline, which began in caps: "MALAS NOTICIAS PARA LOS INMIGRANTES: Congresista Inglis respaldará la posición de inmigración del Presidente Bush." Translation: "BAD NEWS FOR IMMIGRANTS: Congressman Inglis will support President Bush's position on immigration." This is the president who supposedly supports "amnesty!" In other words, if you're a Republican, you just can't win.

Most English-speakers probably do not realize the advocacy role that the Spanish-language media take in the political arena. It would shock most people if English-language outlets did the same. As the Associated Press reported last March, the immigration marches "were organized, promoted or publicized for weeks by Spanish-language radio hosts and TV anchors as a demonstration of Hispanic pride and power."[13] Telemundo Chicago, a Spanish-language TV station, began its coverage blitz ten days before a recent such rally even happened.

In some cases, Spanish-language television has evolved toward a more politically active role beyond just reporting—its top anchors, such as Univision's Jorge Ramos, view themselves as commentators as well, something English-language anchors usually avoid. In his book *The Latino Wave: How Hispanics Will Elect the Next American President* (2004), Ramos certainly has an agenda. On page 219 of that book, he offers his second recommendation for his "Latino Agenda": "We must push for amnesty[.]" Ramos is entitled to his opinion, but on television he styles himself as a neutral commentator.

The fact is that Ramos and many of his Spanish media colleagues are liberals who will never give Republicans a fair shot. On education, Ramos laments in his book how it is President Bush's fault that there is "no specific national program in the works designed to help young Latino students."[14]

Forget about the "No Child Left Behind" law, which raised both standards and funding for *all* students, including Latinos. When I was in the Bush administration, we also set aside $30 million to study the best approaches for teaching young Spanish-speaking children to read and learn English. Ramos misleads his readers, writing as though Bush has neglected every child's education. In fact, to the consternation of his conservative base and many congressional Republicans,[15] Bush has arguably been the most hands-on U.S. president in history with respect to education policy, and certainly more generous than his Democratic predecessor, Bill Clinton, in terms of increased federal funding.[16]

the right message

Amid these obstacles, the situation appears bleak for the GOP. Prejudices like the ones between Hispanics and Republicans can take decades to overcome. And beyond just complaining fruitlessly, there is little Republicans can do about the clear anti-Republican lean of the Spanish-language media. But Republicans can appeal to Latinos directly. Where they have succeeded, Republicans have won Hispanic votes because they found the right message and spoke to our concerns.

Again, we won't be bought with political gimmicks. Don't assume that immigration is our big issue, and that the floodgates will suddenly open and Latinos will vote Republican as soon as Republicans enact a guest-worker program or an amnesty. You might as well eat some tacos for a photo op if that's your plan.

We certainly don't care for a political message like that of Pat Buchanan or Tom Tancredo, who tell us that our cultural heritage is somehow a backward, debilitating pollutant to an otherwise great American culture. But it's also not enough simply to spare us such garbage. We want to hear something *real*. As the most optimistic voting bloc in America, Latinos thirst for ideas and ideals that will improve our lives. And on that front, Republicans have much to offer.

Figure 5.4 The Reality Today: How Parties Speak to Our Values

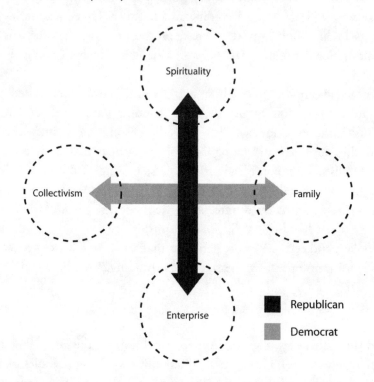

Democrats—and some Republicans—have already learned how to speak to us where we are. In an earlier chapter, I identified four of the principles most important to Latinos: the family, the collective or community, faith, and entrepreneurship. The Democrats already see how they can fit their message to our concerns, but will the Republicans learn as well?

How do the political parties reach out to Hispanics and appeal for their votes? The Democratic message appeals very strongly to two of the four fundamental priorities we have identified as common to the Latino cultures represented in the United States: the family on one side, and the community or collective on the other.

When Democrats argue their point by asserting that a tax hike or a gun ban is necessary "for the children," or that massive social spending is needed "to improve our community," they appeal to a broad number of constituencies. But the message is amplified among Hispanics because of our cultural affinity toward those values.

The liberal Rockridge Institute released a position paper in late 2006 making just this point about the Democratic message, asserting that despite all of the divisions among left-wing interests, they share in common what can be called "nurturant morality."

"The key insight for progressives is that all [progressive] groups express an aspect of nurturant morality," states the institute's position paper. These "nurturant values" include empathy, protection, compassion, equality, fairness, trust, cooperation and community building. As concepts, the paper asserts, they "counter conservative efforts to force Strict Father morality into our society and institutions of government."[17]

As a philosophical expression of an overarching moral system, "nurturant morality" is shallow and unfulfilling. It relies mostly on platitudes and warm feelings, carrying little in the way of substance or overriding rationale. But as a political message, "nurturantism" is nothing short of brilliant. It appeals both to voters' need for love and their fears of failure and shame, and it is particularly effective in reaching our cultural proclivities as Hispanic voters.

Not only do Democrats employ a positive "nurturing" message of love, but also a negative "nurturing" message of fear—a message that says, "*They* will hurt you, but *we* will protect you." This negative theme of "protection"—a message of fear that strikes at the heart of family and community instincts—went so far for the Democratic Party in the 1996 election that they turned the conventional wisdom about positive and negative advertising on its head. "We packaged the message to Latinos in attack ads on the GOP," DNC Latino Outreach Director Andy Hernandez told Stacey Connaughton in her book, *Inviting Latino Voters* (2005).[18] "This is the Party of Newt and Pete Wilson. We tried to package the GOP as anti-Latino."

That is, of course, unsurprising. But normally, negative advertising depresses turnout among an opponent's supporters. In advertising to Hispanics, Hernandez believed he could get *more* of them to vote by playing on fear rather than on love.

"[I]ssue pieces were persuasion messages; negative ads were turnout messages," he told Connaughton. This Democratic operative was amazingly frank about his party's play on fear: "In terms of occasional and swing [Hispanic] voters, they are more likely to go to the polls on the basis of what the GOP would do *to them* as opposed to what the Democrats would do *for them*. That was the theory that we used."

Despite its dark side, the "nurturant" Democratic message is a political message of *mothering*, a pitch for government as the solution to an ever-expanding array of both personal and societal problems, beginning with the widely accepted ones—such as guarantees of physical safety and contractual integrity—and expanding by leaps and bounds into new issue areas as the popular whim identifies new problems with life in the modern world.

Just as a young boy knows that Mom will take care of his skinned knee, the modern citizen can expect his nurturant "Mother Sam" to correct societal inequality, alleviate poverty, guarantee against business failure, root out personal habits inimical to public health (as with smoking bans), and even punish ugly attitudes (as with hate crimes legislation) by giving the kids a time-out. New York City has now banned trans-fats from its restaurants—just how is the progressive government model different from that of your mother, who demanded that you eat your veggies before leaving the table?

The "nurturant" Democrats offer the political and rhetorical equivalent of "comfort food"—it gives the citizens a warm feeling inside, and it assures them that even if there is a Republican boogeyman in the closet, someone in power is looking out for them and can spare them the trouble of solving our everyday problems.

But if this progressive message is the chicken soup of the public discourse, it is being served in a soup kitchen. Its beneficiaries will be back for more next Friday. Its results are institutional dependency and a broad willingness to accept mediocrity as a value, to avoid the personal risks necessary to create a better life for oneself. What the Democrats actually offer is dependency, listlessness, and the restriction of personal freedom.

The Democrats' message speaks to the collective and familial instincts that are so strong in Latino culture. But the message has a serious downside. It does not speak to our aspirations for both material and spiritual fulfillment—our enterprising and religious nature. It causes us to disengage from America as a whole and consider ourselves a special group in need of special treatment. It makes us dependent, isolates us, and de-individuates us.

Figure 5.5 "Hispanic Heart": Creating the Ideal Model

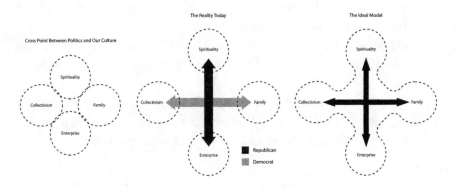

The Democrats offer the warm embrace of a family, but it is a false embrace—the government can never provide a sense of accomplishment or self-worth, nor can it replace the family or give true emotional support.

This is where Republicans can find their opening with Hispanics. As Democrats appeal to the values of family and the collective, Republicans can appeal across the other axis of the Hispanic heart, to the value of entrepreneurship, along with the traditional appeal they make to the religious faith of Hispanic voters.

And as we have seen, the entrepreneurial Latino spirit applies in a broad way, not only to the well-established Hispanic families in the United States, but also—and perhaps especially—to the new immigrants. Among the many reasons President Bush has been so successful with Hispanic voters is his language about entrepreneurship. By talking about an "ownership society," the president is speaking the language of a people that is more optimistic about the future of America than even those higher up on the economic ladder.

If the Democrats' message invites you to a community barbecue, then the Republican message is the opportunity to own your own barbecue. But that's not enough—who wants to barbecue alone? If Democrats appeal to two of the chambers of the Hispanic heart at the expense of the other two, Republicans have to do more. They, too, have to speak to the familial and collective instincts of Hispanic voters. Not only must they soothe the fears Democrats sow in them over "*what they will do to us*," they must also show how Republican ideas and ideals will help Hispanic families thrive. Republicans have to show up and make the case that they can help the community as a whole, by providing opportunities for families to build wealth and to preserve their children's innocence—by helping each individual take responsibility and be an asset to everyone else, not a burden.

We have seen that in Latinos, Republicans have a natural ally, even if neither group sees it yet. The GOP can offer a red-meat alternative to the Democrats' chicken soup—an alternative that needs to be explored.

six

our solutions work

When Republicans talk about growing the "back bench," Ted Cruz, Texas solicitor general, is who they mean. Cruz, a Harvard-educated lawyer, is a fearless purveyor of conservative ideals and he has the rare gift of charisma that inspires others to share his vision.

What I describe as "opportunity conservatism" is the idea that when conceptualizing, articulating and defending conservative policies, the focus should be on easing the means of ascent up the economic ladder. The basic difference between left and right on domestic policy is that the left typically proposes grabbing someone on the lower rungs of the economic ladder and trying to move them up by force of government—which is a perfectly fine aspiration, except it doesn't work. Policies that seek to use government to pick someone up and move them up the ladder systematically fail, and have failed for decades. The data are overwhelming on that. The only things that have ever worked for ascending the economic ladder are instilling individual responsibility and creating an environment that facilitates and encourages people pulling themselves up rung by rung.

> Hispanics have a great record in America of being entrepreneurial, of wanting to work and of understanding why they came to America. They don't come here because they want to be in a third world country ruled by some oligarchy that hands out economic favors but to find a free market economy at every level that serves them.
>
> —*Fred Barnes, executive editor of The Weekly Standard*[1]

Today's political discussion is often more about heat than light. Spend a few minutes watching Fox, CNN or MSNBC, or tune in to any radio talk show—left or right—and you'll conclude that regardless of the issues, politicians and "party strategists" on both sides are more intent on scoring political points than on accomplishing some benefit for the nation. For the sake of full disclosure, I am often one of the pundits.

Unfortunately, Republicans are just as culpable as their Democratic counterparts. In a war of words, unilateral disarmament would be fatal for either party, and so politicians of every stripe line up for the cameras, talking points in hand, offering glib distractions intended to cast their opponents' positions in the worst possible light.

Seldom do we hear any discussion about the common good. Rarer still is the solid, factual analysis that gives voters an objective view of whether a given policy is actually working. Why? Because neither side believes you're interested or smart enough to absorb such complicated discussions. Instead, we hear slogans and see rhetorical smoke.

The cheap shot, the broad generalization, has cost Republicans greatly, because, unlike the Democrats, our agenda is strong enough to stand on its own. In a war of slogans and talking points, the Democrats can win—especially among Latinos, who, as we've already seen, still buy into many unflattering myths about Republicans. Part of the problem is our own political immaturity: Hispanics—even business owners, second- or third-generation families, even activists—have less experience lobbying the government than more politically unified groups. Compare Hispanics to African Americans, or women, or other ethnic or religious groups, and we're still babes in the woods.

My business is based on asking people what they think, then standing back and letting them talk. The answers I get from Hispanic respondents in focus groups reveal monstrous misconceptions about the Republican Party that pose a real obstacle to the GOP getting its message out. Recall the woman who believed, to her core, that President George W. Bush is a "racist." Her basis? His father, President George H. W. Bush, was also a racist, and so the son must be a racist too! That she could provide no evidence for her accusation against father or son mattered not at all. She'd made up her mind based on a misconception, and nobody was going to convince her otherwise.

When I asked Hispanic women in Detroit and California to describe the Republican Party in a word or two, I heard answers like "higher-class," "warriors," "moralists," "support the upper class," "think more about money," "against immigration" and, most troubling of all, "against Hispanics." Though the answers vary by age, length of time in country and other socioeconomic factors, the intensity of the response against Republicans remained consistent. Many of these women were conservative Latinas who said they voted Republican and had only good things to say about President Bush. Yet they were describing Republicans in negative terms, based on what they believed Republicans to be against. If Republicans are going to make progress among these individuals, they must communicate what they are for.

Republicans have a lot of work to do—but the good news is that the misperceptions, while intense, are so vague and have so little basis in reality that they can be unwound and minds can be opened. There is great upside potential in the future.

the right ideas

So what do Republicans stand for? In the climate of the rhetorical food fight that today passes for political dialogue, it's hard to tell. Besides, most families are too busy thinking about things like groceries, mortgages, bills and getting the kids to school to focus on policy debates. Misconceptions provide a handy, if inaccurate, form of shorthand—but if Republicans are to enjoy the full measure of their potential, they must develop a laser-like focus on reversing these political prejudices, especially among Latinos.

It's difficult to disprove a negative, but Republicans are the only ones who can assuage fears among Latinos that they "don't care about the people." They can do so only by demonstrating their commitment to helping Hispanic families and the communities with policies that are effective.

Like the Hispanic families they seek to represent, Republicans believe in lower taxes on working families, not higher ones. They want to make small business owners—including the new family-owned Hispanic grocery store, beauty parlors or contracting business—subject to less government regulation, not more. And just like Hispanics as a whole, Republicans believe in personal responsibility, not government maternalism.

Democrats often respond that such policies benefit the "fat cats." Hispanics—at least those who are "swing" voters, or who are persuadable—understand that "fat cats" employ a lot of people, and all but the most jaded and cynical among us hope one day to become a "fat cat" (or at least an "overweight" cat). Republicans' focus must be on those Hispanics with a positive point of view, who believe it is within their grasp to achieve the dream of starting a business, owning a home, sending a child to college. As with any other group, Republicans' best chance in the Hispanic community is to reach out to the optimists, those who dream, who work diligently and save; such persons don't find much appeal in a government that takes away their money to build a harmful culture of dependency.

Republicans are not the party of the rich, but of those who hope to be rich. They are the voice of those who revere the traditional values of family and faith, who want to preserve the innocence of children in a world that doesn't contradict parental guidance in schools, on television, in movies, in music and on the Internet. They hold that security depends on strength, and they respect and revere the service and sacrifice of those in uniform.

Republican values are the values of working people—even those who are members of organized labor. That's why working-class donors traditionally give far more money to Republicans. And despite a strongly Democratic union get-out-the-vote effort, those earning between $30,000 and $50,000 split their votes evenly between George Bush and John Kerry in 2004.

Republicans are also fortunate to have adversaries who are often so blinded by their own prejudices, so self-righteous, that they cease to think effectively. Consider *The Emerging Democratic Majority*, in which authors Ruy Texeira and John Judis argue that if New Jersey's middle class voted Republican in the 1980s, it must be because they're racists![2] Maybe they should visit the working class neighborhoods in Jersey that were appalled by the Democrats' direction on social issues in the 1970s, which was summed up by a concerned Democratic senator as "Acid, Amnesty (for Vietnam draft dodgers) and Abortion!"[3]

Make no mistake: Republicans will have to do all the heavy lifting themselves—the news media will be of no help at all—and they must do so in a way that is specifically tailored to Latinos.

Republicans and Latinos need each other if we are to strengthen and make secure the nation we all love. Former House Speaker Newt Gingrich likes to say that the best political strategy is to stand by an "80 percent issue"—an issue that most people agree with—and say, "Hey, look at me!" When politicians find common ground this way with large majorities, they can hold voters' attention long enough to explain their views on the big issues they care about, and hopefully to establish a connection. Among Hispanic voters in particular, there are all kinds of "80 percent issues" for Republicans to work with—lower taxes, less regulation, support for families, protection of children against the filth that pervades our culture, protection of the unborn.

Too often, some Republicans run away from their positions. Instead, they should be proud of what they stand for, unafraid to advance their views when they approach the Latino community, because these ideas offer the most hope to Latinos. In this chapter, we will look at a few places where the nexus between Latinos and the GOP is strongest, and offer issues where these two groups can connect for a mutual benefit.

building latino family wealth

The U.S. Census Bureau's last thorough report on Hispanic-owned businesses states that there were 1.6 million of them in the United States in 2002, and that Latinos had been starting new businesses at a rate three times that of the U.S. population during the preceding five years. Today, there are probably upward of two million Hispanic-owned businesses, far more than are owned by any other minority group in America.

These Hispanic business owners and their families represent a natural Republican constituency. Republican ideals on economic and business issues will find a ready audience among these individuals, as we discuss ways of helping Latino businesses grow and create new jobs.

After all, as the fastest-growing segment of the small business community, Hispanics are disproportionately affected by higher marginal tax rates. We're the ones most affected by nit-picking government regulation. In coming generations, we will also be disproportionately affected by the death tax, since so many of these businesses are family owned.

For those who do not own businesses, the best and most common way to build family wealth is to own a home, and more than 50 percent of Hispanics already do, an all-time high. It's an achievement you barely hear of, but one that the Bush administration—and the Republican Congresses from 1994 to 2007—should trumpet from the rooftops. Indeed, surveys show that home ownership is the number one aspiration among Hispanics.

It was Republicans that kept interest rates low, that controlled inflation and made homeownership affordable. And it was Republicans who helped make home ownership so appealing, by creating a $250,000 per person tax exemption for profits from home sales.

For those who own investment property—and Hispanics often find that option a good way to build wealth—Republicans have fought Democratic efforts to raise the capital gains tax.

Just as business and home ownership help Latinos build generational wealth, our nation's retirement system should do the same. In their fight to allow workers to save, invest and have ownership of a portion of the money they currently pay in Social Security payroll taxes, Republicans offer hope for the future, of a nest-egg we can all pass on to the next generation. What's the magic about talking about small entrepreneurship, homeownership and retirement security? They all speak to the natural Latino cultural tendency toward enterprise and risk-taking, and to our strong commitment to sacrifice for family. If Republicans make the case that their ideas help Latino families build wealth and financial security through businesses, homes and investments, they will go a long way toward convincing them of the strength of Republican ideals—and put a dagger into the Democratic myth that Republicans will hurt children, the elderly and families.

marginal tax rates

Incredibly, surveys show that up to *one-third* of the owners of Hispanic businesses don't know they have to pay taxes: They actually believe they can avoid federal taxes by sending their money home to Mexico.[4]

These individuals obviously risk prosecution, but as more Latino business owners are educated about the real impact of the high taxes

Figure 6.1   Hispanic Business Owners' Views on Taxes 79% Believe their Business is Overtaxed

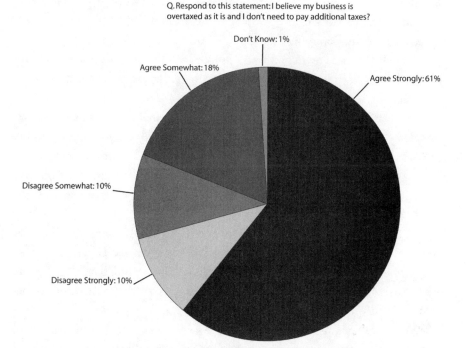

Q. Respond to this statement: I believe my business is overtaxed as it is and I don't need to pay additional taxes?

Don't Know: 1%

Agree Somewhat: 18%

Agree Strongly: 61%

Disagree Somewhat: 10%

Disagree Strongly: 10%

Source: Policy and Taxation Group, *Five-State Executive Interview Study of 100+ Hispanic Family-Owned Businesses on Federal "Death Taxes"*, July 14, 2004

Democrats want them to pay, there's no doubt they will respond politically. Once more, this unusual misconception underscores the need for a truly aggressive outreach effort to Latino business owners, not only in places like Texas and California but especially in the newly established Latino communities of the New South.

In 2004, my firm conducted 100 hour-long, in-depth executive interviews with Hispanic business owners.[5] We found that 79 percent of respondents somewhat or strongly agree their business is overtaxed, and they do not want to pay additional taxes (see Figure 6.1).

The ground is fertile: It is incumbent upon Republicans to educate such business owners about the impact of high marginal income tax rates on small businesses. By lowering top marginal rates, Republicans can help these job creators plough more of their earnings into hiring new employees, buying equipment and otherwise growing their businesses. The result is more jobs, as well as more goods and services at lower prices: Employees win, job creators win, consumers win. And, as more workers pay taxes on *their* incomes, the loss to the government is minimized.

Consider the Republican tax cuts of 2001 and 2003: On average, they saved small business owners $3,235 apiece in 2005—that's not much for Bill Gates or Warren Buffet, but it's a substantial amount for a young, struggling business owner.[6]

Democrats usually respond to the idea of marginal rate cuts by invoking the class-warfare argument: Even when the original 2001 tax cuts made the Tax Code more progressive, Democrats still complained that "top earners" should be denied any form of tax relief. They underestimated the Latino spirit. Remember how negatively Latinos react to the idea of "Two Americas"? At a rate higher than that of Anglos and more than double that of blacks, Latinos flatly reject the idea that America has "haves" and "have-nots."[7] As one Latina small business owner in a Las Vegas focus group put it in 2004, "those wealthy guys were like us one day." Hispanics are the most optimistic voter bloc in America—particularly about our own economic futures.

Moreover, when Democrats talk about the "wealthiest one percent" receiving a benefit from rate cuts, they are pointing directly at small businesspeople, including Latinos. Two-thirds of those paying taxes at the top rate do so on the strength of small business earnings reported as ordinary income.

Particularly beneficial to Hispanic business owners are provisions that Republicans passed after 9/11, which quadrupled the amount businesses can deduct for the purchase of new equipment, from $25,000 to $100,000. "That's trivial to giants, but a major incentive for small fry," wrote *BusinessWeek*'s Peter Coy.[8] President Bush's 2007 budget includes $19 billion in additional tax relief for small businesses.

You, dear reader, may disagree about whether high taxes and regulations harm small businesses, which have fewer resources for compliance than their big business competitors. But Bob, a photographer in a focus group for small, Hispanic family-owned businesses, definitely agrees with me. He was a Latino business owner "going it alone" in Las Vegas who had just learned about the "self-employment" tax he had to pay. When the opportunity came to take on some employees, he was deterred by the mounds of paperwork it would require.

> BOB: I'm at the growth phase, too, so like it was in the next two weeks I had to decide whether I wanted to take another contract and hire employees, so—it's not a lot with one or two employees, because I—
>
> ELSA: But then employee taxes—
>
> BOB: Right, the question is do I want to jump—and that's just the reason why. Do I want to just keep my own contract now and work myself, and be self-employed and not grow because of the impending FICA and Social Security and all that other stuff that goes along with taking on employees? And I'm also debating whether I can actually go on and do this contract, which is basically being handed to me, because I don't know if I can fulfill on that without having to open a whole can of worms, so to speak. And so I guess that is deterring me from growing.

Republicans must make the case to Latino business owners like Bob that lower taxes and less regulation helps their businesses. Americans are *not* undertaxed—our federal government's annual budget ($2.8 trillion) roughly equals the combined GDP of *all* of Latin America[9]—and that doesn't include state and local government spending.

the death tax

Another issue Republicans rarely raise with Latino business owners, but shouldn't be, is the inheritance and gift tax, better known for what it is— the "death tax," since it is paid after the owner of assets dies and passes them along.

This tax will disproportionately affect Latinos in the next generation simply because we are starting more businesses than any other group, and so we will be the ones most likely to leave estates large enough to fall into its trap.

This is an issue of Latino wealth creation. The permanent repeal of the death tax will give more Latino business owners a long-overdue opportunity to pass along wealth to their families.

Democrats have argued that the tax doesn't touch most people, because of the $2 million threshold—but we found in our focus groups that Latino business owners don't buy this when the situation is explained to them. "I have to admit I'm extremely surprised [the lifetime exemption] stopped at one or two million dollars," one of them said to me (the exemption amount depends on whether the taxpayer is single or married). "If you look at the value of a business, it's very easy to get over one or two million." Over the course of 20 years, almost any successful business reaches that milestone. Considering the values of real estate and equipment, it isn't difficult for even a relatively small business these days to amass several million dollars in combined assets.

The death tax is brutal, with rates ranging from 41 to 49 percent. It can cause serious problems, if not a forced sale, for the small businesses whose owners fall into its web.

I have conducted several focus groups on this issue and other pocketbook issues with Hispanic business owners, and the results are incredibly positive for the Republican message. Not surprisingly, most respondents initially don't believe "death taxes" pose a risk to them (after all, up to one in three Hispanic small business owners, as we've already seen, don't think they're even liable for *income* taxes!).[10] But after just a brief, impartial explanation of the tax—including the $2 million threshold—Hispanic business owners, like just about everyone else, are repelled by it: It's fundamentally unfair, and most people outside the House Democratic Caucus believe so immediately.

Here's a sample of the initial responses I got while surveying Latino business owners in Las Vegas:

- "It's a lot of money. I never knew that; it's my first time [learning about the tax]."
- "We live in country supposedly where they tell you [that] you can live the American dream—buy your own house, start your own business. But when the cards are on the table, you know, they pull the rug from under you and say 'whoops you're getting taxed.' "
- "We really haven't prepared for it [death tax], but I think it's unfair that I've already paid taxes on something when I die my children would have to pay it when I've already done it."[11]

Many respondents also expressed fears that owners may have to "sell off their businesses" to pay the penalty. Latina business owners were often strongest in their opposition to the death tax: "I'm disgusted to think the government is living off us people that work hard to make a business for [ourselves] and our family and the generation to come," said Anna, a self-employed mortgage processor.

"There are people that could be employed if we didn't have the 'death tax,' and I think that's more important than paying more government officials," said Alisa, who has run her own consulting business for six years.

These Latinos I interviewed—a real estate broker, an auto mechanic, a photographer, a mortgage processor—are these the ones Democrats are referring to when they speak of the dangers of allowing generational wealth to accumulate? Respondents' number one reason for opposing the death tax was that "government shouldn't take money the family accumulated." This issue strikes at the heart of Latino family values.

Our survey findings stated: "Overall, respondents believed 'death taxes' pose a larger economic burden on Latino family-owned businesses because of the community's lack of awareness and the size and nature of many Latino businesses, e.g., small, service-industry."

Not all of my Latino respondents were surprised to learn about the Death Tax—certainly not Robert, who had just inherited his father's vending machine business. He said he was *currently paying* the estate tax because his father died and left him the business they had run together. "I met with a lawyer," he said. "I was thinking of expanding my business, but don't know if I can do that now."

Can Republicans make the death tax a successful issue with Latinos? As in my other focus groups, these small business owners were asked to compare the merits of two hypothetical political candidates—a conservative named Jones, who proposed repeal of the death tax, and a liberal named Smith, who defended it. When asked to compare the two, 80 percent of respondents said they would support the pro-repeal candidate, Jones, compared to Smith, who said the existing system restores fairness since it affects only the richest 2 percent.

In other words, once they're made aware of it, the death tax becomes the kind of "80 percent issue" where Republicans can approach Hispanic small business owners and offer their help. Latinos will respond very positively, if our focus groups were any indication.

"I think if [Jones] was to do the right campaign and just explain [death taxes] . . . he would win against Smith," one of the respondents volunteered. "Jones is looking out for the small-business owner," said another.

The argument almost makes itself. Republicans have much to gain by reaching out to the entrepreneurial Latino business class, educating them, and showing them how Republican solutions will improve their lives and help them build wealth.

home ownership

For Americans who don't own a business, home ownership is the most common path to wealth in America—and, as we said before, the single greatest aspiration of Hispanic Americans.

By owning a home instead of renting, a person can make sure that a large chunk of his or her living expenses are not being "spent," but rather "invested" in an asset with growing value. Eventually, the home can be sold, and much of those expenses can be regained, plus (hopefully) equity from appreciation. A home is often the single locus of an American family's savings, investment or retirement money.

Again, Republicans must reach out to Latinos to show them how Republican ideals and policies are helping Hispanic families. The Bush administration and Republicans in Congress have increased opportunities for minority homeownership, and Latinos are the ones who have taken the most advantage: In June 2002, Bush set a goal of increasing the number of minority homeowners to 5.5 million by 2010. Since then, 2.5 million minority families have already become new homeowners. By the third quarter of 2006, Hispanic home ownership stood near an all-time high at 49.7 percent.

What did Republicans do for homeownership? Perhaps the most essential pro-homeowner policy was the $500,000-per-couple ($250,000 per person) exemption for the sale of a principal residence owned for at least two years—the idea of Rep. John Kasich (R-Ohio), which passed a Republican Congress along party lines in 1997 before being signed by President Clinton.[12] This, combined with the 2003 cut in capital gains tax rates from 20 percent to 15 percent, ensures that homeowners can walk away from the sale of their home with more cash—that they avoid being crushed by capital gains taxes. This benefits Latinos who are both selling and buying homes by removing government-induced inflation from the price of a home.

In order to achieve the goal of an "Ownership Society," President Bush also started what he called the "American Dream Downpayment Fund." Since 2002, the program has aimed to give grants to 40,000 low-income families each year to help them make down payments on their first homes.[13] By setting $100 million aside for the program this year a

Republican president is helping low-income families—and Latinos on average still have the lowest incomes—to help themselves. Instead of being forced to throw away their living expenses on rent, struggling families can use a down payment to build wealth in a home and thus permanently escape the orbit of government dependency.

RNC Chairman Mel Martinez, the former secretary of Housing and Urban Development, recalls arguments he had with Democrats on Capitol Hill who complained he was not doing enough for renters. "We weren't taking anything away from renters," said Martinez. "It's just that we were initiating programs for home-owners. . . . Why shouldn't you be able to [buy a home], as opposed to someone else approaching you and saying, 'we're going to give you subsidized rent'?"

He added, "Latinos say 'I want to own something.' And if you want to get ahead in this country, then the Republican Party is the party for you, because we understand that you want to own, and you want to be in control, and you want to be an entrepreneur. And that's the connection: family values, education, entrepreneurship. I think those are the three cornerstones of where we connect with Hispanics. It's the politics of dependency versus the politics of aspiration. It's public housing versus homeownership."

These policies, along with a creative new housing counseling program to help families through the complicated home-buying process, are giving low-income families more access to property ownership. The increase in African American and Latino homeownership under the Republicans has improved neighborhoods by giving people a greater stake in their communities; it's reduced crime, and, ultimately, it will help struggling families take the first difficult steps up the economic ladder to the American dream.

social security reform

Many Latinos don't own businesses and haven't yet gotten to the point at which they can afford a home. What can Republicans offer to them, when all they have is one income—producing asset—their own labor?

Think back to when you got your first paycheck. At the top, the stub identified a certain percentage of your pay that was being taken away for

FICA—Social Security. If you're a younger person, you actually may not have had any real expectations that you'd ever see that money again: One famous survey indicated that more young Americans believed in UFOs than believed they'd ever receive Social Security benefits—and judging from the actuarial tables, they may have been right!

To these younger workers, the FICA contribution is just gone. Your paycheck is smaller. Perhaps, when you started working, you never even knew that you were only seeing half of the problem: Your employer has been making an equal contribution on your behalf, money that is factored into the employer's cost of hiring you—money you arguably would otherwise have had in your paycheck.

Since then, you've perhaps begun saving for retirement by other means. But if you're a younger worker, you probably still look at that bite out of your paycheck every week and wish you had at least *some* of that money to spend or save.

What if just a portion of that money, now being spent on such vital government projects as the "bridge to nowhere" in Alaska, could instead be redirected into an account with your name on it? Into an account which waits for you at retirement, and which you could pass on to your spouse or children when you pass away?

Such a proposal would help all workers, but especially lower income workers who otherwise have less to save on their own. It would be particularly beneficial to Latinos, whose average age (27) is the youngest of any large group in the United States, and who therefore are currently paying much more into the system than they are taking out as a group.

The President's Commission to Strengthen Social Security reported in 2001 that "[i]n 1998, Hispanics as a group paid $33 billion in OASDI payroll taxes but received only $18 billion in benefits."

Hispanics represent about 5.6 percent of the elderly population today, but by 2050 the Census Bureau estimates we will account for more than 16 percent of pensioners. But for these people, Social Security is a ticking time bomb. "By the time today's Hispanic taxpayers are eligible for retirement benefits," the bipartisan commission reported, "the current Social Security system would be paying substantially lower returns."[14]

Over his lifetime, the average male born in 2000 will get a pitiful return of 0.86 percent on the money that is taken out of his paycheck for

Social Security.[15] And of course, there is no guarantee that he will live to see any return. Over its lifetime, the Social Security program has become less lucrative for its beneficiaries. A person born in 1936 only had to live until age 82 to get back all the payroll taxes he paid into Social Security, but a person born in 1965 has to live until age 91. Alarmingly, the report continues, "[s]ingle workers paying the maximum tax into Social Security and retiring in 2030 would have to live past age 110 simply to get back what they had paid in."

A change in the system to create personal accounts would especially help Latino workers to save up generational wealth by giving them a better return on their investment than Social Security. It would help Hispanic workers to save without cutting into their take-home pay. Most importantly, it would permit them to *own* the money they save for retirement instead of leaving it in the hands of the government, only to have it evaporate if they die.

A plan that would let younger workers invest just a portion of their Social Security contributions would be a tremendous benefit for Hispanics, as long as it ensures that those in or near to entering the current system would receive the benefits they are expecting—41 percent of Latino seniors depend on Social Security as their only source of retirement income, according to the Social Security Administration. It is all about building family wealth for Latinos.

Democrats flatly rejected this proposal for increased ownership, and again, it was for political reasons. As usual, they expressed doubts about the people's judgment—as opposed to government's—bemoaning the risks of letting ordinary Americans invest their own money. Illinois Congressman Rahm Emanuel's (D-Ill.) recent book seems to make the case that Americans are too stupid to make investment choices: "[T]he sheer number of choices scares many people off altogether, or makes them unduly cautious."[16] Senate Minority Leader Harry Reid (D-Nev.) once compared investments in the nation's financial markets to "gambling"![17]

Democrats also misrepresented the plan—a lot. Sen. Robert Menendez (D-N.J.) told a town hall meeting, "Private accounts simply will not provide the same level of benefits to Hispanics." That's right, Senator: Accounts would provide far *more* in benefits. Others claimed that personal accounts would create deficits—even though yawning deficits already loom under the current system, for which the Democrats offer no solution except perhaps higher payroll taxes.[18]

Needless to say, the bulk of the Democrats' arguments consisted of scaring seniors into believing that their benefits would be affected. The campaign of deceptions was fatal.

Texas Solicitor General Ted Cruz (R) says that Republicans lost this battle because of poor messaging. They must make it an issue of enterprise and the opportunity to build up a poor family's assets, instead of offering dull actuarial talk about Social Security's crisis of solvency:

> The real power of private accounts is that right now, an immigrant comes over from Mexico, spends his or her whole life working as a gardener, pays into Social Security her whole life, gets to retirement age. Then they start to receive benefits for a few years, they die—that's the status quo. Under private accounts, the exact same immigrant works that exact same menial job, and when they hit retirement age they have accumulated an asset such that someone who is only 55 can have an account of $200,000, $300,000 on astonishingly low wages. From that account then, they receive benefits for a few years, and then they die—and that account can be passed on to the kids, and suddenly the kids of the gardener, the kids of the farm worker, start out with a nest egg.[19]

Social Security reform is not just about solvency of a government program: It's about economic opportunity for Latino families and other lower-income groups. "Private accounts don't help the Rockefellers—they don't care, they don't need a private account," says Cruz. "The people it makes a difference for are the working poor, who haven't been able to accumulate assets."

Representative Emanuel and Bruce Reed argue in *The Plan* (2006) that Republicans are just playing politics when they talk about increasing ownership among blacks and Hispanics, because ownership makes them vote more Republican.[20] What they can't explain is how this political logic changes the fact that ownership *actually helps* people in the real world—particularly minorities, who as a whole have less wealth and fewer opportunities to pass something on to the next generation. This is just one place where Emanuel and Reed fall woefully short in their vision. Increased ownership benefits *everyone*, yet Democrats would stand in its way just because President Bush proposes it—just because it could make more people prosperous and potentially more likely to vote Republican. In the place of real "ownership society" programs, Emanuel presents half-baked counterproposals, such as a savings plan that would cost a lot of money and still cut into poor workers' take-home pay—without solving any of Social Security's long-term problems.

When it comes to building Latino wealth, Latinos and Republicans need one another. The Democrats certainly aren't going to help Latinos here: For the sake of politics, they want to preserve an income-transfer system under which "entire generations will receive rates of return below those of risk-free government bonds"—a system in which today's Latino young people "will be forced to lose money through Social Security"[21]—those are the exact words of the bipartisan Social Security Commission.

Even after two months of Democratic nay-saying, 49 percent of Latinos still told the Pew survey in 2005 that they thought Bush's proposal for personal retirement accounts was "a good idea."[22] Only 38 percent said it was a bad idea. Before the campaign of deceptions, Latinos supported the measure at higher levels.

Hispanics may still vote heavily Democratic, but here we are, surprisingly open to what most people think of as a very controversial Republican proposal. Personal accounts would be such a boon to Hispanics that it presents another easy opportunity for Republicans to reach out with a solution that works for Latinos in real life.

commerce and trade

We have looked at three major mechanisms for building Latino families' wealth in this country—businesses, homes, and retirement savings—and in all of them the Republican position is far better for Hispanics than the Democratic one. There is one other economic issue beginning to take life in the Latino community that is critical for bolstering the sense of collectivity we described in chapter three. It will be a major issue in the coming years, affecting Hispanic Americans (and others familiar with Spanish-language and Latino culture) more than anyone else. It is the emergence of Latin American markets. As they increase their commerce with the United States, they will present tens of thousands of new job and business opportunities for Latinos in this country.

Cuban American Rep. Lincoln Diaz-Balart (R-Fla.) formed the Congressional Hispanic Leadership Institute (CHLI) specifically to promote free trade with Latin America. "When you look at the other Latino organizations, they tend to either be silent on the issue of trade, or not favorable," he says. "There was, in our view, a glaring need to fill a void because of the reality of our community, which is two million Hispanic small businesses in the United States. Our community is an entrepreneurial community."

Diaz-Balart notes that increased trade within the Western Hemisphere will not only have a direct impact on the countries of origin of many Latinos in the United States, but it will also present us with numerous job opportunities in the future. As Latin America continues its economic growth and becomes a more formidable market, bilingual Hispanics will be dominant among the importers, exporters, translators, and executives who facilitate this cultural and commercial exchange. It will be like a job factory for Spanish speakers—an affirmative action program for Latinos, only without the affirmative action!

Democrats don't care for this at all. Their union backers spend a lot more money on politics than Latinos do, and so nearly every House Democrat has changed course and united in opposition to free trade over the last four years. Today, the Democratic leadership in Congress has demanded that even lifelong Democratic supporters of free trade—including members of supposedly moderate Democratic groups such as the New Democrat Coalition and the "Blue Dog" group—must reverse course and embrace protectionism. When party leaders cracked the whip in 2005, nearly every member obeyed, as all but 15 House Democrats voted against the Central American Free Trade Agreement. On the basis of flimsy pretexts related to labor and environmental standards, Democrats can now more than ever be expected to curry favor with unions by voting en bloc against free trade with Latin America—all for political reasons. Nowadays, when the rare Democrat like Rep. Henry Cuellar votes for a free trade with Latin America, Democrats try to run him out of the party! Never mind the fact that Cuellar's South Texas district is home to the third-largest international trade hub in the United States, so that free trade immediately creates thousands of jobs there. Cuellar is a Democrat—he is supposed to think first of his party, not his constituents! Isn't he?

*   *   *

Tania, one of my focus group participants in California, expressed the opinion that "the Democrat Party gives more opportunity to Hispanics." Free trade is the last of four clear examples where Democrats do *not* favor opportunity for Hispanics, and Republicans do. Republicans support policies that promote increased Hispanic ownership of wealth and employment in better jobs. Democrats oppose them all, nearly to a man.

Republicans should hold Democrats' feet to the fire when they address the Latino community on issues of building family wealth and creating jobs. The Democrats must come to terms with whether it benefits the country when they obstruct the path to an ownership society, just because it comes in the form of Republican proposals.

say it like you mean it: latinos and education

I love the honesty of children. They say what we're all thinking, unfazed by the fear of embarrassment that later paralyzes us as adults. It reminds me of a tour I took at a suburban elementary school in San Antonio. We entered a first grade class just as a child turned to the teacher and said, "You have a pretty face, but you're kinda fat."

Thankfully, children remind us that it is okay to hear things we may not want to. When it comes to education, the need for an honest conversation is long overdue.

We have a Latino education crisis in America that threatens the economic success we are currently achieving. No one will deny this. For the past three decades, the Hispanic dropout rate has hovered at 30 percent— for some schools along the U.S.-Mexico border the rate is double that. Hispanic (and African American) children underperform educationally compared to their white and Asian counterparts. As a group, Hispanic students have the highest expulsion and suspension rates and the lowest college graduation rates.

Presidential commissions, one of which I worked on, have been created to study the crisis.[23] They have presented reports to the White House

Figure 6.2 Educational Attainment by Hispanic Subgroup Aged 25 Years and Older (by percent)

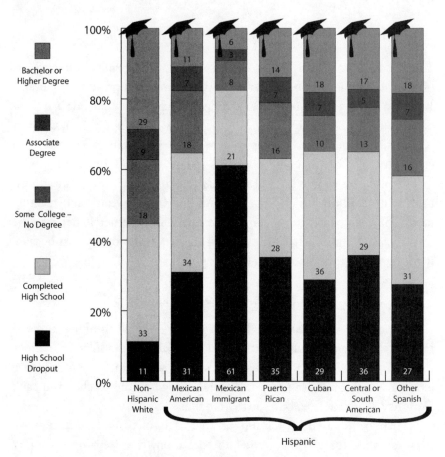

Source: U.S. Department of Education, National Center for Education Statistics: March 2001
*numbers rounded to whole numbers

(a dozen since the first Bush administration), to public and private foundations, chambers of commerce, educators, demographers, state and local elected officials, university heads and an endless array of parents. Although the studies have focused their attention on key areas, misinformation is still rampant. A major movement still exists to protect a government-run education monopoly focused on shepherding generations of Hispanic, African American and poor children through school, with the result that they emerge ill-prepared for the real world and with skills barely sufficient for anything beyond working at a car wash.

Harsh? Yes. But also true.

Democrats and Republicans share a commitment to improving public education for everyone, from migrant children in Milwaukee to second-generation Mexican Americans in East L.A. But the two parties have radically different ways of getting there. The difference between the Democratic and Republican ideas is that the Democratic ones do not work, the Republican ones do. After 30 years of a monopoly on public education under the well-established control of a left-leaning establishment of teacher's unions and bureaucrats, the Democratic strategies on education have gotten us to where we are today—a situation no one can be happy with. Yet most Democrats resist needed reforms because their allies in that establishment want to stick with the same failed solutions.

Latino families face three major problems in education. Their kids are stuck in a system that has no accountability, that doesn't teach them to read, and that they can't escape. Republicans would solve these problems by expanding educational choice and competition, focusing on reading, and measuring achievement to ensure accountability.

At stake is more even than the future of Latino families—the entire country depends on a generation of well-educated young people who will form the backbone of the nation's economic future. Here again, Hispanics and Republicans need one another.

accountability—why "no child left behind" matters

The biggest disagreement between Republicans and Democrats on education is the question of money versus accountability. Democrats often complain that schools are not well funded, and that's the problem—full stop. They resist measures to hold public schools and school systems (or teachers) accountable for poor performance, or to open them up to competition.

Some schools did suffer from a lack of adequate funding in the past, but today this is a myth. Per-pupil spending by American public schools has more than doubled in real dollars since 1971.[24] At the same time, there is no correlation between the amount of money spent per pupil and school performance. No one can seriously argue that our education system has become twice as good since 1971—math and reading scores have remained

Figure 6.3   Education Costs Per Pupil

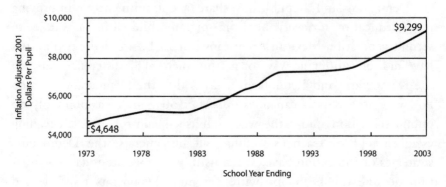

Source: U.S. Department of Education, National Center for Education Statistics, Revenues and Expenditures for Public Elementary and Secondary Education, 1970–71 through 1986–87; The NCES Common Core of Data (CCD), "National Public Education Financial Survey," 1987–88 through 2001–02

flat since that time.[25] Moreover, the District of Columbia school system, the second most expensive in the United States at $13,330 per student, is also by far the worst performing. Just because schools have money doesn't mean they are spending it well or achieving success.

To be sure, the federal education budget has done pretty well under President George W. Bush. Federal education spending has skyrocketed, but now at least part of the money is being used more productively, and scores have actually improved.

The Democratic solution of throwing money at the Hispanic dropout problem produced a "School Dropout Prevention Program" under the Clinton administration that focused on children at the end of the process— once the system had already failed them—rather than at the beginning. It also discounted the fact that by the end, the system had already lost 30 percent of Latino children along the way. It's as though Democrats were waiting at the end of a marathon course with water bottles, ready to help the runners cross the finish line, without addressing the fact that the runners never trained for the race, are all out of shape from eating sugary donuts, and many will never reach the half-way mark.

Accountability is the answer. A system based on outcomes and success is necessary to ensure students get the math and reading skills they will need to go to college if they want to. Lamentably, Latinos and African American students lag behind every other group in this measure of educational success, with only 43 percent of Latinos and 44 percent of African American students assessed as "prepared" to enter college, compared to their white (62 percent) and Asian (70 percent) counterparts.[26]

When President Bush crafted and signed the No Child Left Behind Act (NCLB) in 2002, he implemented a system that required states to test all third- through eighth-grade students for the basic math and reading skills they are supposed to be acquiring in their classes. Aside from the measurement provided by testing, there is no way to tell if schools are doing what they are supposed to do. Although there have been accountability initiatives on the state level, No Child Left Behind is the first national initiative to require us to assess how students perform.

Traditional Democratic allies fiercely criticized this idea of measuring educational success. Teachers' unions, which are poised to look out for teachers' interests and not necessarily students' interests, are never well disposed toward the idea of school accountability. And unions also spend much more money on influencing politics than students will ever be able to. When the unions say "jump," the Democrats have historically asked "how high?"

The unions resisted this reform, arguing that NCLB forces teachers to shape their curricula around testing. President Bush, speaking before Congress two months after taking office, explained why such criticism is unfounded: "Critics of testing contend it distracts from learning. They talk about teaching to the test. But let's put that logic to the test. If you test a child on basic math and reading skills, and you're teaching to the test, you're teaching math and reading. And that's the whole idea."[27]

By measuring achievement, No Child Left Behind seeks to create an atmosphere of accountability. It removes the possibility of "social promotion," which advances students who are not learning into higher grades they are not ready for, just because their peers are advancing. If a school is failing to do its job, more money probably will not change that fact. However, consistently poor test scores will at least reflect the problem and its scope, and send a signal to teachers, administrators and parents that something big needs to change at a particular school.

When I worked at the White House Initiative on Hispanic Education, I often traveled to school districts to study how we could close the achievement gap between white, black and Hispanic students. I stood outside one predominantly Hispanic high school (which will remain unnamed) in southern California in 2003 as one of the school board members pointed at the building and noted that that year's freshman class would have 1,400 students, but only 600 will graduate—as had been the case in years past. That was tough to hear, but it got worse when he added that the school actually made its budgeting decisions on the expectation of losing more than half of each freshman class. If all of the students actually stayed in school, they would never be able to accommodate them! "We don't have enough desks, and there are no plans to buy any," he told me. I was most upset by the fact that this school had such an expectation of failure. This is not uncommon in the same education establishment that bristles at being held accountable for failing the students.

With school accountability comes higher expectations—higher standards for students. Republicans want to be sure Hispanic children know that we expect them to be academically prepared go to college. That's why their platform holds the education system accountable, and does not just keep throwing good money after bad performance and meager success. Republicans have the same expectation of success for Spanish speakers and English speakers, rich and poor children, immigrant and native-born children. Republicans do not believe that we should settle for what we have today, nor will they pretend that adding more money will solve the problem, because it's never worked before.

back to basics—reading

Just as the Hispanic community is itself diverse, so are the reasons we are performing poorly in the educational sphere. They range from poor early childhood development to limited language development, to low expectations, to the fact that some children move often—particularly those of migrant workers. The reasons also vary by ethnic subgroup.[28]

The reasons for the high level of dropouts among Hispanics are many, but the common thread is often that students give up because they can't read English. After the fourth grade, schools stop teaching reading as its own subject. In the normal order of things, students are supposed to be proficient enough by then that they can continue their schooling without a specific reading class. But many non-English speakers, and many lower-income children, find themselves left behind. They cannot read by the fourth grade, and so they never learn.

The Bush administration is the first to have a President and First Lady who are focused intensely on the issue of reading. President Bush announced a major commitment to reading programs after taking office, in his first address to Congress. "Reading is the foundation of all learning," he said, announcing a $5 billion initiative to help children learn to read.

"If children don't read in the early grades, the consequences start to snowball rapidly," said former Secretary of Education Rod Paige.

> They pass a cognitive shelf which makes learning to read much harder. Children who can't read can't do homework or keep up with their other classes. They slide through school until ninth grade, which they repeat until they drop out. Children who can't read are often misidentified as learning-disabled, which means they are put in special ed classes where they don't belong. Every time you hear about a kid who dropped out of school, I hope that will reinforce in your mind the urgency of developing cognitive skills early in a child's life.[29]

Consider what Paige says, and then consider how many Latino English-language learners are mislabeled in bilingual education programs and put into special-needs classes. Is it any wonder the Hispanic dropout rate is so high? A keener and more long-lasting focus on basic reading skills would improve our public school system—especially for Latinos, but really for everyone—by light years. This is why a Republican president and Congress set out to implement the "Reading First" program in 2002.

Students from lower-income families, studies show, tend to be exposed to fewer words than children from higher-income families. "By the age of two years, striking differences in what children know and what they can do begin to distinguish low-income children from their better off peers," said Deborah A. Phillips of Georgetown University, testifying before Congress.[30] "Children living in poverty hear, on average, 300 fewer words per hour than do children in professional families."

Even at such a young age, a poor child's future educational success is being undermined. At the very least, a school system can try to make up for this "vocabulary gap" by focusing more on reading in school and in early learning programs. This is why Republicans tried in 2003 to set educational standards for the Head Start program, making the program's primary mission to prepare poor kids for learning to read in school. The program's main focus before had been teaching poor kids to socialize and providing them with a nutritious meal.

It may sound like a no-brainer: "Kids should read more." How could anyone oppose that? How is this a Republican issue? But Democrats *did* oppose it. No sooner had President Bush tried to solve the problem of the "vocabulary gap" than Democrats decided that they were going to make it a political issue.

"The typical child who enters Head Start as a four-year-old is able to name no more than one or two letters and cannot write a single letter of the alphabet," reads a 2002 White House report. "Despite the efforts to prepare this child for kindergarten, the same child may leave Head Start a year later without significant progress in letter knowledge."[31]

The problems with Head Start needed to be solved, for the sake of the children in the program. The Republican solution began with putting states in charge of the program—since they control most other federal preschool programs—and retraining Head Start teachers to teach young children to read. As one commentator noted, "For too long, Head Start has been merrily rolling along, enjoying ever-more generous increases in funding, without demonstrating its value."[32]

But instead of welcoming an opportunity for these kids to learn, Democrats came to the aid of the Head Start bureaucracy by opposing changes to the program that would benefit poor African American and Latino children.

"This effort [Bush proposal] is destined, in my view, to absolutely destroy this program," Sen. Chris Dodd (D-Conn.) told the *New York Journal News*.[33]

Liberal Rep. George Miller (D-Calif.) growled that putting states in control of the Head Start program was "like handing your children over to Michael Jackson."[34]

The battle over Head Start is just one example of how Democrats are willing to resist positive change in education. Their supporters in the educational establishment would rather let things be as they are, perpetuating a system that is especially failing Latinos, but it really fails everyone. Republicans don't buy the idea that the education system exists for its own sake, independent of the children it is supposed to be serving. Again, Republicans can offer this focus on reading to Latinos as a solution to a real problem facing the Latino community, its families and its future prosperity.

educational choice

We learned from the former Soviet Union that a system with no competition does not work. If the only store in town makes you wait in line for four hours for a loaf of bread, but there's nowhere else to go, they don't have to improve their service or their products.

Monopolies can constantly fail to provide for demand, and the consumer can do nothing about it—that is why we have laws against monopolies. But today's public school system is a monopoly for everyone who lacks the means to get a private school education.

The real benefit of school choice reforms (including charter schools and school choice vouchers) is not necessarily that they give students a way out of failing public schools and into better private schools—although that usually helps too. The real effect of educational choice is that it gives the public school monopoly a *competitor*. Once an alternative exists, and more people—especially African American and Latino families—are given the means to use that alternative, public schools will be forced to improve, whatever it takes.

School choice speaks directly to the Latino educational crisis. It is an issue that Hispanics support strongly. The 2000 Hispanic Business Roundtable survey found that *74 percent* of Florida Hispanics favored a new program there that let kids in failing schools receive vouchers.[35]

A 2005 poll of Arizona voters[36] found that education was the top issue among Latinos, with 38 percent calling it their most important issue. Sixty-four percent of Hispanics said they had a "favorable" opinion of school choice—a higher number than whites or African Americans.

Consider the popularity and effectiveness of charter schools. Started in 1991, charter schools, which receive tax dollars but are independent from their local school districts, have bloomed to nearly 4,000 schools nation-wide. Many represent some of the greatest successes in public-private education. So much so that in 2007 the largest charter school organization, Knowledge is Power Program (KIPP), announced $65 million in donations from well-heeled financiers, including the Bill and Melinda Gates Foundation and GAP retail stores founders Doris and Don Fisher, to open 42 schools in Houston.[37]

Chris Barbic is founder of Houston's YES College Preparatory Schools (YES), named one of *Newsweek*'s top 100 public schools in America. With four campuses and 1,500 students, YES' student body is 80 to 90 percent economically-disadvantaged, Hispanic or African American, first-generation college-bound students and lagging at least one grade level behind in English and math. Despite these setbacks, Barbic contends, "We are proving that every student—regardless of their socioeconomic background—can achieve academic success."[38]

Though not all charter schools are high achievers, they open the door to competition and innovation to ensure each child can succeed.

Democrats oppose school choice for a reason that is all too familiar—the teachers' unions that pull their strings oppose it. The educational bureaucracy, like all other bureaucracies, vigorously opposes change. As long as the unions continue to enjoy a monopoly over the lives of millions of students who can't afford a better elementary or secondary education, they can easily resist change. They continue to allow Hispanic students to languish in schools where there is no discipline, no learning and no accountability.

Some Democrats sense the power this issue has, and they reluctantly go along at the risk of upsetting the unions. Arizona Governor Janet Napolitano (D) had already vetoed a school choice bill twice after it passed out of the Republican state legislature. That was when the Hispanic Council for Reform and Educational Options (CREO) seized the issue. The group launched protests accusing her of betraying the Latino community, and this received much attention from the Spanish-language media. "As a direct result of our activities," CREO's website boasts, "polling data found that the governor's approval rating among Hispanics had dropped a whopping 21 percent."

Napolitano finally conceded and let the bill become law without her signature.

"For those organizations that claim to represent the best interest of Hispanics, the most important issue they can work on is to change the way the system of education serves Hispanic children by leveling the playing field of access to quality schools through school choice," says Robert Aguirre, CREO's president. Aguirre's group is also suing on behalf of several low-income Hispanic families in 96 of New Jersey's worst school districts, to force the state to give families an alternative to failing public schools.

Many, many Latinos feel the same way about education choice, because they are the ones hurt most by the current, failing school system. Again, Republicans have a school choice policy that benefits Latinos and strengthens our economic opportunities in the future.

* * *

The political battle over education has been very nasty, but Republicans have something to show for the fight they've put up against the Democrats and the education establishment since President Bush took office. According to the Long-Term Trend reports of the National Assessment of Educational Progress, the formula of accountability and focus on reading is working. The gap in test scores between Hispanic students and whites is now at an all-time low in both math and reading.[39]

With this early educational success to build on, Republicans can continue by pushing for school choice in new states around the country, increasing school accountability, and making sure every child is learning how to read. When it comes to education, Republicans have something real that will benefit Latino families and improve their economic future. They should reach out with this message, and in the process, they may find a few new voters.

cultural values: strengthening the latino family

On economic and educational matters, Republicans appeal to Latinos' familial and entrepreneurial instincts. But when we turn to social and moral issues, Republicans must appeal to the centrality of faith to the Latino experience, as well as the protection of the family from harmful "progressive" cultural values.

We noted earlier the mobilization of Latinos that various churches are engaging in, urging us all to consider what we believe when we participate in politics. Gradually, this trend will increase over time, but as Latinos begin to think more about cultural issues, Republicans must be ready to give their attention and offer them a choice. GOP candidates must contrast themselves to Democrats when it comes to protecting and preserving the institution of marriage and the human family, and defending human life. Republicans are the party that trusts parents—not the government—to raise their children, and that urges all Americans to behave responsibly.

contemporary issues—abortion and marriage

The conservative stances most Republican voters take on social issues are much more in tune with Latino opinion, as we have seen in surveys cited above, than anything Democrats have to offer. There are always the rare Latino Democrats who stand up for their cultural values when they vote in Congress—Cuellar and Solomon Ortiz (Tex.), for example. But by and large, most Democrats just don't get it. They don't explain the harm that their social agenda has already done to their party.

The fact that so many Democrats oppose a ban on even partial-birth abortion surely says something about their priorities. Even as Sen. Hillary Clinton (D-N.Y.) and Democrats pay lip service to "finding common ground" on the abortion issue, they oppose every meaningful effort that might even slightly reduce business in the abortion industry.

They can't even support a law to prevent adults from transporting minors to another state for an abortion without their parents' knowledge. In the halls of Congress, Democrats have argued and voted against such provisions annually on the assumption that parents cannot be trusted to act in their daughters' best interests when they find out about a pregnancy.[40] This produces their absurd conclusion that the same school-age girl who can't get an aspirin without a signed and notarized waiver should still be allowed to get an abortion with no permission whatsoever.

Republicans can offer Latinos a more compassionate system that respects parents' rights, so that mothers and fathers don't have to worry about their daughters getting secret abortions out of fear.

Just as Democrats lost Italian and Irish allegiance through their radical social agenda, they will lose Hispanics over time, provided that Republicans do the necessary outreach and emphasize their adherence to traditional values. The seeds of Latino opinion are already there for a huge increase in GOP support. I see them among some of the responses in focus groups. Asked to describe the Democrats, some from our group of Latina voters gave as responses words like "liberal" and "immoral."

The media and the Democrats don't give voters enough credit when it comes to these issues. They often write and speak as though people who have values are simply ignorant and filled with prejudices. But I think back to Ella, a Latina in one of our California focus groups, who was easily able to differentiate between the relatively harmless nature of Bill Clinton's sexual dalliances and the extreme danger that comes from Democrats' general support for policies that promote cultural decay: "I wanted to add: I feel Democrats, without talking about private affairs, Democrats allow gay marriages, allow abortions. That contributes to the decline of society. I feel the base for a country is the home, the family."

If they stand with their principles, conservative Republicans can offer Latinos a world where tax-funded sex-ed programs do not encourage experimentation and promiscuity; a world where kids actually get some moral guidance. We saw in an earlier chapter that this was the number-one problem Latinos saw with our current education system: "Students are being taught non-traditional values and are not learning discipline." Indeed, Hispanic parents have ample grounds to worry at the kind of things public schools teach children about sex without parents ever knowing.

This is not just a religious issue but also an issue of promoting public health in an age where sexual libertinism has resulted in 20 to 25 percent of teenagers catching venereal diseases, many of which have long-lasting and/or painful consequences.[41] Adults in authority, such as teachers, often stand aside as this epidemic rages, or else they actually contradict what kids learn from their parents.

As we saw with Proposition 22, which prevented same-sex marriages in California, and in countless opinion surveys, Latinos would appreciate a voice in the political conversation that will not let the Left take away the special status of the traditional family. By decisive margins, Latinos do not want the government to force them to accept a "marriage" between two men or two women as equal to a family of husband and wife.

It was not a coincidence that President Bush adopted the language of Pope John Paul II in calling for a "culture of life," and advocating that every child be "welcomed in life and protected in law." This kind of caring, conservative message on social issues—which rejects harsh, hateful comments about anyone, especially homosexuals—articulates the social conservatism that protects and nourishes the family while bringing Latinos' values and faith into their political decision making. To make a difference on social issues, to preserve the values we share, Latinos and Republicans need one another.

personal responsibility

The innate conservatism of Hispanics is very evident in their answers about welfare and personal responsibility. Hispanics have the highest workforce participation of any major group in America, and so it is little surprise that by a four-to-one ratio, they tell pollsters that they believe welfare is a *temporary* aid, not a permanent condition. The new arrivals in this country—the ones working to send something home—tend to be the least sympathetic toward the "non-working poor."

Latinos, like most other Americans, have an overwhelming sense of fairness. Surveys and focus groups demonstrate that they are just as sickened as anyone else by the idea of anyone—Latino or otherwise—abusing the system and cheating the taxpayer to make an easy life for himself. The Independent Women's Forum allowed me to share insights from focus groups with Spanish-dominant and bilingual Latinas in Southfield, Michigan and Los Angeles, California. They reveal very negative attitudes toward long-term freeloading, but show an understanding that some people do need temporary help:

- "I believe in taking care of people that really need to be taken care of, but I also believe that there's enough jobs out there for people to take care of themselves if they would just take the job . . ."
- "People shouldn't rely on the government. They should rely on themselves."
- "We don't need programs that make them more dependent."
- "People who are in dire straits should be helped, but I think many Americans are more able than they realize."
- "I do not think that government should play parent."
- "There are people that want, want, want. You can't just give them everything. That is not how our country was founded."
- "They need to learn to help themselves. People do need help, but we need to help them to help themselves."

Republicans can remind Hispanic voters that their party passed the historic 1996 welfare reform bill—a bill President Clinton vetoed twice, before political pressure forced him to cave and sign it. This bill made welfare a temporary program—a safety net—instead of a way of life, as it had been previously. Democrats had denounced the reforms, predicting that they would cause millions to starve, but none of their predictions came true. Republicans have also championed policies of ownership, outlined above, that attempt to make the welfare state unnecessary, so that it is used by as few people as possible.

defending freedom

For the average person who works a full-time job and tries to keep up with bills and spend time with the kids, the world of politics can be somewhat opaque. That goes double for Hispanic voters, who are still discovering their place in the nation's political conversation.

When we talk about national security as a political issue, it can therefore be difficult to see the difference between the two parties. But for Republicans, this difference is always worth pointing out with every group of voters.

Hispanic voters, like most others, already give Republicans higher marks than Democrats on the issue of national defense—when I first came to the RNC in 1999, the numbers on this issue were still 53 to 32 percent in the Republicans' favor.[42] This represents another opportunity for Republicans: A successful outreach can demonstrate to Latinos, and remind everyone else, of the historical reasons why Republicans deserve the good rap they have traditionally enjoyed on national security, and why it is too risky to trust Democrats with the issue.

Is it really fair to say that liberals put our nation at risk? Perhaps as a blanket statement it is. Many of the champions of national security during the Cold War were Democrats, such as Sen. Scoop Jackson (D-Wash.). Still, there were others—some of them still in politics today—who fought vigorously against the policies that ended the cold war with American victory. These Democrats' actions made our nation less safe, weakening our military and intelligence capabilities at a time when the United States faced a powerful, well-armed Communist empire that arguably presented our nation's greatest challenge to date. This is part of the reason voters generally trust Republicans more on the issue of national security, even if there is frustration with the Iraq War.

There is one national security issue that Republicans should hit particularly hard in the 2008 election, and it is an argument Latino voters will understand in a debate they have no choice but to care about.

missile madness

In 1983, Ronald Reagan's idea of a missile defense system so worried the Soviets that they were willing to sign almost any nuclear treaty if it would just forbid such a system. This is because such intimidation through fear was the lifeblood of Communism. The Soviets had spent decades using fear to win concessions and expand Communism despite international outrages (such as the invasion of Afghanistan and the coups and civil wars they supported in Latin America). Ever since the Soviets developed the atom bomb, they had kept Western nations in fear of mutual nuclear annihilation, so that everyone was afraid to cross them and interfere with their plans for world domination.

Reagan refused to give up on missile defense, and most writers agree that his steadfastness was critical in hastening the Soviet Union's decline. But Democrats were furious about his plans for missile defense, denouncing it as "Star Wars" and balking at costs. They voted annually to cut off government funding from the program.

Today, the threat of nuclear annihilation remains, only this time the finger on the trigger is much less stable. In 2006, Kim Jong Il's North Korea launched long-range ballistic missiles in the direction of the United States as part of a test to show that they can hit us. North Korea is a rogue state that claims to have nuclear warheads, and now they have demonstrated that their missiles can reach U.S. soil.

Even after the 2006 missile launch, many Democrats had not learned their lesson on national missile defense, which had been a key element in the 2000 presidential campaign of George W. Bush. Every year before and since that election, Democrats tried to eliminate funding for the program—whether directly, as they did during the Cold War, or indirectly, as they did in 2002 by trying to de-fund the parts most likely to make it succeed.[43]

If Democrats had had their way, the United States would be 25 years behind where we are now in developing a functional system to secure our nation from this new threat. Thanks only to Republican persistence, we currently have a system deployed in Alaska and California that can shoot down missiles as they re-enter the atmosphere, but we are still developing a system to destroy them on their way up—when the chances of destroying them is much greater. And even now, after the North Korean missile launch demonstrated that a rogue nation has missiles capable of reaching the United States, Democrats persist in their inexplicable and inflexible opposition to a national missile defense system.

"No, no, no, no, no," said Sen. Joe Biden (D-Del.), who was asked about missile defense shortly after the North Korean launch. "Listen, the national missile defense is not the answer."[44] In 2001, the same man had pooh-poohed the possibility that North Koreans would ever threaten the United States: "The premise that one day King Jong Il or someone will wake up one morning and say, 'Aha, San Francisco!' is specious," Biden had said. He is now a presidential candidate—that isn't going to make voters sleep very well at night!

"Star Wars wouldn't make us any safer today, because we spent a hundred billion dollars and it still wouldn't work," said Sen. Pat Leahy (D-Vt.) when asked the same question.

Sen. Jack Reed (D-R.I.), at that time the ranking member of the subcommittee responsible for missile defense and a longtime opponent of the program, was at least willing to accept national missile defense now—reluctantly. "I think the system is such that we've been committed to deploying it now," he said. "I think that the headlong rush to get anything going might have ironically harmed our ability to proceed."

Republicans are supposed to be a party that supports smaller government, but the GOP has always been willing to spend what it takes to defend the United States from foreign enemies—particularly from the form of nuclear blackmail used by the Soviets decades ago and by Kim Jong Il today. This is a message that resounds with every American, but it is something Republicans have to explain to Latino voters, who consistently rank national security near the top of their priority issues.

* 　 * 　 *

On education and jobs, values and national security, Republicans have all the issues they need to appeal to Latino voters. In each case, the issues are about *family*, they are about *enterprise*, they are about making sure the Hispanic community thrives now and in the future.

Republicans have a lot more to offer on these issues than Democrats ever will—and there are many other such issues as well, including health care, homeland security, and, yes, even immigration! Just one example: Republicans can take a hard line on border security, but why not accompany that with some goodwill toward those who do follow the rules? Reach out to those five million *legal* Hispanic permanent residents in this country by pushing for their expedited naturalization. What an excellent way this would be of reaching out to the community and rewarding those who show respect for our laws.

If Republicans anticipate the political trends of Latino faith, enterprise and geography, if they appeal to the values of family, faith, entrepreneurship and (yes, it's not always a dirty word) collectivism, they will establish a beautiful and long-lasting relationship. Our community is just waiting to be talked to instead of talked at or talked about. If Republicans make the effort, it is within their power to win our votes and hearts. If Republicans do not make the effort, Democrats are more than willing to pick up the slack.

seven

the whining city
upon a hill

Cecilia Ochoa Levine is a born entrepreneur. She designed a line of bags and sold them to one large company—the bags became a hit. To meet demand, she opened small manufacturing plants in El Paso, Texas and Juarez, Mexico. Today she and her husband, Lance, run a global operation with factories in the United States, Mexico and Asia. Appointed to director of the El Paso Branch of the Dallas Federal Reserve Bank, she strongly believes in personal responsibility and having a sense of civic duty.

Drive by Wal-Mart on a Sunday morning in El Paso and you'll see a lady with her trunk open selling tamales. You're in the beauty shop and a guy comes in selling *pan dulce* from his cart.... This man that I know opened up a tiny little place in a pretty poor area of El Paso. He's selling 4,000 burritos per day! Now he's trying to franchise his little place. He has his brothers and now they have places all over El Paso ...

My hardest working employee in the United States works day and night. She told me, "I came here to the United States to give my children the opportunity to grow, but the system has made them parasites. If they're doing drugs, they're considered disabled. The more children they have, the more money they get." She mentioned all the benefits they were receiving, [and that she] felt it wasn't right. She came here to be an entrepreneur, to work hard. Her family was supposed to be productive. Her kids were hooked on the system, getting girls pregnant. One was a drug addict, so he was considered disabled and so he would get more money. So why should he get well? Why should he work if he was getting food stamps? They're trying to keep them poor ...

We don't need their [Democrats'] liberal, give-away programs, we know how to work hard. We should not get preferential treatment because we are poor or because we are Hispanic. To me, that is offensive, because I feel we're at the same level of intelligence. In the United States, we all have the same rights and the same opportunities to become successful and when somebody tells me I need extra help or somebody tells me that Hispanics are not up to par because of their whatever, I don't agree.[1]

> Where's the [drug] problem? It's in the U.S., not Mexico. We should be charging the U.S. for having caused a cancer in our country [Mexico], and also in other countries like Bolivia, Peru, and Colombia. The kids are beginning to use drugs.
>
> —*Enrique Morones, founder of Border Angels and open borders advocate*[2]

In the presidential election of 1920, Democratic candidate James Cox won 127 electoral votes and 11 states—every one of them part of the old Confederacy. He failed to win even 35 percent of the popular vote in what would at that time be the worst performance ever by a major party candidate.

The Democratic Party had become a nearly irrelevant voice in national politics at that point. Exiting President Woodrow Wilson had viciously lashed out at Irish and German Americans for failing to support the League of Nations. "I want to say—I cannot say too often—any man who carries a hyphen about with him carries a dagger that he is ready to plunge into the vitals of this Republic whenever he gets ready," Wilson had said.[3]

Cox's embrace of the unpopular Wilson and his equally unpopular foreign policy cost him any chance of winning over independent voters. Instead, he held on to what was the Democratic Party's base at that time, Dixie. In this environment, Republicans controlled all of the elected branches of government. It took an actual economic catastrophe to return Democrats to power a decade later.

If Republicans choose the wrong path, they will face the ugly prospect of similar long-term irrelevance, and like the Democrats of 1920, they will have brought it upon themselves. They have a chance to offer Hispanic voters a vibrant and optimistic vision of a better America—an America that includes us and to which we can contribute. If they do so, they will continue to attract our interest and win an increasing share of our votes. But if they do not, they run the risk of becoming a southern, white rural party incapable of winning presidential or congressional elections in the future.

Republicans had better have a plan to keep our attention and win our votes—because the Democrats certainly do. Unless the GOP offers Hispanics an appealing choice, a real electoral alternative, Republicans risk letting us slip into the politics of dependency and victimhood.

To date, Hispanics have largely resisted the Democrats' efforts to turn us into a permanent underclass, but Democrats see success in their future, and they already have a model for their plans. Democrats successfully turned the African American community from a group with a Democratic-leaning vote, that gave them as much as 65 percent in each election, into a monolithic constituency. For the future, the Democrats envision a Hispanic bloc that votes the same way, and whose leaders similarly agitate for a "bigger piece of the pie." They look ahead eagerly to a time when we will dutifully report to the polls every November to pull the "D" lever without so much as considering the alternative.

Democrats want to sell the 1960s to the immigrant community. It is not as easy a sell as it sounds, but all it takes is sufficient ignorance and lack of education among the buyers. In their mission Democrats have an ally in the strongly left-wing Spanish language media, and they are helped by the self-destruction of Republican candidates who wrongly believe they can rally their troops and win votes by excluding Hispanics from the political conversation.

"There is a fight for the soul of the Republican party," says former RNC chairman Ed Gillespie, the new chairman of the Virginia GOP. "Are we going to be a party of inclusion, or are we going to be protectionist, isolationist, try to protect ourselves from competition?"

The Democrats also have the labor unions on their side, who would like nothing more than to co-opt an entire class of new arrivals, legal and illegal—bringing them out to march on May Day, perpetuating the idea that the civil rights movement never succeeded and that other Americans consider immigrants inferior.

The Democrats' vision of our future includes a self-policing Hispanic underclass, in which anyone who shows signs of bucking the party line, of thinking for themselves—even of succeeding in broader American society— can be freely denounced as a race-traitor in the most derogatory and hurtful terms: "oreo," "skeeza,"[4] and in the case of Hispanics, "coconut," meaning brown on the outside but white on the inside. A Democratic National Committee official called Rosario Marin a "house Mexican" after she was named U.S. Treasurer.[5] Is that the way to reward success, with public disdain? Will Latinos succeed in America if the Left can convince them that success is shameful?

It's no fluke that Democrats worked so feverishly to defeat Rep. Henry Bonilla (Tex.) last year. Their congressional committee spent nearly a million dollars to bring down the only Mexican American Republican in Congress because it is bad for them to have Mexican American Republicans there. Nor is it surprising that the Left—labor unions, activists, and the left-wing net-roots—tried so hard to defeat one of the few moderate and strongly independent Latino Democrats, Rep. Henry Cuellar (D-Tex.) in his primary of March 2006. A Latino Democrat who doesn't toe the party line sets a particularly bad example. Cuellar, a strong advocate for education, who fended off the left-wing primary challenge, told me that only about 12 percent of Latinos in his South Texas district consider themselves liberals. Yet liberal outsiders organized and gave thousands of dollars to replace him with a left-wing candidate whose 100 percent pro-choice record on abortion was clearly not in line with the district's values, and whose anti-free-trade position was clearly not in its local interests.[6]

"It's a Democratic district, but just because it's a Hispanic district doesn't mean it's a liberal district," Cuellar told me. "In fact, it was almost more than two-thirds of people consider themselves to be moderate-conservative Democrat, and about 19 percent of them consider themselves to be liberal democrat—and these were primary voters. This is what happens to statewide politicians. They say, 'Oh, Hispanic Democrats, let's send our TV commercials, very liberal messages.' I think it's wrong, when people make stereotyped assumptions like that."

Even our major political figures have at times gotten into this act of using scare tactics to discourage Latinos from independent thinking. Before his fall from grace, Henry Cisneros, President Clinton's housing secretary and once a serious prospect to become the first Hispanic president, was playing the same card. The *Rocky Mountain News* documented a typical speech in which he excoriated Republicans for "trying to make Hispanic children 'ashamed of their heritage.'"[7]

One particularly venomous blogger expressed this totalitarian attitude with a nasty and bigoted rant about Republican Rep. Heather Wilson's victory in New Mexico last year. Wilson won with the help of many Hispanic votes—her district is nearly 43 percent Hispanic, and she has always enjoyed a lot of Latino support. Displaying a photograph of a coconut, the Tequila Express blogger launched a tirade that suggests any Latino who does not share his socialist vision of America must be a traitor to his people:

> I am disappointed . . . that she can win off the votes of a select few coconuts . . . who devalue their culture and quite literally abandon all that represents their culture in favor of the dominant American cultural perspectives. . . . How sad that these *Tío Tacos* can quite literally turn their backs on their cultural values because they mistakenly confuse them as being inferior. . . . [T]hey support the oppressors of their people and . . . mistakenly conclude that their rise in social status has nothing to do with the rich cultural values they were given as they rose from their humble beginnings.[8]

Cleverly, the blogger (who pretentiously calls himself "The Voice in the Wilderness") tries to identify Hispanic culture with his extremely narrow, far-left political vision. He writes that Latinos are abandoning their culture, but he is wrong. We're bringing our culture with us into the heart of American society. And every Latino should resent the fact that "The Voice" and his ilk are actually destroying crucial parts of our true cultural heritage, including our natural optimism, our drive to succeed by our own work and our traditional Christian faith. They want to replace our real culture with their cookie-cutter political culture that permits only one view and keeps us all poor and liberal. Why should Hispanics trade our optimism, faith and work ethic to become a bunch of whiny losers?

Often, such rhetoric as that of "The Voice" is cited by the Tom Tancredos of the world as a sign that we do not consider ourselves Americans, or that we are not assimilating or do not want to. Nothing could be farther from the truth. The left-wing haters among Latinos today spring up thanks to efforts like Tancredo's to exclude us from American culture, to shut us out of a conversation in which we have an enormous stake. And these ugly voices are only the tip of the iceberg for what could develop if Latinos become a marginalized group with just one political alternative—the Democrats and their "whining city upon a hill."

Figure 7.1 States Represented by Hispanic Members of Congress

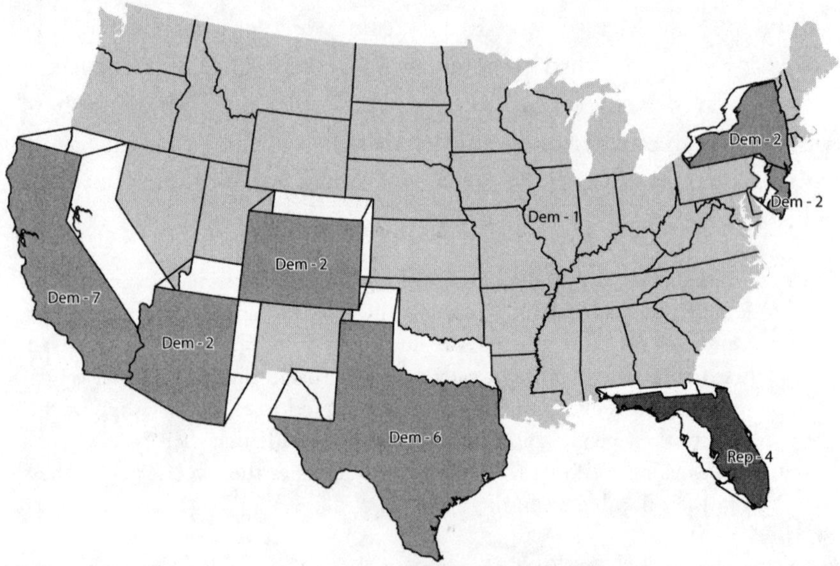

State	Democrat	Republican
California	7	0
Arizona	2	0
Colorado	2	0
Texas	6	0
Illinois	1	0
New York	2	0
New Jersey	2	0
Florida	0	4

Why is that Democrats are satisfied to have every single Latino Democratic congressman representing a district in which minorities make up the majority?

"The attitude among most [state] political parties is, these are your hand outs," says Arturo Vargas of the National Association of Latino Elected Officials. "These are your seats."

Such gerrymandered districts tend to produce leaders whose obsolete civil rights era politics have no appeal outside the poorest Hispanic communities in the country. If their hopeless vision of a permanent Latino underclass takes hold, there will be thousands and even millions of "Tequila Express blogs," working to make Latinos afraid to succeed among a broader electorate.

losing the black vote

If you don't think it can happen, look to the story of how Republicans lost the black vote. It is often said that African Americans' loyalty to the Democratic Party began with a single phone call. It came in October 1960, from Sen. John F. Kennedy, a candidate for president that year. Martin Luther King Jr. had been jailed after an October 2 civil rights sit-in in Atlanta, and the racist authorities detained him longer than the other protestors on the pretext that he had failed to pay an old parking ticket.

Absurdly, King faced four months in prison—over an old parking ticket! But Kennedy called Coretta Scott King, his wife, to pledge his help in freeing her husband. Meanwhile, Robert F. Kennedy, JFK's campaign manager, called a local judge to ask why King could not post bond. He was released the next morning, after eight days in jail.

The 1960 call came at a time when the civil rights movement had captured the attention of Americans everywhere, and just a month before the election. It came with some risk to Kennedy. Democrats had owned the South for a century—thanks in large part to White Democrats suppressing the African American vote. Kennedy showed that he was willing to risk the old Confederacy and its (at that time) 128 electoral votes in order to show good will toward African American leaders in their struggle for equality.

Richard Nixon, the Republican candidate, made no such overtures to King. King's father, a lifelong Republican who had already endorsed Nixon, was so overwhelmed by JFK's outreach that he switched his endorsement.

The effect was not immediately catastrophic for Republicans: In the November election only 65 percent of African Americans voted for Kennedy, who also held on to enough Southern states to win the presidency anyway. But Nixon's support among African Americans did tumble to 32 percent from Eisenhower's 39 percent four years earlier. The GOP had already begun to lose some African American votes during the New Deal, but soon, nearly all African Americans would abandon the GOP entirely. The movement of African Americans toward the Democrats cemented itself in the 1964 election. Sen. Barry Goldwater cited his "states' rights" conservative principles and voted against the Civil Rights

Act of 1964.[9] He may have built the conservative movement, but he also lost the black vote irretrievably—taking just 6 percent—as he carried a handful of Southern states and his native Arizona. Since then, African Americans have never failed to deliver Democrats at least 80 percent of their votes, and Democrats would win few elections without this overwhelming black support.[10] In 2004, 88 percent of African Americans voted for John Kerry, and 90 percent supported Al Gore in 2000.

Such uniformity of opinion within a single racial group is almost eerie, and it is important to remember how it came about. By focusing on civil rights even as the Republicans began reaching out to civil-rights resisters, Democrats succeeded in turning the African American vote into a 90 percent racial bloc vote. Right or wrong, a very large number of African Americans today believe that Democratic votes are in their interests as a race, even though the political situation has changed dramatically since 1964.

"Unfortunately, we vote in monolithic terms and are loyal to a party that has not been loyal to us," says Angela McGlowan, conservative commentator and author of *Bamboozled: How Americans Are Being Exploited by the Lies of the Liberal Agenda* (2007). "The black community gives 90 percent of their vote to a party that solicits our vote by race baiting, scare tactics and the blame game, not by true policy that has created a better America but policy that has led to a near fatherless generation, poverty stricken communities fraught with crime, and a public school system that demonstrates bigotry by low expectations."

Meanwhile, as Latinos surge into America's middle class, we find ourselves pulling even with African Americans economically, and in some areas actually pulling ahead. There were only a handful of Latinos here 40 years ago when African Americans finally won their civil rights, and our population is, on average, four years younger and still starts off in this country making far less money than they do. Yet African American workers currently make the same wages as native-born Hispanics.[11] Add to this the fact that black unemployment in September 2006 was double that of Hispanics, and incarceration rates were nearly *triple*.[12] Race doesn't make people who they are. The story here is the near-total indifference of the Democratic Party toward the real needs of its most loyal bloc of constituents.

It doesn't take a conservative to see the problems with black America's leadership today, and how badly it has misled. National Public Radio Senior Correspondent Juan Williams contrasted today's black leaders very unfavorably with the original civil rights leaders.

"These voices," he said, referring to the old guard, "have always held up notions of empowerment, of taking pride, you know, black manhood, an ability to help oneself and to face tremendous odds and overcome those odds." Now, he continues,

> Instead, we have a generation of leadership that somehow delights in victimhood. And I think, in fact, it's a turnoff for people who might want to contribute, to offer a helping hand. Instead what they see are conspiracy theories. I think it's a terrible signal to our young people about who black people are, to have us constantly wrapped in this cloak of victimhood and to have black leadership that in a knee-jerk fashion defends negative, dysfunctional behavior.[13]

To date, Democrats have never been able to lure Hispanics into this trap, nor have Republicans shown them the kind of hostility that would drive them to the other side—at least not most Republicans, and not in most states. Pollster Matthew Dowd, writing an analysis of the 2000 election for the *Weekly Standard*, pointed out that one key difference between black and Hispanic voters is that their income sharply distinguishes their voting behavior.

"While Democratic candidates by and large have maintained their overwhelming lead among African-American voters, Republicans have managed to increase their share of Latino voters over the years," Dowd wrote. One key to Hispanic disaffiliation from the Democratic Party was income.

> The exit poll data for the 2000 election are quite revealing on this point. Latino voters with incomes under $30,000 voted 31 percent for President Bush; Latinos with incomes between $30,000 and $75,000 voted 37 percent for Bush; and Latinos with incomes above $75,000 voted 46 percent for Bush. As Latinos rise economically they begin to split their votes more between the two parties. This is exactly what happened in the early 20th century with the economic rise of European immigrant groups in America.[14]

Still, some Republicans' strident anti-immigrant rhetoric in today's debate—which is unnecessary regardless of one's position on immigration or border enforcement—is not helping matters.

Figure 7.2   Latino Vote by Income

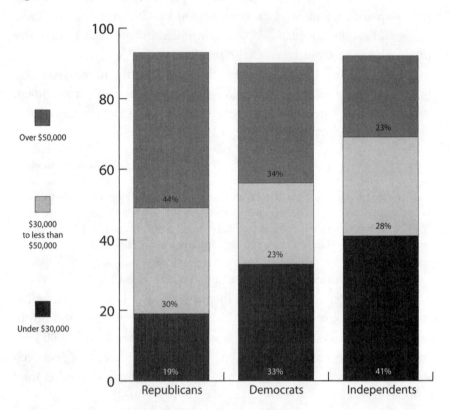

Note: Don't Know/Other responses not included

Source: Pew Hispanic Center/Kaiser Family Foundation National Survey of Latinos: Politics and Civic Engagement, July 2004 (conducted April–June 2004)

The best example of this came in California in 1994 with Proposition 187. To this day, many immigration restrictionists maintain that Hispanics strongly supported Prop 187, and that it had nothing to do with the subsequent collapse of Hispanic Republicanism in California. But they can never explain what killed the state's GOP immediately thereafter, such that it took eight years, an enormous financial and energy crisis, and a movie-star candidate for Republicans to be able to win statewide office there again.

The more conventional view—that the proposition severely damaged Republican performance among Hispanics—rings much truer. "Governor Pete Wilson did in one year what 100 years of Latino activists could not have done," said Gregory Rodriguez, then a research fellow at the Pepperdine Institute for Public Policy, in a post-election wrap-up four years after Proposition 187 passed.[15] "He essentially pushed permanent resident aliens, tens of thousands, hundreds of thousands in the future, off the fence. People who had been reluctant to naturalize are now naturalizing. The rates of civic assimilation, the rates of naturalization, are higher for Mexicans, probably now than ever, as well as the rates of registration and voter participation."[16]

And these people, with the help of the Clinton administration, were (at times illegally) becoming Democratic voters because of the bitter taste Wilson left in their mouth. Daniel Moreno, then an associate professor at Florida International University, contrasted Wilson with the governors of Texas and Florida:

> One of the things that helped George W. Bush with Hispanics nationwide, was he made it very clear after the passing of the anti-immigrant initiative in California, backed by Pete Wilson in 1994, that Texas is not going to follow in these footsteps. In the same way, the Republican Party in Florida quickly backed away from any anti-immigrant initiative. I think the exception in many ways is the Republican Party in California, which under Pete Wilson has done almost everything to insult the emerging Hispanic vote.[17]

It is especially hard to argue that Proposition 187 had no role in alienating California Hispanics when one looks at the contrast between California and those other two states. Gov. Wilson, in wholeheartedly backing the initiative as part of his reelection strategy, took one direction. Gov. George W. Bush took another. Four years later, in 1998, Univision's voter survey found that Texas Hispanics were giving Bush an 81 percent approval rating, versus Wilson's 26 percent approval—with 69 percent disapproval!

el movimiento

There are many reasons for the homogenous and cohesive nature of black Americans as a whole, and its hierarchy of strong, nationally famous leaders. It is easy to name them—King, Ralph Abernathy, and later the more controversial Jesse Jackson and Al Sharpton. Most are ministers, endowed with a divine authority to shepherd their spiritual flocks. The living leaders and the leading organizations in the African American community—particularly the NAACP—all communicate the same political message in favor of Democrats, and the result is the strikingly uniform voting patterns we see in every modern election. Given the historical degradations of slavery and discrimination, one can understand, if not appreciate, why African Americans feel the need to stick together politically.

On the other hand, Hispanics do not stick together at all. Try to name the one or two Hispanic leaders who command the widespread respect of a Martin Luther King Jr. or even just the notoriety of a Jesse Jackson. Considering the Catholic Church's relative lack of direct political involvement on most issues, it is no surprise that there have historically been few prominent pastors to guide the Hispanic flock in a political direction. When Univision surveyed Hispanics in 1999, they asked respondents whom they would consider the most admired Hispanic leader in the United States. The top vote-getter was "Don't know" at 37 percent. The person who scored highest, with a whopping 5 percent, was Chicago-area Rep. Luis Gutierrez (D). He came in far behind "No one" at 16 percent.[18] And in recent national Hispanic surveys, former Mexican President Vincente Fox took top honors with 4 percent.

Nor has there ever been a Hispanic advocacy group prominent enough to organize Latino voters nationwide, as the NAACP works among African American voters. "The organizations that exist for the Hispanic community seem to do a decent job perhaps in lobbying for causes," says Dr. Felipe Korzenny, an ethnic research pioneer and Hispanic marketing professor. "But they don't really represent a lot of the population. If you ask people on the street who the National Council La Raza is, they don't know. And the same thing is true with LULAC (the League of United Latin American Citizens). Nobody knows who they are. The only ones who know who they are are the big companies and the people they approach for money, or the people they are lobbying."[19]

The Hispanic community is more horizontal and less hierarchical than the African American community. It is segmented among various Latin American nationalities whose members do not necessarily share similar experiences or speak Spanish the same way. It is also split between the newly arriving, the less recent arrivals and the native born.

That is not to say that the Left hasn't tried to create a homogenous victim-class among Hispanics. Today, outside of the confines of a few university faculties, the so-called Chicano Movement is a mere footnote. But its substance, and its failure, offers important lessons about the Hispanic experience in America.

El Movimiento, as it was known among its adherents, bears similarity to the slavery-reparations movement, even though its historical premises are far more dubious. At the heart of the movement's perceived past historical wrongs is the failure of American authorities to respect the rights of Mexican property owners who suddenly found themselves on the American side of the border after the conclusion of the Mexican-American War.[20] According to the movement, this and other perceived wrongs entitle Hispanics to a victim status. Chicano ideologues promote an uprising, either through violence or simply through immigration, to reclaim the American Southwest, the mythical land of "Aztlan."

This is, of course, ridiculous, and it has become a straw man for anti-immigration crusaders who allege a conspiracy to return the Southwest to Mexico. After listening to modern-day Chicano academics, fossilized holdovers from another era, one might even be tempted to give Buchanan and others some credit. A sample of their "scholarly work," in which they sometimes express open admiration for the dictator Fidel Castro and other violent Communists, could provide a case study for what is wrong with academia today.[21]

The truth, however, is that the Chicano movement never had much historical currency to begin with, but was rather a tool for inculcating Marxist ideas in yet another ethnic group. Very few of the Hispanics in America today bear any relation to the Mexican families that lost their land in the 1800s. More importantly, El Movimiento short-changes Latinos, ignoring all of their aspirations to something better than perpetual victim status. As Gregory Rodriguez wrote in the *Los Angeles Times*. "The Marxist leanings of so many of the first generation of Chicano Studies professors made it even more difficult for them to admit that millions of Mexicans have come to the United States hoping to one day finally place their families into the middle class."[22]

The Chicano Movement's issues are irrelevant for the vast majority of Hispanics. For one, although Hispanics once suffered from discrimination—the famous signs in San Antonio once read, "No Mexicans, No Negroes,

No Dogs"—there was nothing comparable to mass kidnapping and lifetime enslavement that brought so many Africans to America. Latinos also had Henry B. González, the first Hispanic U.S. Representative from Texas, who long ago contributed to enormous civil rights gains, such as ending the poll tax and ending discrimination in San Antonio's recreational facilities. But America has moved a long way in 40 years. Today, Latinos are an up-and-coming population that does not suffer such indignities, and that includes millions of Hispanics who have immigrated to the United States after 1970.

"I think they're beginning to realize that it doesn't fit," says political commentator Michael Barone. "That the Henry B. González experience is obsolete. That there's never going to be a civil rights issue that was going to be as central for Latinos as the civil rights issue was for the African Americans. Because they're just not excluded that much. Do middle class Latinos have trouble buying a house somewhere? No. Are they not getting served in restaurants? I don't think so. Are they able to get good jobs and work? Actually they do pretty well in the private sector. Do they have segregated military units? I don't think so."

Nor is it in Hispanics' interest to vote all together as a single bloc. As national political coalitions go, groups win only when they are considered a "jump ball"—when they are in play and have a stake in the game. That's a fundamental rule of politics, and true for any group: If you put yourself in someone's hip pocket, you're going to be treated like spare change.

Much has been written about the GOP's attempts to make inroads in the African American community, but these outreach efforts are often dismissed as futile or token efforts. With 80–90 percent of African Americans voting Democratic, few Republican candidates are willing to spend the resources to effectively court their vote.

Most Hispanics have not yet entered the Whining City—how can any group be as successful as we are, and yet buy into the myth that we're failing and disadvantaged? Between Latinos and Republicans, there is still a chance for a connection to be made.

But there is one surefire way to unite us all in opposition, to make sure no such connection is ever made. Just keep hammering home the nativist message, and brown will be the new black. Below is a graph tracking the percentage of Hispanics who cite "discrimination" as their top

Figure 7.3   Percent of Hispanics Dissatisfied with their Treatment Rises

Since 2002…

Q. 7 Next we'd like to know how you feel about the way various groups in society are treated.
For each of the following groups please say whether you are very satisfied, somewhat satisfied,
somewhat dissatisfied, or very dissatisfied with the way they are treated.
Analysis: Since June of 2002, the percentage of Hispanics who are dissatisfied with how Hispanics
are treated in our society has been steadily climbing. In short, almost 6 in 10 Hispanics are
dissatisfied with how Hispanics are treated.

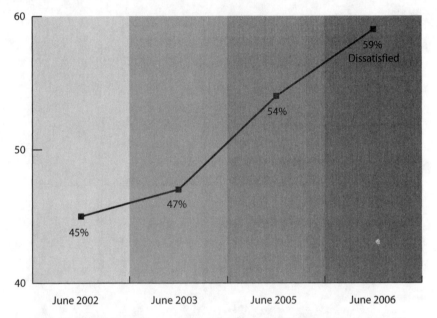

Source: Gallup Poll Social Series: Minority Rights & Relations/Black-White Social Audit Annual Survey
June 2002, 2003, 2005 and 2006
* 2004 Data Not Available

concern, and on the following page a timeline of key happenings in the
immigration debate over the last two years. The results are striking.
Between 2002 and 2006, the number of Hispanics saying they felt
Hispanics were badly treated grew steadily and consistently.

For Democrats, "discrimination" is a magnet issue, serving the same
purpose "national security" often serves for Republicans in the political
arena. When people worry about it, they come flying back to the party.

Republicans cannot allow this to happen. They can either listen now
and enter into a relationship that will benefit them and the country, or

158

Figure 7.4 Immigration Timeline

Sept. 11, 2001	Attacks on the World Trade Center and the Pentagon cause the country to reexamine immigration policies
Mar. 12, 2002	President Bush releases a statement about immigration bill applauding House for working in bipartisan fashion to pass comprehensive reform
Jan. 30, 2003	United States Immigration and Naturalization Service (INS) institute an electronic reporting system to track international students and exchange visitors in U.S.
Mar. 1, 2003	Service and benefit functions of the INS transitioned into the Department of Homeland Security (DHS) as the U.S. Citizenship and Immigration Services (USCIS).
Sept. 23, 2003	Legislation is announced by Senators Larry Craig (R-ID) and Edward Kennedy (D-MA) and Representatives Howard Berman (D-CA) and Chris Cannon (R-UT) addressing legal immigration status available in the agricultural sector of the economy
Oct. 1, 2003	Visa Waiver Program nationals are required to obtain either a Machine Readable Passport or a United States non-immigrant visa to enter the United States
Oct. 4, 2003	Immigrant Workers Freedom Ride concludes in New York City. Over 100,000 people attended to show support for a new immigration policy
Jan. 7, 2004	President Bush proposes new temporary worker program
Jan. 12, 2004	President Bush makes proclamation: To Suspend Entry as Immigrants or Nonimmigrant of Persons Engaged in or Benefiting from Corruption
Feb. 9, 2005	Congress proposes to amend the Immigration and Nationality Act with HR 698 (bill to eliminate birthright citizenship)
Oct. 18, 2005	President Bush signs Homeland Security Appropriations Act for 2006
Dec. 16, 2005	United States House of Representatives passes the Border Protection, Anti-terrorism, and Illegal Immigration Control Act of 2005 (HR 4437) by a record vote 239-182; plan focuses on border security first
Mar. 25, 2006	750,000 march from Olympic and Broadway to the City Hall in Los Angeles in "La Gran Marcha" (The Grand March), a protest of the proposed HR 4437
Apr. 7, 2006	Sen. Arlen Specter (R-PA) introduces Senate Bill 2611 (Comprehensive Immigration Reform Act)
Apr. 28, 2006	"Nuestro Himno," a Spanish translation of the "Star Spangled Banner" is played simultaneously on about 500 Spanish radio stations
May 1, 2006	"The Great American Boycott" or "El Gran Paro Americano," is timed to coincide with the traditional May Day communist celebration of the worker; an estimated 2,000,000 participate. Organizers include liberal groups such as ANSWER (Act Now to Stop War and End Racism), union organizers and fierce political partisans
May 3, 2006	In response to the pro-immigration reform boycott, the Minuteman Project begins a caravan across the United States
May 15, 2006	President Bush addresses the nation on immigration reform
May 25, 2006	Senate Bill 2611 is passed with amendments by Yea-Nay Vote: 62 to 36
Sept. 14, 2006	Secure Fence Act passed in House by recorded vote: 283 to 138
Sept. 29, 2006	Secure Fence Act passed in Senate without amendment by Yea-Nay Vote: 80 to 19
Oct. 26, 2006	President Bush signs Secure Fence Act

they can become a permanent minority. And Latinos will be better off having a real alternative. Fifty years from now, today's young generation of Hispanic voters will tell their children and grandchildren their political experiences. It will be a shame if they say, "I remember where I was when the Republicans tried to build a wall around America."

eight

the credit card

Writer, actor and comedian Carlos Mencia has rocked the world of comedy with his refreshing, though politically incorrect (consider yourself warned!) take on being Latino in America. No stereotypes are safe here. After starting his career as an electrical engineer at California State University, he left to pursue an even tougher line of work on the comedy circuit, eventually landing his own show, Mind of Mencia, *on* Comedy Central.

[T]ake, for example, the Hispanic vote in this country, all right? It's mostly Democratic. Yet, if you talk to them based on issues, just issues and politics, they're very conservative.

I remember my dad was like, "I vote Democratic." And I was like, but dad, everything that you say is conservative. Why do you vote Democratic? And he was like, well, I mean I identify with the Democrats. And I go, "Dad, you're for spanking people at school, you're for, you know, everything that was not Democratic."

And he was like, "Yeah? But who gives us the cheese?"

And I was like, "All right, great . . ."

—June 12, 2006, Excerpt from NPR's Morning Edition

Obviously, Latinos have the ability to move anywhere from 12–15 points in an election cycle. People were surprised that Kerry got so low a Latino number; I was not. Yet after that, the Republicans were saying exactly what the Democrats are saying now [in 2006]—"Oh, the Latinos came home." No, they didn't come home. They gave you a political credit card that can come due at any time.

—Marcelo Gaete, deputy director of the National Association of Latino Elected and Appointed Officials (NALEO), Nov. 30, 2006

In just a paragraph, Marcelo Gaete offers perhaps as precise a summary of today's Latino vote as anyone can. Our vote is volatile because it is winnable, because enough Latinos still keep an open mind and vote on a case-by-case basis. This is the same lesson I learned when I worked at the Republican National Committee in the run-up to the 2000 presidential election.

The year was 1999, and people at the RNC were perplexed about the demographic changes the nation was experiencing. The numbers told us then that Democrats owned the Hispanic vote, and they were tightening their grip with each passing election.

In 1996, the last presidential election, Bob Dole had won the lowest percentage of Hispanic votes of any Republican presidential candidate since the advent of exit polling. His miserable 21 percent showing among Latinos represented the tail end of an unmistakable downward trend—a straight line headed from Ronald Reagan's 37 percent showing toward zero at some future date.

Fortunately, we did not just bury our heads in the sand. The GOP could ill afford to let Democrats radicalize and monopolize the Hispanic vote as they had done with the African American vote.

The Republican Party, which had been the natural home of black voters until FDR, was no longer viewed as the party of Lincoln, but as the party of white America. So thoroughly have Republicans lost the African American support that their strategists had long ago adopted a "harm reduction" approach to it. "[E]ven though we cannot departisanize the Democratic orientation," wrote Republican pollster Lance Tarrance in a private 1983 memo, "[we must] make sure the black population does not feel that they are 'going to be hurt' by the Republican label."[1] Prophetically in the same memo, Tarrance had suggested Republicans "[r]edouble efforts to attract the Mexican-American population as a long-term 'offset' against the black Democratic partisanship. In other words, we need to 'double our budget' in this area if we stand any chance for the future."

The election of 2000 also promised to be the first election in which Hispanics had a significant impact on national politics. More Hispanic voters had participated in 1996 (making up about 5 percent of turnout, or almost two million people) than in any other presidential election in history.

And more of them voted for the candidate who "felt their pain" and wanted to "build a bridge to the 21st century," than the one who waxed nostalgically about middle America as typified by Russell, Kansas, circa 1930. Even I could see that if the Republicans continued with a message like that, the party was in trouble.

The RNC had hired me as the number-three spokesperson in the press shop, working directly below Clifford May, the former *New York Times* reporter, and Mike Collins, known as the junkyard dog of Republican politics. Two days into the job, Chairman Jim Nicholson called me into his office and asked me to grade the GOP on how well it was doing with Hispanics.

I thought for a moment—if I answered truthfully, I might be fired. I took the safe road, answering hesitantly, "I'd give us a C."

Nicholson did not hesitate at all. "I'd give us an F," he quickly responded. By this time, we already had Univision's 1998 survey of U.S. Hispanics, which gave us some clue of just how badly we were doing. Whether or not the RNC deserved an "F," a large plurality of Hispanics felt completely ignored by the GOP[2]:

Table 8.1   The Republican vs. the Democratic Party

The Democratic Party . . .		The Republican Party . . .	
Takes me for granted	18	Takes me for granted	22
Ignores me	18	Ignores me	41
Reaches out	47	Reaches out	26

Source: Univision Communications, Inc., *The Power of the Hispanic Vote,* April 23, 1998.

I offered to help the party formulate a national plan to better target Hispanics, even though I was not sure how to do this. It had never been done on this scale, but with Nicholson's support, I recruited a brain-trust of the best Republican Hispanic marketing consultants, starting with Frank Guerra, a respected San Antonio advertising man who had a long history with the party, and Lionel Sosa and his wife Kathy, a top creative director. I also reached out to political strategist Mike Madrid of California, as well as Lance Tarrance, Jr., a leading Republican pollster and strategist who was convinced to come out of retirement to join us.

This was our dream team, and we were working at a critical time. By entrusting us with this study, the Republican Party was clearly beginning to look more at Hispanics as a base, and now felt the need for a new Hispanic Strategy to replace the Southern Strategy of the 1960s and 70s. Tarrance was quoted discussing this change in a Salon.com article at the time:

> Republican consultant Lance Tarrance, a chief architect of the GOP's 1960s and '70s "Southern strategy," sees big changes ahead for the Grand Old Party. "For the last three decades, we've had a Southern strategy," Tarrance said Wednesday. "The next goal is to move to a Hispanic strategy for the next three decades."[3]

We developed a plan over the next 30 days and presented it to Nicholson and his chief of staff, Tom Cole—now a congressman from Oklahoma. We warned that Republicans would have to embark on a crash course of outreach to the Hispanic electorate. If the GOP did not get more than 25 percent, it would be statistically impossible to win a presidential election after 2008. Over the past 30 years, the GOP had averaged 30 percent of the Hispanic vote. We identified 37.5 percent as the target Hispanic percentage needed both to win the presidency and contribute to down-ballot victories.[4]

We walked out of that meeting with $80,000 to do a comprehensive analysis—"The New America Study"—about shifting Hispanic demographics. It may not sound like much now, because such things have become more common in politics. But it was rare then for a political party to invest that kind of money in such a study. In fact, it may have been a first in American political history. Parties did not invest such resources lightly, and we were emboldened by this show of support.

This seminal study, I believe, was a big step in changing the trajectory of modern Republican politics. It gave us the opportunity to survey 2,200 Hispanic voters with detailed questions, the answers to which would form our strategy.

Later in 1999, Tarrance reiterated our message at an RNC consortium of Republican governors, warning of America's developing demographic realignment. Republicans, he said, could not afford to miss this demographic change the way they missed out on bringing new Irish and Italian Catholic immigrants into the Republican Party. Nor could Republicans afford to let this entire demographic go to the Democrats, as happened after half of all African Americans left the South for the industrial jobs available in the North. "If we're not careful, we're going to miss it again," he said.[5]

We knew that Texas Gov. George W. Bush, then considered the likely presidential nominee for 2000 (although it later became a close race with Sen. John McCain), had tremendous appeal with Hispanic audiences nationwide. He had also won 49 percent of the Hispanic vote in his 1998 reelection. We needed to make sure we had an active plan in place to capitalize on his natural popularity with Hispanics and bring more of them into the party from around the country.

The RNC strategy focused on developing a Hispanic component for every function of the RNC, including grassroots activities, state party operations and press relations. It became one of the most intense outreach campaigns ever directed at Hispanics. We created the first-ever Hispanic communications program to distribute Spanish-language press materials to over 700 television, print and radio outlets. We formed a first-of-its-kind "Hispanic Speakers' Bureau," which trained and coordinated over 35 Hispanic surrogates to speak on behalf of Bush and the GOP. Among the speakers was George P. Bush, son of Jeb and Colomba Bush. Over the next year and a half, these speakers would conduct more than 2,000 Spanish- and English-language interviews promoting Bush's candidacy.

At the time, there was no Spanish-language RNC website—something we remedied immediately (thanks in large part to a dedicated GOP operative, Ana Gamonal). Working with the state parties, we also produced bilingual campaign brochures and materials.

We trained Republican members of Congress and press secretaries in the basics of how to reach Hispanic constituents—in many cases this was as simple as contacting ethnic media outlets, which some had never tried. With RNC co-chair Patricia Harrison, we organized Hispanic coalitions for Bush in 25 states, and we opened campaign offices in areas Republicans had not been in for over a generation—such as East Los Angeles and Philadelphia. In California, we recruited 5,000 Hispanic volunteers for grassroots organizing, including literature drops, phone banking and knocking on doors.

Finally, we launched a $2 million dollar television and radio advertising campaign, consisting of six Spanish-language ads aimed at appealing to Latino swing voters in a dozen states. That was part of a total $5 million in Spanish-language advertising spent by the RNC, state parties and the Bush campaign combined. In 2000, we would spend more than twice as much advertising to Hispanics as the Democrats did.[6]

Nicholson announced the new initiative with optimism, declaring that Hispanic votes "are up for grabs—if Republicans are willing to include Latinos, embrace Latinos, compete for Latinos, and to fight for Latinos. I'm here to tell you that we are and we will—more aggressively than ever before."[7]

The result, of course, is history: The contentious, razor-thin 2000 presidential race saw George W. Bush defeat a sitting vice president in a time of peace and relative prosperity, and a handful of Hispanics in Florida made the difference. The significance of this must not be underestimated: It was easy enough for Bob Dole to lose big among Hispanics in a year when he was losing big with most groups of voters. But for Bush to do so well among Hispanics in a tight 50–50 election was phenomenal and important.

Bush managed to reverse the Republican slide among Hispanics, dramatically increasing their GOP percentage on the presidential ballot (to 35 percent)—the first increase since 1984. The estimated 2.5 million Hispanic voters who supported Bush nationwide in 2000 represented an increase of nearly 1.5 million votes from four years earlier. Significantly, the exit polls showed that Bush won Florida not just among Republican-leaning Cubans, but within the overall Hispanic vote, estimated at 656,000 ballots cast. If not for the combined Hispanic vote in Florida, Al Gore could be finishing his second term as president today.

Even more importantly, the change in the Hispanic vote lasted beyond the 2000 election. In 2004, Hispanic voters increased their support for the president just like non-Hispanic Republicans did, giving him an impressive 44 percent of their votes versus 53 percent for Sen. John Kerry (D-Mass.). This result, which came despite discontent over the Iraq War and a difficult economic recovery from the terrorist attacks of 2001, had major conse-quences down-ticket, as Republicans gained seats in both the House and Senate—including the Florida Senate seat of Mel Martinez (R).

Florida was also key to Bush's 2004 reelection. He was able to improve on his narrow 2000 margin there thanks largely to Puerto Rican voters, who by most estimates gave President Bush nearly half of their vote. Their support in the "I-4 corridor," which runs from Tampa through

Orlando and on to the Atlantic coast of Central Florida, allowed Bush to increase his margin of victory in the state, sparing the nation another agonizing recount.

"When the I-4 corridor in central Florida went for the President, the campaign knew that the President had carried Florida," said Luis Fortuño, the Republican who was elected to represent Puerto Rico in Congress that year. Bush's numbers among Puerto Ricans in Florida, he told me, "hovered around 48 percent, which was even above the 44 percent attributed to Latinos throughout the country. In terms of voting for Senator Martinez, in that race the number was in the high 50s."

Democratic pollster Sergio Bendixen described to me the nature of Bush's success among Hispanics: "Latin America is one of those places you hear about when there are revolutions or earthquakes or drug problems. To think they would have a culture you can learn anything from is a foreign concept. The Bushes are the only ones that truly got it. They saw how powerful it was in a way that changed the future of Hispanic politics in America at least for a generation. They understood the most important concept about working in the community."

None of this is meant to imply that Republicans have already done the job with regard to Hispanic voters. Election 2006 is proof of Latino independence, as many of those who supported Republicans before went to the polls in support of Democrats. But at the very least, the positive experiences of 2000 and 2004 demonstrate conclusively that the Hispanic vote is there to be won, if Republicans are willing to work for it.

And there is still more to the story: Our work left us with data suggesting that if they work for it, Republicans will someday begin winning Hispanic majorities. That is, as long as they effectively reach out and avoid insulting Hispanic voters with anti-immigrant diatribes.

The results of the RNC research helped us to develop a detailed plan for the future. Based on our working group's findings, we believed that Latinos were fertile ground for our party's message. We had only to plough and cultivate it sufficiently to translate an obvious cultural conservatism into Republican strength among Hispanics—but the process would take some time.

Based on our pre-2000 study, we estimated that the Hispanic base vote for Republicans is approximately 30 percent. Although a weak candidate like Dole—who was out of touch with most other Americans anyway—can always underperform, we surmised that any reasonable candidate will receive this vote no matter what. The fact that Republican candidates received 30 percent of the Hispanic vote in a year as bad as 2006 confirms our estimates at that time.

We believed that in the election of 2000, we could improve upon that 30 percent base, bringing more Hispanics to vote Republican in the short term with a strong election campaign. These, of course, became the targets of our outreach work in 2000. They were predominantly Mexican (partly because of the large number of Mexicans in Texas), and mostly female, since men already provided two-thirds of the base Hispanic Republican vote.

Beyond that, we identified a large additional group as "approachable" by the Republican Party, so long as the party could engender a "comfort level" with their communities. Nicholson referred to this group when he spoke to the press: "There's a block of 25 percent of Latino voters who through the recent survey have sent us this message: 'We're open to change. We don't want to be taken for granted by any political party. We want policies and programs that really work for us and for all Americans. So persuade us. Make your best case. We're listening.'"

Looking forward, we conduced a major post-election study to see where we were with Hispanics. Combining those who voted Republican already—the base—with the group we had won in 2000, plus this other 25 percent Nicholson referred to, our maximum GOP performance among Hispanics could be almost two-thirds—63 percent. These voters said they would be comfortable voting for a Republican candidate if Bush, as President, showed national interest and genuine concern for Hispanics during his administration. That is not to say that we thought we could win nearly that many votes—rather, this was our ceiling, the best we could possibly do with the Hispanic vote in the long term. We were taking into account the fact that about 30 to 35 percent of Hispanics were staunch Democrats who would vote against us no matter what.

The estimates proved to be very accurate for the November 2000 election, and we analyzed them carefully afterward. After our post-election survey of Hispanic voters, we believed that we could take 45 percent of the Hispanic vote in 2004. President Bush came just short of that when he took 44 percent of the Hispanic vote.

Figure 8.1 Hispanic Vote Breakdown by State, 2004

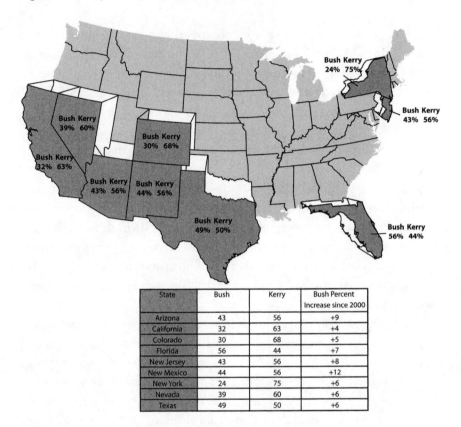

State	Bush	Kerry	Bush Percent Increase since 2000
Arizona	43	56	+9
California	32	63	+4
Colorado	30	68	+5
Florida	56	44	+7
New Jersey	43	56	+8
New Mexico	44	56	+12
New York	24	75	+6
Nevada	39	60	+6
Texas	49	50	+6

Notably, the race in Florida that year was not nearly as close as it had been in 2000—with a margin of 400,000 votes, there would be no recount. Part of the reason is that even as he slipped slightly among Cubans—traditionally the most Republican Hispanic group—Bush improved among other Florida Hispanic groups. The result was a seven-point improvement and a decisive 56 percent finish among all Hispanics. In Florida, Hispanics voted nearly the same as whites, who gave Bush 57 percent of their votes.

The numbers Bush produced in these key states (see Figure 8.1 above) put the thesis of *The Emerging Democratic Majority* on thin ice. They reveal conclusively that the Hispanic vote is a genuine "swing vote," much more comparable to the Catholic vote than to the union vote.

It is not a vote Democrats can easily count on to build their "permanent majority."

Texeira, however, refuses to concede the point. Appearing at a Washington, D.C. forum in February 2007, he denied that Hispanics are or will be a swing constituency, minimizing the "instances in which Hispanics have voted fairly heavily for progressive Republican candidates," and asserting that they will never support conservatives.

"Jeb Bush!" chimed in Democratic pollster Sergio Bendixen, offering the obvious response. Bendixen made a conclusive case that Hispanics will vote for either party under the right circumstances. He added, "[a]bout Hispanics not being swing voters, in New York City in 2000 Hispanics voted 80 percent plus for Hilary Clinton, a Democrat. A year later the same exact group of voters voted 50 plus for Michael Bloomberg, a Republican." Bendixen also noted Al Gore's strong performance among Puerto Ricans in Central Florida in 2000. "Just two years later," he added, "they voted for Jeb Bush at 64 plus. . . . If Hispanics are not swing voters, there are no swing voters in America."

Gary Segura, an associate professor at the University of Washington and co-principal investigator of the Latino National Survey, added shortly afterward: "I can't help but disagree with the entire gist of Ruy's presentation. . . . There is substantial change in the Latino electorate from election to election. . . . By contrast, the African American electorate, it's big news when the Republican share goes from 10 to 11 percent. That's not the reality we're describing for Latinos."[8]

"The good thing about it is that increasingly we're beginning to demonstrate how far we will swing," says Gaete of NALEO. He was even inspired to tell one Democratic Latino consultant that this Republican success could make him rich. "I told a Democratic operative the same thing. Look, if you keep arguing to the Democratic Party that Latinos are in your base, you are going to get less money. If you point out that Latinos just swung 15 points in 2 years, you should just increase your fees, and tell them 'you got lucky this time but don't expect it in the future.'"

Latino partisanship is based more on where we live and how the candidates speak to our concerns than it is on racial issues. And for many of us, evidently, we really make up our minds how to vote on a case-by-case basis. Some ask why, if Hispanics are such natural Republicans, they don't vote that way. The best answer is that they will if the GOP approaches them with respect and speaks to their concerns.

But after the tremendous gains of 2004, many Republicans threw out the respect part, and their share of the Latino vote suffered accordingly. Our vote is indeed like a credit card—eventually the bill comes due.

nine

dis-inviting the *familia*

The son of Mexican migrant farm workers, Gaddi Holguin Vasquez rose to become director of the U.S. Peace Corps, where he brokered the first-ever agreement for volunteers to serve in Mexico. In 2006 he was confirmed as the U.S. representative to the United Nations Food and Agriculture Organization in Rome, Italy.

I was asked by a Democratic friend, "Why are you one of them and not one of us? Based on your upbringing, you fit the profile of a Democrat, not a Republican." Says who? When I turned 18, I did what most young people do and analyzed the two parties. I was thinking, we want a future without nuclear war. Who can sustain peace? Nixon was President and I saw these images of him opening dialogue with China and the USSR. It sent a signal to me that peace could be at hand. I do not always agree with the Party, but I agree more than I disagree. I have a pragmatic approach. I don't want any more and I don't want any less than an even playing field.

Latino voters are pragmatic voters. We are good for a time but it's a window of opportunity. Our vote is not like concrete that begins to harden. Latinos want a fair and responsible shot at living on America's main street. The problem is some Latinos have no voice. They are multilingual, multicultural. We are of the same fabric but different weaves. The best hope we have is that someone in the faith movement, a preacher, a pastor, or someone with profound conviction, will step up and be an advocate for our community. The good news is we are starting to see the fishers of men.[1]

> America is in BIG trouble—Congress is preparing to pass AMNESTY for *illegal aliens*! Help stop Illegal aliens from murdering 12 Americans daily.
>
> —*A recent "Alert!" from the Minuteman Project, Dec. 1, 2006*

Before the election of 2006, the RNC acknowledged publicly the need to build on its 2004 level of Hispanic support. "We cannot maintain majority status in America without a growing share of the Latino vote," RNC strategy director Adrian Gray told the *Los Angeles Times*. "When 44 percent of Latinos supported President Bush in that last election, it opens the door for many of them to vote Republican in the future."[2]

But Republicans lost badly in the midterm. For all the positive spin the party tried to apply, to it, they were clobbered for a loss of 30 House seats and six Senate seats, giving control of both chambers of Congress to the Democrats—to say nothing of six governorships and control of nine state legislative chambers.

Nationwide, Democrats took 52 percent of the congressional vote to 46.5 percent for Republicans. In the last midterm election of 2002, Republicans had taken a plurality of 49.6 percent, and they had taken 49.1 percent in 2004.

Republicans lost ground with every group, whether divided along lines of race, gender, religion, education level or income. And one of their worst performances was with the Hispanic vote.

In 2004, as they approached parity with Democrats in the presidential contest, Republicans convinced more Hispanics than ever before to support them. Hispanics accounted for 8 percent of the national congressional vote in 2004, according to exit polls, and 44 percent of them backed Republican candidates, compared to 55 percent for Democrats. But in 2006, Republicans returned to rock-bottom with the Hispanic vote—still 8 percent of the national electorate—with a 30 percent showing just two years after their national apex.

To accept the data on its face, as a simple 33 percent decline in Hispanic support, would be overly simplistic. In 2006, Republicans lost ground with nearly every group, and so it is natural they would lose some support from Hispanics over concerns about the Iraq War and Congressional corruption. But why so much?

immigration in 2006

"Many politicians will incorrectly presume that ethnic appeals, or a focus on supposed 'Hispanic issues,' hold the key to attracting more Latino votes," Democratic consultant Mark Feierstein wrote in 2001. The "Hispanic issues" model, he explained, includes "speeches peppered with Spanish, events with salsa music, and an emphasis on immigration and defense of bilingual education, rather than on broader issues of concern."

This is the wrong approach, he warned at the time. "Hispanic voters, like voters overall, are most impressed by substantive proposals. And they respond best to messages designed for the general electorate."[3]

Feierstein wrote that he and Stan Greenberg had performed a survey during the 2000 election suggesting that Hispanic voters ranked immigration the least important among ten issues they tested—just 6 percent of voters saw it as a top priority. This squares with what several other surveys have found, including the Pew survey and our own RNC survey of Hispanic attitudes in 1999, in which immigration came in fourth with 7 percent.[4]

Feierstein continued:

> Research in 2000 showed that initiatives that focused on supposed Latino issues like immigration or made reference to Hispanics were generally less effective among Latino voters than messages that stressed education, health care, and retirement . . . The politicians that win over Hispanics will be those who speak to their concerns principally as Americans, not as Hispanics.

So immigration usually means little—but what if a candidate or a party does not treat, or barely treats Hispanics as Americans? This is where the election of 2006 provides the exception that proves the rule. Immigration doesn't matter to most Hispanic voters, at least not until the issue becomes a platform for bashing immigrants in general and Hispanics in particular. Candidates who talked the tough talk on immigration—who demonstrated through their rhetoric that they resent the influx of Latino culture and that they do not see a shared future for Anglo and Hispanic Americans—were defeated in the competitive races they ran.

Naturally, the hostile Spanish-language media tarred the Republican Party with a broad anti-immigrant brush. Their news reports downplayed President Bush's commitment to immigration reform and attributed enormous (and undeserved) importance to marginal anti-immigration figures such as Tom Tancredo.

Not only was the anti-immigration chatter offensive to some Hispanics, it also proved utterly useless in turning out the "base vote" that conservatives had expected in reaction to unfettered immigration.

Indeed, Election 2006 gave the lie to the idea that immigration is a powerful issue that motivates "middle America" to vote.

"It is important to note that immigration in the Latino population is never a top-tier issue," said Gabriel Escobar, associate director of the Pew Hispanic Center, in an interview with the *Houston Chronicle* in 2006. "Nor is it for the rest of the population."[5] Indeed, at least the latter proved true. Despite nationwide polling that shows support for many restrictionist immigration measures, Republicans have now discovered over the course of two elections that almost no one—not even their hard-core base supporters, who turned out in record numbers to back the "pro-amnesty" President Bush in 2004—hangs their vote on immigration. Support for restrictionism may be a mile wide, but it is also an inch deep.

When it comes to the immigration issue per se, the results among Hispanics are nuanced and even counterintuitive. Even as some of the most vocal immigration blow-hards went down to defeat, both Hispanics and non-Hispanics in Arizona quietly supported ballot initiatives regarding immigration restriction and acculturation. The lesson appears to be that Hispanics are not so much averse to tough border-control policies—including fences, English-only laws and apparently even some benefit cut-offs—as much as they are to immigrant-bashing politicians.

the blow-hards

Candidates across the country, running for every level of elected office, tried to capitalize on the contentious immigration debate that dominated the national conversation in the summer of 2006. In nearly every case, their rhetoric and advertising had the obvious goal of frightening voters into action—sometimes with the side effect of demeaning and offending Hispanics and other people who heard them.

Their ads ranged from the silly ("When it comes to immigration, Matt Knoedler is a wet Knoodle!"[6]) to the shocking ("Since 9/11, more Americans have died at the hands of illegal immigrants than died in the terrorist attacks and the war in Iraq combined"[7]).

Most of these immigration-related attacks had a few things in common. Many were demeaning toward immigrants—sometimes even legal ones—and most of them blamed immigration for the nation's everyday problems.

Nearly all of them included the same kind of scary music and foreboding voice discussing the threat posed by illegal immigrants. It was nearly always an attempt to use the issue to *scare* voters into taking action. But voters apparently did not like being frightened and manipulated in this way.

An ad from Numbers USA, a self-proclaimed immigration-reduction organization, was typical. It gave the threatening—and absurd—impression that there is not enough *space* in America for immigrants, with no distinction between the legal and illegal variety: "Nearly 50 million immigrants and dependents are already crowded into our communities."[8]

North Carolina's Vernon Robinson, a repeat candidate for congress in 2006, became famous in 2004 for running ads calculated more to be creative (and often offensive) than to win him votes. Robinson's campaign focused heavily on immigration, just as it did when he lost in 2004, with one ad decrying today's America as a "Twilight Zone" overrun with Spanish-speaking foreigners. Robinson's campaign placed robo-calls against his Democratic opponent, Rep. Brad Miller, that consisted of a song to the tune of "The Beverly Hillbillies," accompanied by a banjo:

> Come hear me tell about a politician named Brad,
> He gave illegal aliens everything we had.
> Gave 'em Social Security and driver's licenses too!
> Free healthcare, free lawyers, and free lunch at the school.[9]

After another verse about Brad Miller and "illegals," a narrator with a drawl intones, "Hey y'all illegals, put your shoes on and go home! Don't come back now, hear?"

Not all of the ads bashed immigrants so lightly—some portrayed them as grave threats to public safety. An ad by Len Munsil, the Republican gubernatorial nominee in Arizona, began by mentioning that 9/11 hijacker Hani Hanjour boarded his final flight with an Arizona driver's license. The ad then goes on—again, delivered in a threatening voice—to compare the terrorist to illegal immigrants in general: "Unbelievably, Janet Napolitano supports giving driver's licenses to illegals like Hanjour."[10]

Democrats have only held New York's First Congressional District in Long Island since 2002, when an incumbent Republican blew his easy reelection after his own negative ad backfired. Republicans, hoping to take back the seat, tried to field a serious candidate against Democrat Rep. Tim Bishop in the person of Italo Zanzi, the the Vice President of Hispanic Marketing for Major League Baseball. Zanzi ran his campaign almost as if immigration was the only issue. In one radio ad, narrated by a man with an angry, threatening voice, Zanzi identified immigration as the cause of all of Suffolk County's local problems, even those barely or not at all related: "Sky high property taxes. Dangerous, overcrowded housing. Deteriorating quality of life. Illegal. All are ways to describe the illegal immigration problem we have in Suffolk County."[11]

In a follow-up ad which he narrated himself, Zanzi continued to hammer away at people's fears over illegal immigration. "I'm running to become your Congressman, to stop the illegal immigration problem that is plaguing Suffolk county," he said. "You've heard my ads since the summer, talking about the illegal immigration crisis, and how our Congressman has had four years to get the job done, but has failed us miserably . . . This year you have a choice. Elect me, Italo Zanzi, as your congressman, to give you the leadership you deserve, or vote for my opponent, who has allowed the illegal immigration problem to spiral out of control, costing you hard-earned money."[12]

In Tennessee, Jim Bryson, the Republican nominee for governor, ran a heart-wrenching ad in which a woman described how a drunken illegal immigrant, after being arrested and released 20 times, killed her parents in an auto accident. The ad concludes, once again, with the characteristic threatening voice: "For the toughest illegal immigration laws in the nation, vote Jim Bryson."[13]

The immigration obsession did not do much good for any of these candidates. In Tennessee, incumbent Gov. Jim Bredesen (D), whose negligence on illegal immigration supposedly caused the car crash (which was a bit of a stretch), trounced the tough-on-immigration Bryson by 40 points, carrying every county in the state. The other candidates who ran these ads fared little better. Munsil lost by 30 points. Voters were neither frightened nor impressed enough to give gave Zanzi more than 39 percent of the vote in a district that had been recently held by a fairly conservative Republican.

"It isn't what you say, it's how you say it," said Allan Hoffenblum, a Republican political strategist in Los Angeles. "You had these Republicans sounding mean. . . . It's an angry tone that all American problems are because of illegal immigrants. There's little doubt that when you go around acting as if you don't like a group of people, they don't vote for you. So Latinos stopped voting for Republicans."[14]

* * *

In 2002, Republicans received about 38 percent of the Hispanic vote for Congress. That means that from one midterm election to the next, roughly one in four Hispanics willing to vote Republican abandoned the GOP.

There were certainly many reasons for their doing so, but the large presence of the immigration debate over the summer of 2006 cannot be written off as insignificant in the November results. This is particularly true in light of what Hispanic voters told exit pollsters after listening to the immigration debate raging around them. "In exit polls, 37 percent of Hispanic voters ranked illegal immigration as an issue that was 'extremely important' to them, compared with 29 percent of all racial demographic groups."[15]

Suddenly, immigration had become a more important issue to them than it normally was. It is a sign that the debate was on Latino voters' minds. After the election, some fingered the Republican message on immigration as the culprit for the defeat. "This time there is no doubt [Hispanics] felt Democrats were on the right side of the immigration issue," Republican media advisor Lionel Sosa told *USA Today* after the election.[16]

Rev. Luis Cortés had similar words for the *The Washington Post* two weeks after the election. "A lot of the Republican candidates chose immigration as the wedge issue, and polls seem to bear out that it was an error for them to do that," he said.[17]

Others made a more subtle point: It's not that that Republicans and Hispanics could not find common ground on immigration and border security, but rather that many Republicans had spent the summer insulting and denigrating Hispanics in their campaign against illegal immigrants.

In October 2006, BBC correspondent Lourdes Heredia asked a Mexican American student at George Washington University, "Lorena," about "how the heated immigration debate would affect her vote." The response was much more than the reporter bargained for.

"I am fed up with stereotypes," Lorena responded. "I do not care a bit about immigration issues. I am a U.S. citizen and I am very proud to be here. I don't care too much about one law or the other. That wouldn't change my life or my family's opportunities. I am a second-generation [American] and frankly, I might feel sympathy for the [new immigrants] who are struggling, but . . . not really," she said.[18]

But importantly, Lorena also noted that "she doesn't like the anti-immigrant rhetoric and wouldn't vote for representative or a senator who says she, or her parents, do not have the right to be here."

Lorena's concerns were widely shared. Tamar Jacoby, a supporter of open immigration, asserted that the rhetoric turned off even Hispanics who agreed on the need for immigration curbs and a border fence.

> The problem was as much about tone as substance—many Latinos are also worried about illegal immigration. But the hard-liners' grandstanding added up, and there was no mistaking the message: Not only illegal immigrants but 30 million Latino voters heard Republicans saying, "We don't like you." The results were hardly surprising.[19]

Democratic pollster Sergio Bendixen voiced a similar note in an interview with the *Wall Street Journal.* "They're upset about the tone of the debate. They did not see it as a debate about immigration policy. They saw it as a debate about whether Hispanics are welcome in the states and whether Hispanics are appreciated."[20]

Many Hispanics rejected the Republicans for the same reasons other voters did: Iraq, scandal, and out-of-control Congressional spending. Hispanics appear to have disapproved more strongly of President Bush (63 percent disapproval) than the electorate at large (57 percent disapproval). A full 37 percent of Hispanics supported an immediate withdrawal of troops from Iraq, as opposed to 29 percent of all voters. And whereas 36 percent of all voters said that they cast their vote as a rebuke to Bush, 45 percent of Hispanics said the same.[21] It is another sign of the volatility of Hispanic electorate—Bush had been Latinos' favorite Republican.

But as we have seen, there is ample evidence that Hispanics were turned off or even riled up by the immigration hard-liners' rhetoric.[22] I can offer as an example my mother, whom after years of work I had finally convinced to start voting Republican. Democrat though she had always been, she came to Washington in 2001 to attend the presidential inauguration. I was working for the Inaugural Committee, and we had access to great parties and seats for the duration of the event.

After four days of freezing temperatures and endless security checkpoints, Mom was ready to return to Sugar Land, Texas, and as she boarded the plane I saw former Majority Leader Tom DeLay, who happened to be her congressman, in line. I said hello and introduced him to Mom before she entered the terminal.

Later she called to let me know she had sat next to "Tom" for the three-hour flight and talked extensively about her inaugural experience, my career and other unending details I was sure I'd be embarrassed about later.

"Tom is such a nice guy," she gushed. "I told him all about you. I shared photos of you."

Ugh! How humiliating!

"He said call if you need anything."

Years passed, and I would frequently hear mom talk fondly about "Tom" and his work in the community. She'd even save his congressional newsletter to share with me on visits. But in the fall of 2005, Mom was apoplectic when she called my cell phone. "Tom DeLay wants to put the Mexicans in tents!" she said. "I don't like him anymore!"

I groaned on the inside, wondering what he had said. Did he have any idea how long it had taken me to get Mom to vote Republican?

DeLay's remarks had come in the midst of the illegal immigrant backlash on Capitol Hill. In the southern border-states, Republican legislators were taking sides, responding to the roar of constituents to "do something about the illegals problem." In the heat of the debate, Congressman Tom DeLay gave a speech to Fort Bend County Republicans, the county in which I grew up, and charged that he does not support educating illegal immigrants and encouraged local police to round them up.[23]

"If you pick up 50 or 100 of them," he said, "put them in tents."

A few months later, my husband and I visited Mom for the holidays. Again, she anxiously turned to my husband with the news, "Tom DeLay wants to round up the Mexicans and put them in tents."

"Good thing you're an American," he responded.

"Oh, yeah. You're right," Mom said with a sudden look of relief. Unfortunately, Mom had shared this story with many of her friends and committed not to vote for her former friend "Tom" again. She, like many other Hispanic Americans, believed that DeLay singled out Hispanics. Of course, DeLay never specifically spoke of targeting "Mexicans." But because Texas is a state where Mexicans are by far the largest minority and the largest immigrant group, it was easy to infer.

The problem, again, is with the *tone* of the debate. Further evidence for this comes from Hispanic voters in Arizona, who proved to be fairly conservative on immigration *issues*. Hispanics made up 12 percent of Arizona voters, and 48 percent of them voted for a ballot proposition making English the state's official language. The measure, Proposition 103, received 74 percent of the vote. It won everywhere except for Apache County, which has almost no Hispanic presence—the Navajo Indians, who comprise a large majority of that county's population, voted against the measure en masse in order to protect their ancestral language.[24] The Voter News Service did no exit polling on Proposition 300, a more draconian measure that cut off certain state benefits for illegal immigrants, but that measure must have performed very well among Hispanics. It carried every county, including those with large Hispanic populations, on its way to a 71.4 percent victory.[25]

Interestingly, the backers of the immigration-related propositions spent almost nothing to promote them, and that may have actually helped those ballot propositions among Hispanics because the issue did not become so heated. At the same time these initiatives were passing, however, Tempe area Rep. J. D. Hayworth (R) was running a re-election campaign with an almost myopic focus on illegal immigration and the U.S.-Mexican border.

In his first ad of the campaign, threatening music played in the background as Hayworth stepped in front of the camera, a white family having a conversation in the background. "I'm J. D. Hayworth," he began, "and I approved this message because we must secure our borders with beefed up enforcement, no amnesty, English as our official language, and no Social Security for illegal aliens—none!" The ad proceeded to fault his opponent for being weak on the issue, and ended with a dramatic setup:

ANNOUNCER: "J. D. Hayworth: He's drawing the line . . ."
HAYWORTH: ". . . at the border."

When a *Wall Street Journal* reporter asked him about the news that business groups were cutting back their financial support for Republican border-hawks, Hayworth responded with a flourish befitting his talk-radio past. "The oath of office I took was not to hand-hold business," he said. "It was to protect the citizens. . . . That is a responsibility I'm not going to abdicate."[26]

The citizens evidently did not feel threatened enough by the insecure border to re-elect Hayworth. He lost on November 7 by just over 8,000 votes.[27] If immigration restriction is such a winner for Republicans, why did Hayworth take just 46 percent of the vote in a district where the "pro-amnesty" George W. Bush had taken 54 percent in 2004?[28]

Meanwhile, a few hours to Hayworth's south is the eighth congressional district, stretching from eastern Tuscon to Sierra Vista and the Mexican border. The district was vacated by the retiring moderate Republican Jim Kolbe, a champion of open-border policies and a robust guest-worker program. In the race to replace Kolbe, former state Rep. Randy Graf received the Republican nomination against state Sen. Gabrielle Giffords (D) and proceeded to run an immigration-focused campaign in which he took reporters to the border in order to show them just how unguarded it was.

No one ever gave Graf, one of the original members of the Minuteman Project, much of a chance. The district's moderate makeup, Graf's own inability to raise money, and a clear lack of support from an already weak local party made his an uphill run. Still, if a hawkish position on immigration is to have grassroots support anywhere, one would expect it to be a place like this, where thousands of illegal immigrants make the crossing from Mexico every night and the Border Patrol makes its presence felt on every roadway leading from the border. Graf was crushed, taking only 42 percent and losing by nearly 31,000 votes.

The tough-on-immigration stance of Rep. John Hostettler (R-Ind.), chairman of the House Judiciary Immigration and Border Security

Subcommittee, did not help him much as he approached his crushing loss. A rare conservative who had opposed and voted against the Iraq War, Hostettler was defeated 61 to 39 percent by a local sheriff, Brad Ellsworth (D) of Evansville.

During his campaign, Hostettler had focused on immigration, making appearances with the Minutemen and spending his small war-chest on ads denouncing his opponent as "wrong on illegal immigration, wrong for America." None of this helped the already outmatched congressman, who had never run a conventional congressional campaign before. In Hostettler's case, there is no question of whether Hispanics had anything to do with his defeat—they make up less than one percent of his district. But border-hawk ideology was clearly not an effective way for Hostettler to rally his white voters, either.

"Certainly, if you look at the people who ran the most aggressive on just law, just border security they didn't do well," says Ken Mehlman, the RNC chairman who presided over the 2006 election. "Three of the most aggressive proponents of that approach all, unfortunately, lost. One of the lessons of Hayworth, Graf and Hoestetler, in my judgment is, that while a strong border security is necessary it's not sufficient to address the issue."[29]

Republicans in Virginia had learned the same hard lesson in 2005 about just how ineffective the immigration hawk's rallying cry can be. Attorney General Jerry Kilgore (R) ran a campaign for governor that emphasized immigration along with other issues, particularly the death penalty. His immigration ad fit precisely into the hawkish playbook, and appeared calculated to outrage voters over Democrats' plans to build day-laborer centers, which would mostly service illegal aliens, with taxpayer dollars. "What part of 'illegal' does Tim Kaine not understand?" bellowed the announcer, in an attempt to scare immigration-wary voters away from supporting the Democratic candidate.

Immigration certainly wasn't the only factor in the race—and of course it never is. Kilgore also ran a series of extremely cynical death-penalty ads that most everyone agrees backfired on him. But the result of this election was interesting because the immigration-focused candidate was the clear loser once the votes were tallied. Not only did Kilgore lose, he was the only Republican on the ticket to lose that year. The GOP swept the down-ticket, keeping both the attorney general's office and the lieutenant governor's spot, so it wasn't merely a bad year for Republicans. In fact, among the six major-party candidates running for Virginia's top three statewide offices— three Democrats and three Republicans—Kilgore received fewer votes than anyone else.

The immigration issue did not kill the candidacies of most hawks, but it does not look like it added to the bottom line even of the winners. House Homeland Security Chairman Pete King (R-N.Y.) made immigration a centerpiece of his campaign, championing border fence legislation and even appearing on Lou Dobbs's CNN program to discuss immigration. He was held to just 56 percent in 2006 against Cuban American county legislator David Mejias (D). In the last two races in his Long Island district, King had received majorities of 63 and 72 percent in years when immigration was not an issue.

"Republicans were warned that the lack of distinction between legal and illegal immigrants, coupled with occasionally overheated rhetoric, sent the wrong signals to the Hispanic, Asian, and other important immigrant communities," writes Dr. Frank Luntz in his new book, *Words that Work* (2007). "This was definitely one rule Republicans didn't follow."[30]

There are counterexamples to these stories of hawkish immigration rhetoric proving divisive or at least impotent, but there is nothing that suggests hawkish immigration rhetoric can win close elections for Republicans in the future.

As Hayworth and Graf were going down to defeat in his state, Arizona Sen. Jon Kyl (R) was outperforming national Republicans with the Hispanic vote, taking 41 percent against his well-funded challenger, former Democratic state chairman Jim Pederson (D). Kyl had opposed the Bush immigration plan, but proposed a compromise guest-worker program that required illegal immigrants to leave the United States before applying. Throughout the debate, he avoided harsh rhetoric, sticking to calm and at times wonkish expositions on how one policy or another bill contained many fatal defects.

Meanwhile, a few Republicans softened their immigration position and did well with Hispanics. One of the clearest cases of a Republican candidate who won Hispanic votes this way is California Gov. Arnold Schwarzenegger (R).

At one point, after he offered public praise for the Minuteman patrols, Schwarzenegger's internal polls showed him suffering badly with the Hispanic vote, taking just 12 percent. His campaign responded by bringing Hispanics into his cabinet—including Rosario Marin. He noticeably softened his hard line on immigration and played up his immigrant roots in the last few months before the election.[31] He was also blessed to have in his opponent one of the worst candidates in the state. In the end, Schwarzenegger won 39 percent of the Hispanic vote—a good performance by California standards—as he blew out State Treasurer Phil Angelides (D) to receive a full term. It remains to be seen whether someone like Schwarzenegger can heal the wounds created by Proposition 187, but earning so many Hispanic votes is at least a good start. Anyone who voted Republican in a year like 2006 is more likely to consider doing it again in the future.

Other Republicans who performed reasonably well among Hispanics included a long list of Republicans who mostly avoided the immigration issue, even if they did deal with it in the sphere of policy. Their success testifies to the fact that the 2006 election did not completely destroy any relationship between Latinos and Republicans:

- Attorney Gen. Charlie Crist (R) tied Rep. Jim Davis with 49 percent of the Hispanic vote and won his race for governor. Crist took 70 percent of the Cuban vote and 33 percent of non-Cuban Hispanics in Florida.
- Jim Gibbons (R-Nev.) lost the Hispanic vote in Nevada but took a healthy 37 percent, to his Democratic opponent's 55 percent, in what was a very close race, hinging on last-minute accusations of an impropriety by Gibbons.
- On the same ballot, Sen. John Ensign won 45 percent of the Hispanic vote as he cruised to reelection. This is a strong number for Nevada Latinos. Ensign had fought in the Senate to prevent the proposed guest-worker program from giving Social Security benefits to illegal immigrants for the time they were working illegally, but he did not make immigration a major issue in the campaign.
- Texas Gov. Rick Perry won only 31 percent of the Hispanic vote, but that was in a four-way race. The Democrat, former Rep. Chris Bell, took just 41 percent of the Hispanic vote, while independent candidate Kinky Friedman took 9 percent. Carole Keeton-Strayhorn, a Republican turned independent, took 18 percent.
- Sen. Kay Bailey-Hutchison (R-Tex.), in her uncompetitive reelection race, snapped up 44 percent of the Hispanic vote.

Although a broad majority of Americans tell pollsters that they care about illegal immigration and want it stopped, the issue does not scare voters enough to affect how they vote. Immigration restriction has broad but extremely shallow support, "political fool's gold" for Republicans that fails to rally their base and in some cases hurts them seriously with the Hispanic swing group.

None of this necessarily means that Republicans have to embrace a policy of amnesty or open borders in order to win the Hispanic vote. But as Sosa told *USA Today*, "It means Republicans need to have a much higher sensitivity about how Latinos feel about their worth and the worth of immigrants." Republicans who show respect to immigrants and court them, instead of bashing them, can win their votes, regardless of their position on immigration.

Rep. Henry Bonilla's loss was something that I felt personally, because he'd done so much to keep this Latina interested in politics when I had all but given up. He probably did not lose his election because he had voted for the tough House border security bill—the analysts say that his run-off election campaign was poorly run and poorly supported by the national GOP after the November 7 loss. But the border measure may have helped stoke turnout against him.

His unusual late election arose after the Supreme Court decided that the 2003 round of redistricting in Texas had removed too many Hispanics from his district and diluted their voting power. The newly drawn district brought in many new Hispanic areas of the south San Antonio suburbs that he had never represented before, bringing the district population up to over 60 percent Hispanic and 55 percent Democratic.

On November 7, Bonilla needed 50 percent in a crowded field of seven opponents to avoid a special-election runoff, but he received just 48 percent. In that first round, as in the December 12 runoff, his support collapsed in some border counties where he had won decisive majorities in the past. Many people along that part of the border—the Rio Grande valley, stretching from El Paso to Laredo—view a fence as a very bad idea. Maverick County, a 95 percent Hispanic border county that Bonilla had carried with 59 percent in 2004, gave him just 29 percent on November 7 and 14 percent in the two-way runoff.

For one reason or another—perhaps they were Christmas shopping or just tired of politics for the year—an estimated 28,000 of Bonilla's base voters from a month earlier failed to show up on December 12 for the runoff, and he fell short by a 6,039 votes.[32]

is Hispanic turnout already making a difference?

Hispanics accounted for just 8 percent of the national electorate in 2006, which may tempt one to think that they remain a future electoral force whose relevance is not yet upon us. But that may be a mistake. According to the U.S. Census Bureau, Hispanics represent 10 percent or more of the population in 8 of the 30 U.S. House districts that switched from Republican to Democratic control in 2006.[33]

Every House race is different, and in some situations, no number of Hispanic votes could have made the difference. Shelley Sekula-Gibbs (R-Tex.), for example, was doomed when the courts ruled she was not allowed to have her name on the ballot. On the other hand, Rep. Joe Negron (R) in Florida, who had been forced to run under the name "Mark Foley" after that congressman dropped out late amid accusations of cybersex with

Table 9.1   Districts lost by GOP with large Hispanic Population

District	Candidates (incumbents in bold)	Democrats' margin of victory	Percentage of Hispanic population
Arizona–5	**Hayworth (R)**, Mitchell (D)	4% (8,023 votes)	13.3%
Arizona–8	Graf (R), Giffords (D)	12% (30,866 votes)	18.2%
California–11	**Pombo (R)**, McNerney (D)	6% (10,612 votes)	19.7%
Colorado–7	O'Donnell (R), Perlmutter (D)	13% (22,999 votes)	19.6%
Connecticut–5	**Johnson (R)**, Murphy (D)	8% (27,016 votes)	10.5%
Florida–16	**Negron (R)**, Mahoney (D)	1% (4,404 votes)	10.1%
Florida–22	**Shaw (R)**, Klein (D)	4% (8,102 votes)	10.7%
Texas–22	Sekula-Gibbs (R, write in), Lampson (D)	10% (14,833 votes)	20.3%
Texas–23[34]	**Bonilla** (R), Rodriguez (D)	9% (6,039 votes)	65%

Table 9.2 Close GOP Saves in Districts with large Hispanic Population[35]

District	Candidates (incumbents in bold)	Republicans' margin of victory	Percentage of Hispanic population
Arizona–1	**Renzi (R)**, Simon (D)	8% (16,955 votes)	16.4%
Colorado–4	**Musgrave (R)**, Paccione (D)	3% (7,206 votes)	17.0%
Connecticut–4	**Shays (R)**, Farrell (D)	3% (6,645 votes)	12.8%
Illinois–6	Roskam (R), Duckworth (D)	4% (4,810 votes)	12.5%
Nevada–2	Heller (R), Derby (D)	6% (12,587 votes)	15.3%
Nevada–3	**Porter (R)**, Hafen (D)	2% (3,971 votes)	15.6%
New Mexico–1	**Wilson (R)**, Madrid (D)	< 1% (879 votes)	42.6%

House pages just a month before election day, came heartbreakingly close to winning anyway.

A serious, perennial effort in some other districts to court Hispanic voters could have helped in some of the other close losses as well. In the future, a boost in Hispanic GOP support—or in some cases a slackening of Hispanic hostility—could put Republican House candidates over the top.

But beyond the question of Republican losses, and equally relevant to the Republican Party's continued survival, is the number of narrow Republican saves in Hispanic-heavy districts. In many of the closest House races, just enough Hispanics voted Republican to save endangered incumbents. It is a sign that in election cycles to come, they could well determine the outcome of future elections because of their heavy presence in key districts that could someday decide who has the House majority.

The race of Rep. Rick Renzi (R) only tightened late, when there was a hint of a federal investigation of one of his land deals. But his district is drawn to be competitive. With the exception of Rep. Marilyn Musgrave (R-Colo.), who underperformed in a district that went 58 percent for President Bush in 2004,[36] all of these seats are by nature competitive.

Between the close wins and the losses in Hispanic-heavy districts, there are 15 competitive races that could determine who controls the House after the 2008 elections. Republicans in these 15 districts have everything to gain by making an earnest attempt to appeal to Hispanic voters.

Republican politicians cannot wait for the next election wishing away the Latin surge in population. Their congressional districts are the ones picking up most of the immigrants, according to a recent census study by the Associated Press. "Republican congressional districts are becoming magnets for immigrants—legal and illegal," writes AP's Stephen Ohlemacher. "Of the 50 House districts nationwide with the fastest-growing immigrant communities, 45 are represented by Republicans." Republican congressmen nationwide have seen three million new immigrants settle in their districts since 2000. Across the country, Republicans are confronted with the need to reach out to the newly arriving communities and be a positive influence in shaping their political culture.[37]

Will Republicans follow the lead of Rep. Bob Inglis, who has embraced the Hispanic community in South Carolina, or that of Tom Tancredo, who frequently insults Hispanics and views them as a backward influence?

securing america

The immigration issue has become so politicized that almost no one is interested any longer in seeking a sensible policy. The casualty in this heated debate is the nation's ability to do anything about an immigration system that everyone agrees is broken.

As we have seen, some Republicans embrace an anti-immigration position on the mistaken belief that it will help them win elections. Democrats are also opportunists on the issue, but in a different way. Now that they control Congress, they can delay passing immigration reform because they benefit politically from having Republicans continue to argue over it. The tendency toward delay is strong enough that Hispanic Democrats in Congress recently complained of the absence of immigration reform from the top priorities of their Democratic leaders.[38]

As this circus goes on, we remain literally in the worst possible situation on immigration—the status quo. We do not know who is here, and we do not know their intent. This dangerous situation will persist as long as this political game is played. The only way to end this mess is for people to open their minds a bit. We should not ignore the arguments of those who truly want to restrict immigration—whose motives are more than just political. They employ three key arguments for their position, based on economics, culture, and security. Each of these arguments can be made in good faith, and some of them must be accommodated in any new immigration policy. By the same token, however, many of these arguments are simply meritless and must be refuted.

Conservatives who argue that immigration is economically destructive should take stock of the company they are keeping. Liberal *New York Times* columnist Paul Krugman expresses concern that the Left's support of immigration is hurting American workers by driving down their wages and benefits.[39] Krugman—while typically making sure to disagree in vague terms with anything Republicans support—nonetheless comes off a lot like Tom Tancredo when he hits specifics on immigration.

> Because Mexican immigrants have much less education than the average U.S. worker, they increase the supply of less-skilled labor, driving down the wages of the worst-paid Americans. The most authoritative recent study of this effect, by George Borjas and Lawrence Katz of Harvard, estimates that U.S. high school dropouts would earn as much as 8 percent more if it weren't for Mexican immigration.

To Paul Krugman, immigrants who flee poverty and corruption in order to find a better life are capitalist-opportunists. They're coming to the states to make money at the expense of poor Americans!

It is actually little surprise that Krugman should find himself in agreement with restrictionist conservatives here. The problem with the economic argument against immigration is that it begins with the same mistaken premise that the economy is a pie with a defined size, and that any piece taken by one person is taken at the expense of another. This is a Marxist premise that fails to take the growth of market economies into account. In a growing, dynamic market economy that spurs new innovations and investments, the masses can improve their lot simultaneously without damaging anyone else. This is a key principle of the conservative supply-side economic model embraced by President Ronald Reagan.

The most common economic objection is that immigrants drive down wages and take away jobs from natives. Yet most studies show there is little or no correlation between immigration and the wages of unskilled natives, and the explanation for this is fairly simple.[40] One recent study, by David Card at Berkeley, notes in the summary, "Overall, evidence that immigrants have harmed the opportunities of less educated natives is scant." Among the numerous reasons, he notes, is that "the fraction of natives with less than a high school education has fallen sharply, more than offsetting the inflow of less-educated immigrants."[41] It is only natural that as more and more Americans attain higher levels of education, this should open up opportunities for uneducated immigrants, because someone still has to do the unskilled jobs in society. Even among the less-skilled Americans who compete directly with immigrants, Card continues, "there is a surprisingly weak relationship between immigration and less-skilled native wages."

A recent example in Colorado illustrates the problems with the assumption that immigrants are stealing jobs Americans would otherwise do. A dearth of immigrant laborers (due to a crackdown on illegal aliens there) has not raised American workers' wages at all, because there aren't any Americans freely stepping forward to do the work. Instead, the disappearance of the migrants has spurred a new program that will place low-risk state prisoners at farms where they will work for 60 cents an hour—much less than most of the illegal workers were making. If anything, this solution should actually put more downward pressure on U.S. wages for farm workers.[42] Some economists also point to the benefits of immigration for American skilled tradesmen. A lack of unskilled workers could actually hold back investments and projects that result in more highly skilled Americans having work. To give a rough example: Without a sufficient number of low-wage workers ready to hang drywall, American electricians would have fewer houses to wire each year.

Many immigration restrictionists argue that immigrants consume too much in the way of government services. There is a legitimate concern here, but the related argument that illegal immigrants come to the U.S. to go on welfare is preposterous, considering how little they actually get. According to the Center for Immigration Studies, a restrictionist think-tank, the average government payout to a household headed by an illegal immigrant is less than $1,000 per year, and only about 20 percent of such households are estimated to receive payments. Even then, this money does not pay the bills or put food on the tables of illegal immigrants. Nearly all of the payouts come from medical expenses through Medicaid and uninsured medical care.

The question of preserving American culture also looms large in discussions of immigration. Now, as in the days when waves of Irish and then Italian and Eastern European immigrants reached our shores, fears are rampant that all these immigrants will not, cannot, ever assimilate to our unique American values—they will more likely change America for the worse.

History, of course, has proven those fears to be unfounded, as immigrants have historically not only assimilated but also made positive contributions to American society. As we saw earlier, surveys show that Hispanics are indeed learning English as earlier immigrants did, contrary to the uninformed opinions of many anti-immigration writers and activists. The market tells us the same story: the single largest U.S. Spanish-language advertiser is Lexicon Marketing, the purveyor of English-learning tapes and DVDs. The company's advertising budget was $180 million in 2005, greater than the Hispanic ad budget of Procter & Gamble![43]

Other writers posit that immigrants are causing greater harm to America through their lack of values than through their lack of English. Take, for example, *City Journal*'s Heather MacDonald, whose arguments on this subject typify the sloppiness of much anti-immigration argumentation. Based largely on vague anecdotal evidence, MacDonald wrote in *National Review Online* last summer that Hispanics in the United States, both young and old, have no sexual morals and view single motherhood as a desirable status in life:

> Talk to any social worker and she will tell you that illegitimacy has become completely normalized among her Hispanic clients. . . . The mothers of teen mothers are themselves completely on board with single parenting, say the social workers, having often been single parents themselves. And they have no qualms about hooking their daughter and grandchildren into the public-benefits apparatus: "It's now culturally OK for that population to be served by the welfare system," says a case manager in a Santa Ana, Calif., home for teen mothers.[44]

With one stroke, MacDonald characterizes an entire ethnic group as lacking any trace of family values, offering no hard numbers to back up her assertion.

Moreover, she takes her definitive evidence on the word of someone who deals every day with the worst cases. The U.S. Census—probably a more reliable indicator than the one social worker MacDonald appears to have interviewed for her piece—tells us that 65 percent of Hispanic children under 18 live with both parents, compared to 67 percent in the population at large. The illegitimacy rate among young urban Latinas is a serious problem indeed, but it doesn't seem to be destroying the Hispanic family any faster than the national average. And what of MacDonald's unsupported assertion that vast numbers of older Hispanic women—the grandmothers—were "single parents themselves," something she has published more than once now without offering any statistical evidence?[45] Was this trend completely missed by American social scientists during the 1980s? Or is MacDonald suggesting that it began in Hispanic countries of origin, meaning that Latin American women aspire to the Murphy Brown lifestyle, and hope their children can enjoy the same? MacDonald, in her zeal to make Latinos look as bad as possible, does not need to specify.[46] But her unsupported assertions do not square with most people's experiences in those countries, nor with mine in South Texas. My family was *very* conservative when it came to such things. I got a training bra when I was 12, and I would sleep in it, because my Mom told me in no uncertain terms that I was *never* to take it off! (It took my Aunt Blanca, one night when I stayed over at her house, to tell me it's okay to take it off at bedtime.)

Another common "values and culture" argument originated with John Tanton, a radical environmentalist and population-control advocate who was the intellectual godfather of the modern anti-immigration movement.[47] Tanton argued that Mexicans "bring corruption with them" from foreign lands. But as we've seen, many of them—particularly Mexicans, but also others—fled to *escape that corruption.*

It's more than just a matter of officials soliciting bribes—a daily fact of life in Mexico that is routine and totally unchecked. Mexicans are also hurt by the kind of corruption that lets politicians dole out as favors what we consider necessities of life. When Mexico City's mayor launched public demonstrations over his loss of the presidential election last year, word emerged that his city government had compelled all of its employees, under threat of losing their jobs, to participate in the protests (the city government, of course, denied this). My friend Claudia was forced to attend political meetings for the PRI (the old ruling party) several days a week or else, she was told, she would lose her ability to buy one of a group of homes owned by a prominent official—and because Mexico has no reliable system for rating and evaluating credit, there was no other way for her family to buy property!

Such unofficial corruption is augmented by left-wing economic policies that fail to reward risk and skilled labor. Last year, in northern Virginia, I had an Argentine aircraft pilot in one of my focus groups who said that instead of flying planes back home, he is now a day laborer for an American construction company. As it happens, the latter profession pays much better, and so all of his pilot training goes to waste! Is it any wonder that many immigrants view our immigration laws the same way most of us view the 55 MPH speed limit?

The strongest argument for curbs on immigration, both legal and illegal, centers on national security concerns. This argument must be addressed and accommodated by any immigration reform plan.

But again, the worst outcome for national security is no reform plan at all. Even if amnesty is an undesirable policy, the status quo is *more dangerous* to our national security than an amnesty would be if it could at least identify everyone illegally present within the United States.

In the end, the solution will be a combination of border enforcement—probably including a physical security barrier—and legalization for some illegal immigrants to match with U.S. labor needs. Otherwise, the underground economy of labor and all of its accompanying vicissitudes—including the trade in false identification documents—will persist.

"A legalization program will not only serve our economic needs but our security needs," said Daniel Griswold of the CATO Institute, "We could concentrate our enforcement firepower on the smaller numbers coming across intending criminal actions. We'd start to drain the swamp of smuggling and document fraud that's spawned by our enforcement efforts. We would have a better idea of who's in the country."

We tend to worry about illegal immigration because it could bring terrorists into the United States. But what of the concern that some conservatives have that Hispanics in the United States represent a fifth column? In *The Death of the West* (2002), Pat Buchanan compares the influx of Hispanics and Hispanic culture to the influx of Muslims into Europe from Turkey and other Middle Eastern nations. Perhaps events have borne out Buchanan's view of Europe, where unchecked immigration has created a dramatic cultural clash resulting in riots and unrest in France. But can any of this be said of the United States?

There are surely similarities between America and Europe, including the fact that the new immigrants in both places are needed to sustain the pension systems of aging populations that are not reproducing. But there is one enormous difference that Buchanan completely overlooks: He's writing about the *death* of the West, but Mexicans and other Latinos *are* Westerners. Muslims in Europe find themselves cultural aliens to their new homeland—sharing neither its traditional religion nor its world outlook, cultivated over centuries of Christianity and Enlightenment philosophy. Mexican and Latin immigrants to America, on the other hand, are already Christian and Western in their cultural worldview, and share far more in common with their new compatriots.

In October and November of 2005, Americans were shocked to watch on television the rioting in France, and to hear of Islamic extremists threatening (and sometimes more than threatening) political opponents with violence in the Netherlands and other European countries. By contrast, as much as the pro-immigration rallies of 2006 rankled the sensibilities of some Americans—and in spite of very few random cases of violence—the protests here were remarkably peaceful and tame compared to the European experience.

The United States, far more than Europe or any other country in the world, has a history of assimilating immigrants, who go on to contribute significantly to our economy and our society. In Hispanic immigrants, we are absorbing immigrants who are easily assimilable—Westerners, Christians, and capitalists who appreciate the value of a free and law-based society.

Aside from the fact that they do not persuade voters, many of the arguments for ending or sharply curtailing immigration to the United States are simply bad arguments that employ faulty logic or begin with bad data.

The relationship between America and the immigrants should be understood as a win-win situation. Those who abuse foreigners as a menace to our society, and who stoke the flames of nativism for their own political advantage, will never succeed in making America whiter or closer to what it was in the 1950s. They may, however, benefit the Left by driving away a potential voting bloc that shares many of their worthy 1950s values and ideals.

ten

"reaganismo"

When you meet political newcomer Rep. Luis Fortuno (R), Puerto Rican Resident Commissioner to the U.S. Congress, it's easy to recognize why he's the recipient of numerous accolades ("Man of the Year" by Caribbean Business or "Public Servant of the Year" by business groups.) He's a maverick with endless energy and a vision of economic growth for Puerto Rico. But what influenced him?

I knew that I would go back to Washington at some point in life. I didn't know when and how, and I never expected that it would be this way, but I knew I would go back. That city has something that really leaves a mark on you. At that time, at the beginning of my college years—that was 1973—the country was in terrible shape. And then came along this visionary leader, that really actually turned me into a Republican, and that was Ronald Reagan. . . .

First of all, everything he said just made sense—pure common sense put into words. And he was an optimist, an eternal optimist.

My feeling is that he understood the contributions that we Hispanics were going to be making to the rest of the country. He was inclusive—remember that he was governor of California, and California, already back then, was clearly the Hispanic state to a great degree. You could tell by the way he referred to the contributions of Hispanics. That he wanted to be the person who started really trying to work together very closely with Mexico.

I would say that he is the predecessor of the efforts to adopt NAFTA. If you look back at his first meeting with the President of Mexico as President-elect, he was saying so many things that made sense, that Hispanics could relate to.

First, the importance of accountability in education and parental choice. Secondly, the importance of getting the government off our backs and allowing individuals' innovation and creativity to take over, to create jobs and to build small and medium-sized businesses—that's the backbone of the Hispanic community. Thirdly, the importance of the family—the cornerstone of our society. And fourth, taxes. With Reagan it was very clear. There were the failed policies of the Democratic Party: to tax more and spend more, and that was the way we were going to solve our problems. Whereas that was in total contrast to Reagan's perspective, which was to lower taxes and allow people to keep as much as possible of their hard-earned money. That just made so much sense to me that I knew right there and then that I was a Republican.[1]

> I have six sons—five of them are Republicans. I don't preach politics. I just try and make them understand the difference between right and wrong and our historical cultural patriotism. They ask me, "who did you vote for and why?" I go through the whole thing with my kids. I think it's an obligation that parents have to do these things. They ought to be thankful to God that they live in a free country.
>
> —*Jess Quintero, American patriot and president of the*
> *Hispanic War Veterans of America*

I never met Ronald Reagan. The closest I ever stood to him was 20 feet away, as he delivered his last major address at the 1992 Republican Convention. I connected to the ideas of this man at the twilight of his career, though it was the dawn of mine. I have rarely thought about how many other Latinos of different backgrounds had the exact same life-shaping experience connecting with the same man. In the course of researching and writing this book, I interviewed more than 100 experts and Latino leaders. I found an entire generation of Latinos like myself, whose ideological grounding had been formed by him.

That Reagan should have had such an impact seems logical enough. But who imagined that the people who would stand on the shoulders of Reagan's legacy would bear names like Cruz, Rodriguez and Duran? These are young men and women who were in high school or college at the end of Reagan's presidency. Twenty years later, this young generation of *Reaganistas* (mostly under 40) are deeply committed to conservative principles. They are intelligent and educated—in many cases, the first in their families to earn professional credentials in campaigns, as government appointees and as elected officials.

In the world of employment, Hispanics still remain predominantly in low-skilled positions, yet our numbers continue to rise in the corporate and professional worlds. In 2003, 66 percent of white employees in the private sector held white-collar jobs, compared with 39 percent of Hispanics.[2] But with this new generation of Youngbloods, everything is changing. These Latino professionals are entering the corporate or private sector, using their skills, expertise, and networking prowess to expand Hispanic educational and employment opportunities in the private sector.

Many of them will move to politics in the future, part of a new wave of Hispanic Republicanism. These are not your father's Latino politicians— the civil rights activists who began in union halls and Hispanic advocacy organizations. They are something else entirely. They are adopted a hybrid approach, moving through the world of money and power, but never forgetting where they came from. Now they are lowering ladders from their high places to pull others up behind them.

"The movement is going to be exponentially strong for one reason," says Dan Garza, a former migrant farm worker who went on to work in the Bush White House and now leads CONFIA, a newly formed faith-based group that mobilizes Hispanic voters. "As Hispanics, we see ourselves as a generation of young leaders who know and owe much to our communities. Now we're graduating. Our lack of knowledge has started to dissipate. Now we have access, and can look from the inside out. We have no fear. We can swim in a world that we are very comfortable in, and now we are the trainers."

These young leaders are forming their own conservative-minded organizations such as CONFIA, Hispanic CREO, and The Latino Coalition in Washington, D.C. They each have the potential to draw like-minded Latinos of various races and cultures to mobilize on a mass scale on their core issues.

"We knew we had to either offer a platform for young, bold leaders to represent us or sit down and be quiet," said Manuel Lujan, a former Member of Congress from New Mexico who served as a cabinet secretary for George H. W. Bush. He formed the Hispanic Alliance for Progress Institute, a nonprofit group aimed to promote traditional Hispanic values, economic prosperity, and entrepreneurship.

One of the most successful young professional political organizations in the late nineties was called Young Professionals for George W. Bush (YP4W). A 30-something investment banker in New York, Jose Fourquet, said, "We started as three guys with an idea, and we finished with 50 chapters, 5,000 members, dedicated staff in Austin and several hundred thousand dollars raised.

"In New York, when I was working for Goldman Sachs, I recruited a group of 15 friends and acquaintances from the major law firms, investment banks and from different ethnic groups." he told me. "Together we became the steering committee of YP4W in New York. My two friends in D.C. (Ken Mehlman and Joe Bogosian) did the same thing in Washington. However, our NY steering committee probably had the highest component of extremely sharp, well-educated, and upwardly mobile Latinos of any other YP4W group. We had Latinos from Morgan Stanley, Goldman Sachs, Credit Suisse First Boston and Prudential Securities, among others. These Latinos were just top notch professionally and personally."

And we continue to rise up. Consider Michael Montelongo, whom Bush appointed assistant secretary of the United States Air Force for financial management and comptroller. In 2005, after leaving the government, he was appointed to the board of directors of Denny's restaurants. He is currently a senior vice president with Sodexho, Inc., an international provider of food and facilities management services in Gaithersburg, Maryland.

Charles Garcia, a successful financier who focuses exclusively on Latino clients with high net worth, speaks of the newfound power Hispanics have as they enter the top levels of American business. "What happens when you get the CEO of Winn Dixie to call the governor of Florida and say, 'I want to hire more Hispanics, but they're dropping out of school'?" he asks. "That's powerful. Now imagine if you have ten CEOs doing the same thing. Now you have impact."

We are now seeing Hispanics who are engaging at a much higher corporate level than before—on the board level, on the foundation level— to increase Hispanic opportunities for education, building businesses, building wealth. All of the things that go with the American dream.

They are also running for office, and they are winning in places where you might not normally expect to see Hispanics run. In 1996, Latino elected officials served in 34 states; by 2006, that number had increased to 43. Marilinda Garcia, 23, is a bright young example of Republican Hispanics moving into the mainstream. In a year when Republicans had their clocks cleaned, she was newly elected to the New Hampshire state house of representatives on a straight conservative platform that included signing a pledge never to support a tax hike. Likewise, Virginia delegate Jeff Frederick, a Colombian American, has fought the good fight on a vast array of fiscal and social conservative issues. Democrats targeted him in 2005 to no avail. Thirty other Republican state legislators and seven Republican state senators are Hispanic as well. Those numbers will increase in the future.

Latino Republicans have also enjoyed statewide success both in terms of elections and appointments. Of the seven statewide offices held by Hispanics, three are held by Republicans. Still in office are Florida senator Mel Martinez, Texas railroad commissioner Victor G. Carrillo and Idaho's newly elected superintendent of public instruction Tom Luna. Others have given up their statewide offices for higher offices, such as U.S. attorney general Al Gonzales, and Brian Sandoval, the Nevada attorney general who went on to become his state's first Hispanic U.S. district judge and one of the youngest U.S. district court judges in the country.

Although the number of Latino Republican elected officials continues to lag behind that of the Democrats, Republicans from our ranks are being appointed to high positions and winning elections to office. They are finding success in nontraditional areas and they are coming from non-traditional backgrounds, entering public service from business and professional life, not professional activism. They aren't just winning because of their heritage or their last name, they're winning elections on their ideas—Reagan's ideas—with votes from people from all backgrounds.

"If we are going to increase our Latino members, we need crossover candidates to attract nonlatino voters," said Arturo Vargas, the nonpartisan NALEO's executive director. Particularly in areas with only small Hispanic populations, Republican Hispanic candidates can offer that crossover appeal. "We saw growth in non-traditional states, in non-Latino districts," he said.

Florida offers the most telling case study for success, says Al R. Cardenas, the former two-term chairman of that state's Republican Party. He is credited with building a farm team of qualified Hispanic candidates: "We have three Hispanic Republicans in Congress, 15 Members of the state legislature, including a Puerto Rican and a Colombian, and all of

Figure 10.1   Occupations of Hispanic Republican Federal and State Elected Officials

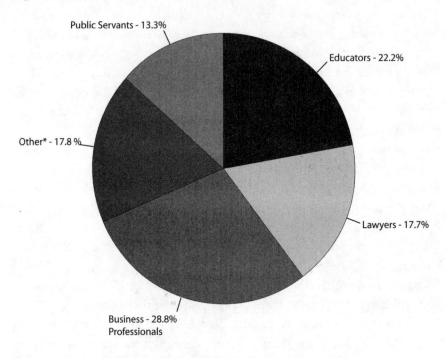

Public Servants - 13.3%

Educators - 22.2%

Other* - 17.8 %

Lawyers - 17.7%

Business - 28.8%
Professionals

*Real Estate, Banker, Engineer, Rancher , Technician, Doctor, Administrator

Source: National Association of Latino Elected and Appointed Officials

them are Republican." Cardenas also points to the rise of 35-year-old Marco Rubio, the son of Cuban exiles, who became speaker of the Florida House of Representatives. He is the first Hispanic and second-youngest person in Florida's history to preside over a legislative body. While the GOP's success in Florida centers around Cuban Americans, it has already begun its expansion to other Hispanic groups as well.

"The best way to achieve this is through the election of leaders like Jeb Bush, Mel Martinez and others who voters can begin to identify with," says Cardenas.

As Mexican Americans, Puerto Ricans and Central and South Americans advance in greater numbers into the middle class and build alliances within the non-Hispanic marketplace, is it likely they will replicate the Cuban success story in other Republican-leaning states?

"It can be done, but it will take time." Cardenas adds. "We didn't have to deal with two and three generations of Hispanics traditionally voting Democratic."

Meanwhile, at the top levels of the Republican Party, the leadership seems to get it—particularly the top dogs running for president in 2008. With the exception of Tancredo, who threw his hat into the ring in January, the serious Republican candidates—right, left and center— understand the value of working with Latinos and building a long-term coalition that will win in the future.

Sen. John McCain (R-Ariz.) is a favorite of Latinos in his home state. His sponsorship of a guest-worker program will probably win him some Hispanic votes across the country, but his real support comes from the years he spent courting Latinos in Arizona, and not just a single bill he has sponsored.

Former Massachusetts Gov. Mitt Romney seemed to have the right idea when I spoke to him last November. "Hispanic Americans bring a great vitality of culture, family values and love of freedom, and so naturally the Hispanic voter will be inclined to the Republican Party," he told me. "But we're going to have to make a real effort as a party to communicate our values and to connect with Hispanic voters." He was the first candidate, Republican or Democrat, to announce a Latin American policy advisory group and to begin advertising to Hispanics, airing Spanish-language radio ads nearly a year in advance of the Iowa Republican Caucus.[3]

New York City mayor Rudy Giuliani clearly connected with Hispanic voters in New York City when he delivered on promises to stem the city's crime epidemic, which was disproportionately affecting Latino families and businesses in places like the Bronx. Despite the extreme Democratic tilt of Latinos in New York, he won 42 percent of their votes in his reelection race.[4]

Conservative Sen. Sam Brownback (R-Kan.), more of a long shot than the others, hopes to connect with Hispanic voters on values issues. In the unlikely event that former Gov. Jeb Bush jumps in, he would have the potential to do even better among Hispanics than his brother before him.

Democrats will not always enjoy the political environment we saw in 2006, with a Republican president in an extremely unpopular war and a small group of corrupt Republicans in Congress whose antics kept the political conversation as far away from ideas and ideals as possible. In the future, the parties will have to win voters over with issues, and Democrats face a serious challenge here. With the number of union members and FDR-generation seniors declining, it is clear that Republicans are not the only ones with a long-term crisis on their hands. Democrats *must* increase their base share of the vote with women, professionals and Hispanics to make up for the decreases in their structural base. Otherwise, they will have to fight on issues. And since the emergence of the New Left in 1968, Democrats have *never* won a presidential election by dint of the left-wing issues that dominate their leadership today.

Anything Republicans can do to increase their share of the Hispanic vote cuts at the very heart of a coalition Democrats must build in order to survive as a viable party. Only a few Democrats seem to understand this— their national party already wants to take Latinos for granted, and the sparsity of the Democratic outreach program in 2004 confirms that fact— we saw that they spent much less than the Republicans did.[5]

The Democrats appear most likely to field as their presidential candidate a woman that a senior Democratic consultant offhandedly called "*la fria*"—meaning "the cold one" or "the iceberg." Hillary Clinton's lack of warmth poses a challenge for her in winning Hispanics not unlike the one John Kerry faced in 2004. "She does need to break through that cold image, too worried about showing her emotions," the consultant said. "With Hispanics, that will be her challenge."

Sen. Barack Obama (D-Ill.) would be a much warmer choice, and he is a proven winner of Hispanic votes in Illinois. But some fear that he still lacks the experience it would take to run for or serve as president. He has never even faced a difficult election before. Sen. John Edwards (D-N.C.) comes from a state with very few Hispanic residents, and he preaches a message of class warfare that, as we have seen, Hispanic voters just don't buy.

Latinos are optimistic about our own future and that of the nation. Those of my generation think back to Reagan, but what about the next generation of Latinos who are now in high school or entering college? What will their first political memory be? As we find our place in the political debate of tomorrow, what will frame the new Latino political identity?

There are two paths for us, and which one we take will be determined by the first impressions of Latino young people today. One is the path that begins with the bitter memory of "when Republicans tried to shut us out." Along that path, Republicans become the people who neither envision nor desire a common destiny with Hispanics. It leads to a place where Hispanics lose all the gains we have made in America. We stop putting our enterprising spirit and our fathers' faith into practice in our politics. It leads to a place where we view ourselves as "disadvantaged" and "victimized," where we embrace a paradigm that enslaves us to our ethnicity.

The other path leads to a much more hopeful and prosperous future for Latinos in America. It begins where Republicans embrace them as brothers who share many of the same ideals. It continues with Latinos maintaining their independence and bringing Latino culture into every part of society, not just keeping to ourselves. Along this path, we remain a swing vote whose center of gravity drifts gradually to the right as the years go by.

I have written this book on the belief that Republicans and Hispanics need one another in order to make a better America. The Hispanic spirit of optimism and enterprise, of faith and family, is a spirit that fits naturally with the beliefs I hold as a Reagan Republican. I am excited as I look forward to Latinos bringing these values to the voting booth, forever breaking that last stereotype that says we will march in lock-step with a Democratic Party that looks forward to the day it can take us for granted.

As Latinos grow and mature in our political participation, we ask ourselves the tough question: How hard are we willing to work for ideas that work for us?

Republicans, however, must first ask themselves their own hard question: Do they really take Reagan's ideas seriously? Do Republicans want to create an exclusive America—an America that's "just for us"—or was Reagan right that our neighbors are welcome in the Shining City upon a Hill, no matter their background? I am optimistic that the latter is the case. I think back to Reagan's radio address on Christmas Day of 1982, when he quoted from a letter written by a patriotic U.S. sailor named John Mooney:

> I hope we always have room for one more person, maybe an Afghan or a Pole or someone else looking for a place . . . where he doesn't have to worry about his family's starving or a knock on the door in the night . . . and where "all men who truly seek freedom and honor and respect and dignity for themselves

and their posterity can find a place where they can . . . finally see their dreams come true and their kids educated and become the next generations of doctors and lawyers and builders and soldiers and sailors."[6]

This is the America I have come to know. There has always been room. And, *ojalá*, there always will be.

postscript

My gratitude goes out to everyone who took time to share with me their experiences and unique ideas. In all, I interviewed more than 150 people. Remarkably, all of their stories came together to create this book, which I believe offers a new hope for what America could become. This living snapshot will continue to grow on the Internet in a new website (www.losrepublicanos.net) to showcase new and extended interviews, explore insights about Republican-Latino experiences and continue the dialogue about how issues affect a *diverse* Hispanic electorate.

This conversation must transpire not solely among Latinos but among other bands of immigrants desperately seeking to "learn the ropes" and understand how they too, can belong.

notes

introduction

1. Thomas B. Fordham Institute, "Simon Bolivar? Hernando Cortez? Kids Don't Know—and States Aren't Asking," *The State of World History Standards, 2006.* The study notes, "At a time of intense national debate about immigration and assimilation, many states do not seem aware that there are countries and cultures south of the Rio Grande," and finds that "30 states have 'significant gaps' in standards for teaching Latin American History." Available at http://www.edexcellence.net/institute/publication/publication.cfm?id=356&pubsubid=1287. Accessed Dec. 29, 2006.
2. The term itself is an inadequate generalization of all persons of Hispanic descent eligible, or soon to be eligible, to vote in this country. After all, we don't say "European" vote. However, for purposes of speaking to our shared cultural identity, these terms will be used interchangeably.
3. The anti-immigration group Federation for American Immigration Reform (FAIR) reports that more than 40 percent of the city's foreign-born population had become naturalized citizens. This does not include foreign-born Latinos with a pending immigration status or U.S. citizen Puerto Ricans.
4. Among Hispanics concerned about terror (defined as organized terrorists entering the United States secretly to smuggle nuclear, biological or chemical weapons into the country), 70 percent favor a physical barrier along the U.S.-Mexico border. Findings based on a nationwide RT Strategies National Omnibus Poll conducted Feb. 23–26, 2006 for Let Freedom Ring, a non-profit, grassroots public-policy organization in Pennsylvania.
5. Press release from the Office of Rep. Nancy Pelosi, Democrats Unveil Hispanic Agenda, July 10, 2003. Available at http://www.house.gov/pelosi/press/releases/July03/prHispanic Agenda071003.html. Accessed May 1, 2007. The agenda title is *Compromiso Demócrata con el Pueblo Latino.*

two   a changing america

1. Excerpt from speech delivered at Capital Life Church in Washington, D.C. on May 14, 2006.
2. Art Moore, "Is Mexico Reconquering U.S. Southwest? Illegal immigration fueling aims of Hispanic radicals," *WorldNetDaily.com*, Jan. 4, 2002. Available at http://www.worldnetdaily.com/news/article.asp?ARTICLE_ID=25920. Accessed Oct. 1, 2006.
3. National Vital Statistics Reports, volume 55, number 1, Sept. 29, 2006.
4. Sharon Jayson, "Society switches focus away from children," *USA Today*, Jul. 12, 2006, based on Whitehead and David Popenoe, "The State of Our Unions: The Social Health of Marriage in America," *National Marriage Project*, July 2006.

5. U.S. Census Bureau, 2004, "U.S. Interim Projections by Age, Sex, Race, and Hispanic Origin," http://www.census.gov/ipc/www/usinterimproj/, release date Mar. 18, 2004. Accessed Mar. 14, 2007.

6. "Hispanic Fact Pack: Annual Guide to Hispanic Marketing and Media," *Advertising Age* (2006 edition), p. 10.

7. Jeffrey M. Humphreys, "The Multicultural Economy 2006," *Georgia Business and Economic Conditions* vol. 66, no. 3 (Third Quarter 2006), p. 6.

8. From *Letters and Journals of James, Eighth Earl of Elgin*. Available through the Gutenberg Project at http://www.gutenberg.org/etext/10610. Accessed Mar. 10, 2007.

9. U.S. Central Intelligence Agency, "*The World Factbook: Mexico.*" Available at https://www.cia.gov/cia/publications/factbook/geos/mx.html. Accessed Mar. 19, 2007.

10. Larry Schweikart and Michael Allen, *A Patriot's History of the United States* (New York: Sentinal, 2004), p. 15f, 21–23.

11. The Latino Coalition, *National Survey of Hispanic Adults*, Oct. 2, 2006. This is a poll of adults that disproportionately surveys non-English speakers.

12. Sarah Lueck and Joel Millman, "Vote is a Blow to Republican Pursuit of Hispanics: Party Forfeits Recent Gains As Harsh Immigration Talk Appears to Have Backfired," *Wall Street Journal*, Nov. 9, 2006, p. A8.

13. Joseph Carroll, "Whites, Minorities Differ in Views of Economic Opportunities in U.S." *Gallup News Service*, Jul. 10, 2006. Sixty-four percent of Hispanics surveyed rejected the notion of an America consisting of "haves" and "have-nots," compared to 57 percent of whites and 31 percent of blacks.

14. Oral history of the U.S. Census, interview with Conrad Taeuber, former associate director for demographic fields, conducted Oct. 12, 1989, p. 9. "The most dramatic case was, again, the matter of Hispanics. The 1970 schedule was ethnically oriented when the order came down that we were to ask a direct question, have the people identify themselves as Hispanics. We argued that we had native-born of foreign parentage; that gives us Mexicans of first and second generation, gives us some Puerto Ricans of first and second generation, but we couldn't get away from the people in New Mexico, Arizona, and South Texas. There were to be three schedules]: There was a 100-percent schedule, 20-percent schedule and a 5-percent schedule. The 5-percent schedule had barely started at the printers when we pulled it back and threw in the question which hadn't been tested in the field—under orders." Available online at http://www.census.gov/prod/2003pubs/ oh-Taeuber.pdf. Accessed Mar. 10, 2007.

15. Oral history of the U.S. Census, interview with Conrad Taeuber, p. 6. "The descendants of those people are still to a large extent speaking Spanish, and still to a large extent in Spanish-speaking churches," said Conrad Taeuber, who was then the chief of demography for the U.S. Census. "They preserve their culture. Identifying them as native born of native parentage didn't quite do it."

16. Tony Castro, *Chicano Power: The Emergence of Mexican America* (New York: E.P. Dutton. 1974).

17. "Mexican Republicans of Texas," *Handbook of Texas Online*, s.v., http://www.tsha. utexas.edu/handbook/online/articles/MM/wembf.html. Accessed Dec. 29, 2006.

18. "Campaign Notes: Reagan Team Seeks 50% of Coast Hispanic Vote," *Associated Press*, Sept. 23, 1984.

19. "Sen. Pete Domenici Discusses the Battle Over the Budget," CNN transcript of Evans, Novak, Hunt and Shields, aired Sept. 30, 2000.

20. Author interview with Sergio Bendixen, Dec.18, 2006.
21. Peter Wallsten, "Immigrant Issues are Personal for Bush," *Los Angeles Times*, Apr. 2, 2006.

three   the latino moment

1. Jorge Ramos, *The Latino Wave: How Hispanics Will Elect the Next American President* (New York: Rayo, 2004) p. 97.
2. *Television Weekly*, a trade publication for the television industry, warns that it is a myth that the Hispanic market is Spanish dominated: "For starters, about one-fifth of the assimilated Hispanic population of the United States speaks only English and so is unreachable in Spanish. On top of that, several studies suggest that U.S. Hispanics watch roughly half of their television in English. The most recent U.S. Census figures show that 70 percent of those who say they speak Spanish at home also understand English 'well' or 'very well.'" Keith Rosenblum, "*Breaking Down the Market Myths: To Reach Latino Viewers, Separate Fact From Fiction,*" *Television Week*, Oct. 10, 2005.
3. Republican National Committee, *Hispanics in the New Millennium: A Real Political Picture*, Jan. 13, 2000. Significantly, the finding means that 80 percent is probably the *floor* for English-speakers among the Hispanics who actually vote in U.S. elections—the real number could be even higher.
4. We also found that 47 percent favored making English the official language of the United States, which squares with the results among Hispanic voters in Arizona for an official English ballot initiative.
5. The one-third figure comes from social scientist Richard Alba, interviewed in "Immigrants Reshape American Society—and Vice Versa." *Chronicles of Higher Education*, Feb. 11, 2004. Alba, author of *Germans or Foreigners? Attitudes Toward Ethnic Minorities in Post-Reunification Germany* (Palgrave Macmillan, 2003). Alba states that this is "much higher than the interracial marriage rate for African Americans. It suggests that, for a substantial portion of Latinos, racial barriers are not very high." Available online at http://chronicle.com/colloquylive/2004/02/immigrants/. Accessed on Mar.1, 2006. The one-fourth figure comes from Sharon M. Lee and Barry Edmunston, Barry, "New Marriages, New Families: U.S. Racial and Hispanic Intermarriage," *Population Bulletin*, June 2005. They write that the rate "has been fairly stable since 1980."
6. "Latino Cultural Identity Project," a speech delivered in Miami by Carl Kravetz, president of the Association of Hispanic Advertising Agencies, Sept. 20, 2006.
7. Lydia Saad and Alec Gallup, "Gallup Poll Social Series, Minority Rights and Relations/Black-White Social Audit," *Gallup News Service*, Jun. 8–25, 2006. The breakdown for Hispanics is 49 percent weekly attendance or more frequently, and 17 percent more at least monthly; for the general population the number was 44 percent at least weekly, 10 percent at least monthly.
8. More than one Catholic commentator noticed that the 2000 *Bush v. Gore* decision came down on December 12, the feast of Our Lady of Guadalupe.
9. Gaston Espinosa, Virgilio Elizondo, and Jesse Miranda, "Hispanic Churches in American Life: Summary of Findings," *Interim Reports* by the Institute for Latino Studies, University of Notre Dame vol. 2003.2, second edition (March 2003): p. 14.

10. Gaston Espinosa, Virgilio Elizondo, and Jesse Miranda, *Latino Religions and Civic Activism in the United States* (New York: Oxford University Press, Inc., 2005).

11. D. P. Moynihan, "The Negro Family: The Case for National Action," U.S. Department of Labor, 1965.

12. Lydia Saad, "Blacks Committed to the Idea of Marriage," Gallup News Service, Jul. 14, 2006.

13. Ibid.

14. Ibid.

15. Among women the percentage of divorcees is 8.8 for Hispanics, 11.0 for non-Hispanic whites, and 10.9 for blacks. U.S. Census Bureau, *Marital Status: 2000.* Available online at http://www.census.gov/prod/2003pubs/c2kbr-30.pdf. Accessed Nov. 25, 2006.

16. U.S. Census Bureau, *Hispanic Owned Firms: 2002.* Released August 2006. Available at www.census.gov/prod/ec02/sb0200cshisp.pdf. Accessed Jan. 30, 2007.

17. Hispanic Business Round, *A National Survey of Hispanic Opinion,* conducted Jan. 7–17, 2000.

18. Badillo gives a dropout rate of 50 percent, without providing a source. He may be referring to New York City, because that is far out of sync with U.S. Census estimates nationwide. "Among all Hispanics ages 16 to 19, about 21 percent, did not graduate from high school or were not enrolled in school, down slightly from nearly 21.6 percent in 1990. Among blacks of that age, the dropout rate was 12 percent, down from 14 percent. For whites, it was just below 7 percent, down from 9 percent." "Census: Hispanic Dropout Numbers Soar," *Associated Press,* Oct. 11, 2002. The piece notes that a substantial portion of the 528,000 Hispanic high-school dropouts are actually new immigrant teenagers who never set foot in school. " 'For some, it may not be that they are dropping out of school, but rather that people are coming here and not going to school to begin with,' said Jennifer Day, an education analyst with the Census Bureau."

19. Richard Alba, interviewed in "Immigrants Reshape American Society—and Vice Versa." "[T]he concern about changes in economic structure tacitly assumes that socioeconomic advance by the contemporary second generation must somehow mirror that in the past, and it loses sight of the greater opportunities that exist today in the educational system. Some of my recent research shows that 40–50% (the lower bound applies to males) of U.S.-born Mexican Americans now attend college for at least a year. The figures are lower, certainly, than those for non-Hispanic whites, but high in an absolute sense. They imply that a substantial fraction of the second and third generations are prepared for white-collar jobs, including those requiring technical skills." *Chronicles of Higher Education,* Feb. 11, 2004.

20. Karen Brulliard, "Hispanic Unemployment Down, Study Finds," *The Washington Post,* Sept. 28, 2006, p. A13.

21. Pew Hispanic Center, *Latino Labor Report, 2006: Strong Gains in Employment,* Sept. 27, 2006. Available at http://pewhispanic.org/files/reports/70.pdf. Black unemployment was 10.1 percent during the same period, which also tends to skew the black median wage upward. Accessed Dec. 29, 2006.

22. Alan Korwin, "The Uninvited Ombudsman," *Gun Laws of America,* May 11, 2006. Commentary is available online at http://www.gunlaws.com/PageNine-2.htm. Accessed Mar. 18, 2007.

23. Pew Hispanic Center, *National Survey of Latinos: Politics and Civic Engagement,* July 2004.

24. "The Power of the Poor: Capitalism's Moment of Truth," Institute for Liberty and Democracy video narrated by Hernando DeSoto, 2005. Available online at http://www.ild.org.pe/eng/articles.htm. Accessed Mar. 19, 2007.

25. Steven A. Camarota, "Back Where We Started: An Examination of Trends in Immigrant Welfare Use Since Welfare Reform," *Center for Immigration Studies*, Mar. 2003. Available at cis.org/articles/2003/back503.html. Accessed Dec. 10, 2006.

four   the emerging latino republican majority

1. Robert Novak, "Harkin Hollering," *Chicago Sun Times*, Jun. 5, 2005. ". . . Harkin said Christian broadcasters are 'sort of our home-grown Taliban.' He added: 'They have a direct line to God. And if you don't tune in to their line, you're obviously on Satan's line.' " Other examples abound, including Howard Dean's statement three days later that the Republican Party is "pretty much a white Christian party." Former Sen. John Edwards (D-N.C.) did not back away from the claims of two viciously anti-Catholic bloggers when their obscene rants came to light in Feb. 2007.

2. The increase in conservative self-identification is pronounced among Hispanic men, going from 32 percent in 2004 to 36 percent in 2006. Special thanks to Gallup for providing me with the full cross-tabs for this survey over the three-year period.

3. Republican National Committee, *Hispanics in the New Millennium: A Real Political Picture*, conducted Dec. 5–15, 1999. The RNC authorized the release of these findings for this book.

4. Tamar Jacoby, "Hispanic Leadership Out of Touch," *New York Sun*, Aug. 6, 2002.

5. "Republican National Committee, *Hispanics in the New Millennium: A Real Political Picture*, conducted Dec. 5–15, 1999." The responses among the specially targeted group of Hispanic voters for the 2000 election did not vary significantly. Univision's 1998 survey *The Hispanic Voter* found that a plurality of 48 percent of Hispanic respondents agreed with the statement that "the U.S. allows too many people to immigrate to this country."

6. Let Freedom Ring, *Four-State Qualitative Research Assessment to Test Messages Related to the Border Security and Immigration*, Feb. 16, 2006 combined with RT Strategies National Omnibus Poll conducted Feb. 23–26, 2006.

7. Hispanic Business Roundtable, *A National Survey of Hispanic Opinion: Results of the HBR Survey*, conducted Jan. 7–17, 2000.

8. Linda Chavez, "Hispanic Like Me?: Racial games, racial tags—the way the Left plays—identity politics," *National Review*, Mar. 10, 2003.

9. President George W. Bush, speech in East Room for Hispanic Heritage Month celebration, Sept. 15, 2004.

10. "Does God Want You to Be Rich?" *TIME*, Sep. 10, 2006.

11. Gastón Espinosa, Virgilio Elizondo, and Jesse Miranda, *Latino Religions and Civic Activism in the United States* (New York: Oxford University Press, 2005).

12. "TIME Names the 25 Most Influential EVANGELICALS in America," Jan. 30, 2005. Available online at http://www.time.com/time/press_releases/article/0,8599,1022576,00.html. Accessed Mar. 20, 2007.

13. http://www.greatergreenville.com/neighborhoods/historic_greenville.asp.

14. Judith S. Prince, "Educational gap for minorities exposes big problem," *Greenvilleonline.com*, Feb. 17, 2006.

15. Adrian Wooldridge and John Micklethwaite, *The Right Nation:Conservative Power in America* (New York: The Penguin Press, 2004).

16. William Frey, "Melting Pot Moves to the Suburbs," *Newsday*, Aug. 4, 1999.

five disconnect

1. Interview with author on Nov. 30, 2006.
2. Republican National Committee, *Hispanics in the New Millennium: A Real Political Picture*, conducted Dec. 5–15, 1999. Findings provided by the Republican National Committee.
3. Univision Communications, Inc., *The Power of the Hispanic Vote*, Apr. 23, 1998. Survey conducted by Penn Schoen and Berland Associates and Edelman Public Relations Worldwide. Limited survey results available at http://www.lulac.org/programs/civic/voter/univpres.html/ Accessed Mar. 20, 2007.
4. Joe Kovacs, "Bush doesn't think America should be an actual place," *WorldNetDaily*, Nov. 19, 2006. http://www.wnd.com/news/article.asp?ARTICLE_ID=53023. Accessed Dec. 3, 2006.
5. The Michael Savage Show, Mar. 28, 2006.
6. Rona Marech, "Rights Groups Want Latino Media to End Gay Pranks, on-Air Ridicule," *San Francisco Chronicle*, Apr. 16, 2005.
7. Interview with Dr. Robert M. Entman, Dec. 11, 2006.
8. Leslie Jackson Turner and Chris W. Allen, "Mexican and Latino Media Behavior in Los Angeles: The 1996 Election Example." *American Behavioral Scientist* vol. 40, no. 7 (June/July 1997).
9. HR 4437, Amendment 18, roll call vote number 655, Dec. 16, 2005. Shortly after passage of H.R. 4437 in December 2005, *Impacto The Latin News* ran an article with the following headline: "Republicanos convierten a millones en delincuentes; Proyecto de Ley anti-inmigrante califica de delito penal presencia ilegal en Estados Unidos." Translation: "Republicans turn millions into delinquents; Anti-immigrant bill makes illegal presence in the United States a felony."
10. Victor Caycho, "Escándalo sexual involucra a republicano antiinmigrante," *Washington Hispanic*, Oct. 6, 2006. The piece does at least mention that Foley is a former Democrat who switched parties.
11. Undocumented Alien Emergency Medical Assistance Amendments, HR 3722, roll call vote number 182, May 20, 2004.
12. Department of Homeland Security appropriations, HR 5441, Amendment 968, roll call vote number 224, Jun. 6, 2006.
13. Gillian Flaccus with contributors Emily Fredrix and Carla K. Johnson, "Spanish-Language Media Organized Protests," *Associated Press*, Mar. 28, 2006. Available at http://www.signonsandiego.com/news/state/20060328–1051-immigrantrallies-deejays.html. Accessed Mar. 18, 2007.
14. Jorge Ramos, *The Latino Wave: How Hispanics Will Elect the Next American President* (New York: Rayo, 2004), p. 230.
15. Jonathan Weisman and Amit R. Paley "Dozens in GOP Turn Against Bush's Prized 'No Child' Act," *The Washington Post*, Mar. 15, 2007, p. A01.
16. Budget of U.S. Government; Fiscal Year 2005, Historical tables, Table 5.2-Budget Authority by Agency, 1976–2009: ". . . [F]unding for the Department of Education is up 58 percent in the first three years of Bush's term and is set to rise further under the budget he proposed in January. It's already gone up more under Bush than it did during all of Clinton's eight years, in fact." Available at http://www.factcheck.org/article162.html. Accessed Mar. 20, 2007.

17. The Rockridge Institute, *Creating a Progressive Values Movement*. Dec. 7, 2006. Available online at http://www.rockridgeinstitute.org/research/rockridge/valuesmovement. Accessed Mar. 20, 2007.
18. Stacy Connaughton, *Inviting Latino Voters: Party Messages and Latino Party Identification* (New York: Routledge, 2005), p. 45. Italics in original.

six   our solutions work

1. Interview with the author Dec. 20, 2006.
2. John B. Judis and Ruy Teixeira, *The Emerging Democratic Majority* (New York: Scribner, 2002), p. 90. Texeira and Judis offer a typical example: "Blue collar Middlesex (county) voters, many of them pro-New Deal Irish Catholics, began voting Republican as part of the racial backlash."
3. The phrase originated in Rowland Evans and Robert Novak, "Behind Humphrey's Surge," *Chicago Sun-Times*, Apr. 27, 1972. Novak reveals the source of this famous anonymous quote in his new memoir, *The Prince of Darkness* (Crown Forum: New York, 2007).
4. Policy and Taxation Group, *Five-State Executive Interview Study of 100+ Hispanic Family-Owned Businesses on Federal "Death Taxes"*, Jul. 14, 2004.
5. Ibid.
6. Department of the Treasury, "Fact Sheet: Millions of American Families Are Benefiting From Tax Relief," released Apr. 14, 2005.
7. Joseph Carroll, "Whites, Minorities Differ in Views of Economic Opportunities in U.S." *Gallup News Service*, Jul. 10, 2006. It is worth asking just how much John Edwards' "Two Americas" speech hurt John Kerry among Hispanics in 2004. Kerry had the worst performance among Hispanic voters since pollsters began keeping track of our vote.
8. Peter Coy, "Right Place, Right Time: Small Businesses Aren't Just Surviving," *BusinessWeek*, Oct. 13, 2003.
9. International Monetary Fund, World Economic Outlook Database, April 2006.
10. Policy and Taxation Group, *Five-State Executive Interview Study of 100+ Hispanic Family-Owned Businesses on Federal "Death Taxes"*, Jul. 14, 2004.
11. Ibid.
12. [105th]: Taxpayer Relief Act of 1997, HR 2014, roll call vote number 245, Jun. 26, 1997. Available at http://clerk.house.gov/evs/1997/roll245.xml. Accessed Feb. 11, 2007. Two Hundred Twenty-Six Republicans voted for the bill, joined by just 27 Democrats. On the House floor, Democrats opposed this middle-class tax benefit as being aimed only at the rich.
13. Department of Housing and Urban Development, "Martinez highlights President Bush's Initiative to Expand Homeownership Opportunities." Press release, Jun. 24, 2002. Available online at http://www-domino4.hud.gov/NN/nn_news.nsf/ArticlesByDate/835A4186876D8AB985256BEA0072591F?OpenDocument. Accessed Dec. 28, 2006.
14. President's Commission to Strengthen Social Security, "Interim Report," Aug. 2001, p. 27.
15. Ibid., p. 28.
16. Rahm Emanuel and Bruce Reed, *The Plan: Big Ideas for America* (New York: Public Affairs, 2006), p. 90.
17. Nancy Pelosi and Harry Reid, Response to President Bush's 2005 State of the Union Address, Feb. 2, 2007.

18. Emanuel's book restates a falsehood from an erroneous 2005 *The Washington Post* report suggesting that investment gains in private accounts would have to be paid back to the Social Security system. Emanuel and Reed, *The Plan*, 13 and 85. The *Post* story by Jacob Weisman first ran on Feb. 3, 2005. The *Post* issued a correction the next day (Feb. 4, 2005) in another Weisman story titled "Benefit Cuts Would Offset Contributions." "*The Washington Post* incorrectly reported Thursday that the balance of a worker's personal account would be reduced by the worker's total annual contributions plus 3 percent interest. In fact, the balance in the account would belong to the worker upon retirement . . ." The fact that it was false didn't stop Nancy Pelosi from repeating it that weekend on television (Feb. 6, ABC's *The Week*), nor did it stop Emanuel from including it in his book 18 months later. It is telling that Democrats must distort the truth to explain to poor people and minorities why they won't allow them this source of wealth.

19. Author interview with R. Ted Cruz, Dec. 5, 2006.

20. Rahm Emanuel and Bruce Reed, *The Plan: Big Ideas for America* (New York: Public Affairs, 2006), p. 12–13. "As Rove openly explained to anyone who would listen, the real beauty of the Ownership Society was not substantive, but political."

21. President's Commission To Strengthen Social Security, "Interim Report," Aug. 2001, p. 28.

22. Richard Fry, Rakesh Kochhar, Jeffrey Passel and Roberto Suro, "Hispanics And The Social Security Debate," *Pew Hispanic Center*, Mar. 16, 2005.

23. President's Advisory Commission on Educational Excellence for Hispanic Americans.

24. U.S. Department of Education, *Digest of Educational Statistics*, 2004. Table 163.

25. U.S. Department of Education, *Digest of Education Statistics*, 2004. Tables 110, 120.

26. The Final Report of the President's Advisory Commission on Educational Excellence for Hispanic Americans, "From Risk to Opportunity: Fulfilling the Educational Needs of Hispanic Americans in the 21st Century," Figure 8, p. 34. Available at http://www.yic.gov/paceea/reports.html. Accessed Mar. 15, 2007.

27. President George W. Bush's first address to Congress, Feb. 27, 2001.

28. For instance, "Mexican immigrants experience nearly twice the dropout rate (61 percent) of other Hispanic subgroups." Part of the problem with that group in particular is that so many of them are entering school late, at the age of 15 or 16, with low English proficiency. At that point, graduation is a very difficult proposition, and pressure mounts within the family to take a job instead.

29. Secretary of Education Rod Paige, speech at the White House Summit on Early Childhood Cognitive Development, Jul. 27, 2001.

30. Testimony before the House Committee on Education and the Workforce, Jul. 31, 2001.

31. The Final Report of the President's Advisory Commission on Educational Excellence for Hispanic Americans, "From Risk to Opportunity: Fulfilling the Educational Needs of Hispanic Americans in the 21st Century," Figure 8, p. 14. Available at http://www.yic.gov/paceea/reports.html. Accessed Mar. 15, 2007.

32. Ron Haskins, "Competing Visions: President Bush Proposes to Refocus Head Start on the Teaching of Academic Skills. Should Democrats Go Along?" *Education Next*, Jan 1, 2004.

33. Andrea Rubin, "Bush Plan May Alter Head Start," *The Journal News* (Westchester County, NY), Mar. 4, 2003, p. A1.

34. The Brookings Institution, forum Head Start's Future: Perspectives from the Bush Administration, Congress, States, Advocates and Researchers, May 7, 2003. Transcript available at http://www.brookings.edu/comm/events/20030507wrb.pdf. Accessed Nov. 30, 2006.

35. Hispanic Business Round, *A National Survey of Hispanic Opinion*, conducted Jan. 7–17, 2000.
36. Hispanic Council for Reform and Educational Options (CREO), *Arizona Likely Voter Survey on Proposed Legislation to Enhance School Choice*, March 2005, Survey sponsored by the Milton and Rose D. Friedman Foundation.
37. Jay Mathews, "$65 Million to Help Build 42 Houston Charter Schools," *The Washington Post*, Mar. 20, 2007, p. A01.
38. YES College Preparatory School press release: "YES College Preparatory School Achieves Texas Education Agency's Top Ratings for Unprecedented 8th Consecutive Year," Aug. 9, 2006.
39. U.S. Department of Education release, "Spellings Hails New National Report Card Results," Jul. 14, 2005. Available at http://www.ed.gov/news/pressreleases/2005/07/07142005.html. Results for the long-term trend are available at http://nces.ed.gov/nationsreportcard/ltt/results2004/. Both accessed Mar. 13, 2007.
40. One hundred forty-five House Democrats voted against the Child Interstate Abortion Notification Act (roll call vote number 144, Apr. 27, 2005). In the Senate, Democratic leaders then filibustered to prevent a House-Senate conference from forming a final bill. Only six Democratic senators supported a motion that would have allowed the bill to become law, effectively killing it. (Senate roll call vote number 263, Sept. 29, 2006.)
41. Meg Meeker, M.D., *Epidemic: How Teen Sex is Killing Our Kids* (Washington, D.C.: Lifeline Press, 2002).
42. Republican National Committee, *Hispanics in the New Millennium: A Real Political Picture*, Jan. 13, 2000. The RNC authorized the release of these findings for this book.
43. David Freddoso, "Levin Tries to Kill Missile Defense," *Human Events*, Jul. 1, 2002.
44. Amanda Carpenter, "Democrats Don't Regret Filibustering Missile Defense." *Human Events*, Jul. 17, 2006.

seven   the whining city upon a hill

1. Interview with author Dec. 15, 2006.
2. Interview with author June 20, 2006.
3. Woodrow Wilson, Final address in support of the League of Nations, delivered Sept. 25, 1919 in Pueblo, Colo.
4. Former New Jersey Poet Laureate Amiri Baraka denounced Condoleezza Rice with this vicious insult—"street slang for a prostitute." David Zucchino, "Poet's Words Viewed as Harsh as Sticks, Stones: Work seen by many as anti-Semitic has led to a bill seeking end of New Jersey's laureate post," *Los Angeles Times*, Feb. 9, 2003. The poem is about the white man, and has insulting comments directed at a wide variety of independent-thinking blacks, including Colin Powell, Clarence Thomas and Ward Connerly.
5. Richard Marosi, "Marin Draws a Contrast to Past GOP Candidates," *Los Angeles Times*, Feb. 25, 2004. "'She makes a good house Mexican for the Republicans,' read a mass e-mail by Steven J. Ybarra, a Democratic National Committee official." Ybarra's hate-filled remark did not prevent him from becoming a delegate at the Democratic convention that summer, and he was still a member of the DNC as of September 2004. See Josephine Hearn, "Dean Tried to Nix Early Becerra Nod," *The Hill*, Sept. 27, 2006.

6. Excerpt from author interview with Rep. Henry Cuellar, Dec. 18, 2007. "CAFTA, in my opinion, was not a Republican issue," Cuellar said. "I just looked at what was good for the district . . . It was a no-brainer . . . Laredo is the largest inland port in the whole U.S. The biggest ports for total trade are LA, New York, Detroit and right behind is Laredo. So trade is extremely important . . . so when people attacked me on the trade issue, it actually helped me in my area . . . Trade is good for my home town and good for the border area."

7. "Cisneros blasts GOP policies: Republicans target Hispanics, immigrants, housing secretary says," *Rocky Mountain News*, Jul. 17, 1996.

8. Available at http://tequilaexpress.blogspot.com/2006/11/democrats-win-nationwide-however-new.html. Accessed Dec. 9, 2006.

9. In fact, Goldwater had been a civil rights leader, his efforts brought about the desegregation of Phoenix schools prior to his 1952 election to the Senate. But his inflexibility on the Senate floor spelled disaster for the GOP among blacks.

10. DeWayne Wickham, "Focus on blacks, but voters of all races need to get to polls," *USA Today*, Oct. 24, 2000.

11. U.S. Census Bureau, *Black-Owned Firms, 2002*, and *Hispanic-Owned Firms, 2002*. Both published August 2006. Hispanic-owned firms stood at 1.6 million, and black-owned firms at 1.1 million.

12. Bureau of Justice Statistics, *Prisoners in 2005*. Abstract available online at http://www.ojp.usdoj.gov/bjs/abstract/p05.htm. Accessed Nov. 12, 2006.

13. "Juan Williams on African-American 'Victimhood'" National Public Radio's *Morning Edition*, Aug. 8, 2006.

14. Matthew Dowd, "Doing the Latin Swing: Latino voters are the Soccer Moms of the new decade," *The Weekly Standard*, Dec. 3, 2001.

15. "New Americans Emerging: The Immigrant Vote in the 1998 Elections and Beyond," *National Immigration Forum*, November 1998. Transcript available at http://www.immigrationforum.org/DesktopDefault.aspx?tabid=275. Accessed Mar. 2, 2007.

16. William Branigin, "INS Says it May Never Find Naturalized Criminals," *The Washington Post*, May 1, 1997.

17. "New Americans Emerging: The Immigrant Vote in the 1998 Elections and Beyond," *National Immigration Forum*, November 1998.

18. Univision Communications, Inc., *The 2000 Elections: A New Opportunity for America*, Sept. 17, 1999.

19. Author interview with Dr. Felipe Korzenny, Nov. 10, 2006.

20. General Accounting Office, "Treaty of Guadalupe Hidalgo," June 2004. This detailed analysis of the U.S. government's handling of land claims deriving from Mexican or Spanish grants can be found at http://www.gao.gov/new.items/d0459.pdf. Accessed Mar. 12, 2007. To give some context from pop culture, the historical issue of Mexican families being cheated out of their land factors into the spaghetti western *Joe Kidd*, starring Clint Eastwood.

21. See, for example, Adolfo A. Bermeo, UCLA Chicano Studies, http://www.today.ucla.edu/2001/010522bermeo.html: "Which living person do you most admire? '*Fidel Castro, because he transformed his country and used its wealth to teach people to read and write and to provide medical care for the humblest of Cubanos. I admire Subcomandante Marcos and the Zapatistas, as well*.'"

22. Gregory Rodriguez, "Taking the Oath: Why We Need a Revisionist History of Latinos in America," *Los Angeles Times*, Aug. 20, 2000.

eight   the credit card

1. Memo from Lance Tarrance, Jr. to political friends and campaign technicians, dated Mar. 17, 1983. Also important in Tarrance's memo was his dismissal of what were then standard GOP attempts to win black votes: "The use of 'black symbolic candidates' and black symbolic assistants has absolutely no value whatsoever in the political system today to attract black voters. Secondly, the continued 'p.r. play' of the Republican Party as 'the party of Abraham Lincoln' is now seen as a joke by black voters."
2. Univision Communications, Inc., *The Power of the Hispanic Vote*, Apr. 23, 1998. Survey conducted by Penn Schoen and Berland Associates and Edelman Public Relations Worldwide. Limited survey results available at http://www.lulac.org/programs/civic/voter/univpres.html/ Accessed Mar. 20, 2007.
3. Anthony York, "The GOP's Latino Strategy," *Salon.com*, Jan. 14, 2000.
4. After we conducted our survey, we would set a higher bar: "If the GOP captures about one-half of this 'swing' group (reaching 42 percent of the Hispanic vote nationally), they will achieve Reaganesque wins. This could change the political landscape of American politics." Lance Tarrance at the unveiling of the Republican National Committee's survey *The New America Survey*, in San Jose, Calif., Jan. 13, 2000.
5. From Anthony York, "Drop the Chalupa, Al Gore!." *Salon.com*, Nov. 19, 1999. Available online at www.salon.com/news/feature/1999/11/19/gop. Accessed Jan. 2, 2007.
6. Ira Teinowitz, "Amount Spent on Hispanic Political Advertising Triples: Both Parties Heavily Target Latinos in Swing States." *Ad Age*, Aug. 19, 2004. In 2000, the Gore campaign and the Democratic Party spent $960,000 on Hispanic advertising.
7. Press statement by former RNC Chairman Jim Nicholson at RNC Winter Meeting, San Jose, Calif., Jan. 13, 2000.
8. Testimony from "Latino Voters: Misconceptions and Reality" Forum, Center for American Progress, Washington, D.C., Feb.16, 2007.

nine   dis-inviting the *familia*

1. Author interview on Jul. 14, 2006.
2. Peter Wallsten, "Latino and black voters reassessing ties to GOP," *Los Angeles Times*, Oct. 24, 2006.
3. Mark Feierstein, "Don't Pander to Latinos." *Christian Science Monitor*, May 10, 2001.
4. Republican National Committee, *Hispanics in the New Millennium: A Real Political Picture*, conducted Dec. 5–15, 1999. The RNC authorized the release of these findings for this book.
5. Michelle Mitteldstadt, "Immigration alone didn't sway Hispanics from GOP: Exit polls cite economy, Iraq war in higher rate of defecting Latino voters," *Houston Chronicle*, Nov. 28, 2006.

6. Clear Peak Colorado (a Democratic political 527 organization) produced and funded this ad for a state legislative race. Available online at http://www.youtube.com/watch?v=WcOJJeZkYIU. Accessed Nov. 29, 2006.

7. Dick Mountjoy for U.S. Senate (Calif.). Available at http://www.youtube.com/watch?v=FZfoKkJ7utU. Accessed Nov. 29, 2006.

8. Numbers USA, available online at http://www.youtube.com/watch?v=Qiw85f5fYGY&NR. Accessed Nov. 29, 2006.

9. Vernon Robinson for Congress. The complete robo-call can be heard online at: http://www.youtube.com/watch?v=4yUn_fT__mM. Accessed Nov. 29, 2006.

10. Available at http://www.youtube.com/watch?v=BVQ_z9aKu18&mode=related&search. Accessed Feb. 21, 2007.

11. Available at http://www.youtube.com/watch?v=SrRSuhMQzvE. Accessed Nov. 27, 2006.

12. Available at http://www.youtube.com/watch?v=AXH0DHCryjI&mode=related&search=. Accessed Nov. 29, 2006.

13. Available at http://www.youtube.com/watch?v=fvSVddby00Y. Accessed Nov. 28, 2006.

14. Teresa Watanabe and Nicole Gaouette, "Anti-Immigration Rhetoric by GOP Cited in Hispanic Vote for Dems," *Los Angeles Times*, Nov. 10, 2006.

15. Jeanne Cummings, "Hispanic Voters Shift Allegiance to Democrats, Republicans Lose Ground With Minorities After Call For Immigrant Crackdown," *Wall Street Journal*, Nov. 8, 2006.

16. Kathy Kiely, "Republicans Lose Ground Among Hispanic Voters." *USA Today*, Nov. 13, 2006.

17. Darryl Fears, "After Gains in 2004, GOP Stumbled on Immigration." *The Washington Post*, Nov. 18, 2006. Cortés, whose group serves as an umbrella for more than 10,000 churches, had given an interview to the *Los Angeles Times* in late October, expressing frustration over the immigration debate. "That group in the Republican Party said, 'We want your parents, your grandparents, we want anyone here without documentation, regardless of why—we want them out,'" he said. "If voting is about personal interest, how are Hispanics to vote? They will vote against those guys." From Peter Wallsten, "Latino and black voters reassessing ties to GOP," *Los Angeles Times*, Oct. 24, 2006.

18. Lourdes Heredia, "Latino Surprise," *BBC.com*, Oct. 19, 2006. Available at http://www.bbc.co.uk/blogs/thereporters/lourdes_heredia. Accessed Nov. 1, 2006.

19. Tamar Jacoby, "GOP can't lose Latinos," *Los Angeles Times*, Nov. 17, 2006.

20. Sarah Lueck and Joel Millman, "Vote Is a Blow to Republican Pursuit of Hispanics," *Wall Street Journal*, Nov. 9, 2006, A8.

21. Ibid.

22. Andres Oppenheimer, "Immigration Stance Doomed GOP," *Orlando Sentinel*, Nov. 10, 2006. "[T]he anti-immigration hysteria spearheaded by Republicans in the House—and by cable-television fear mongers such as Pat Buchanan and Lou Dobbs—irked many U.S.-born Hispanics who normally don't care much about immigration."

23. Edward Hegstrom, "DeLay criticizes Houston's policy on illegal immigrants: He favors idea of withholding federal funding from cities that offer 'sanctuary,'" *The Houston Chronicle*, Aug. 5, 2005.

24. U.S. Census, 2004 estimates for Apache County, Ariz. Available online at http://quickfacts.census.gov/qfd/states/04/04001.html. Accessed Nov. 27, 2006.

25. Arizona Secretary of State. Available online at http://www.azsos.gov/results/2006/general/BM300.htm. Accessed Nov. 27, 2006. In 2004, Voter News Service exit polls indicate that 47 percent of Hispanics in Arizona backed Proposition 200, a measure that required proof of citizenship in order to register to vote or to receive some non-federal benefits given by the state of Arizona.

26. Sarah Lueck, "Cracks in a Republican Base: Hard-Line Immigration Stance Angers Some Business Groups." *Wall Street Journal*, Aug. 24, 2006, p. A4.

27. Arizona Secretary of State. Available online at http://www.azsos.gov/results/2006/general/GEN-1005.htm.

28. Michael Barone and Richard Cohen, *The Almanac of American Politics, 2006* (Washington, D.C.: National Journal Group; rev ed edition, 2005).

29. Author interview with RNC Chairman Ken Mehlman, Nov. 22, 2006.

30. Luntz, Frank, *Words that Work: It's Not What You Say, It's What People Hear* (Hyperion: New York, 2007), p. 175.

31. Richard Marosi, "Gov., Rival Spar but Step Lightly; Most of the rhetoric on immigration has been voiced at partisan events. The candidates are not far apart on key issues, political analysts say." *Los Angeles Times*, Oct. 7, 2006.

32. Author interview with Bonilla campaign operative Eric Fox, Dec. 13, 2006.

33. U.S. Census Bureau, 2000 Census.

34. This result is for the Dec. 12 runoff election. Bonilla received 28,000 more votes on election day, Nov. 7.

35. Michael Barone and Richard Cohen, *The Almanac of American Politics, 2006* (Washington, D.C.: National Journal Group; rev ed edition, 2005).

36. Ibid.

37. Stephen Ohlemacher, "Immigrants flocking to GOP districts," *Associated Press*, Oct. 21, 2006.

38. Alexander Bolton, "Hispanic leaders call for reform on immigration within 100 days." *The Hill*, Jan. 9, 2007.

39. Paul Krugman, "North of the Border," *The New York Times*, March 27, 2006. See also Michelle Goldberg, "The Left Splits Over Immigration," Salon.com, Apr. 20, 2006.

40. Nell Henderson, "Effect of Immigration on Jobs, Wages Is Difficult for Economists to Nail Down," *The Washington Post*, April 15, 2006.

41. Card, David, "Is the New Immigration Really So Bad?," presented January 2005 before the Philadelphia Federal Reserve Bank.

42. Dan Frosch, "Inmates Will Replace Migrants in Colorado Fields." *The New York Times*, Mar. 4, 2007.

43. "Hispanic Fact Pack: Annual Guide to Hispanic Marketing and Media," *Advertising Age*, 2006 edition, p. 12.

44. Heather MacDonald, "Myth Debunked: A Latin conservative tidal wave is not coming," *National Review Online*, Jul. 24, 2006. Available at http://article.nationalreview.com/?q=YzkxMDk1MTQ3Yzg2MzdjZDA0NmFkODhiOWI1NjhjNjE=. Accessed Nov. 3, 2006.

45. See Heather MacDonald, "Hispanic Family Values?", *City Journal*, autumn 2006. "A lot of the grandmothers are single as well; they never married, or they had successive partners. So the mom sends the message to her daughter that it's okay to have children out of wedlock."

46. Nor does MacDonald entertain the idea that Latinas are hesitant to choose abortion because of their religious heritage, and that Hispanic mothers are supportive of their

pregnancies for the same reason. A *New York Times* editorial and an *El Diario* article cited by MacDonald both list this as a factor, but MacDonald omits any mention—perhaps because it could undermine her politically charged thesis that Hispanics are unusually licentious.

47. Tucker Carlson, "The Intellectual Roots of Nativism," The *Wall Street Journal* Interactive Edition, Oct. 2, 1997.

ten *"reaganismo"*

1. Author interview conducted Oct. 31, 2006.
2. U.S. Equal Employment Opportunity Commission, Table 1. Occupational Employment in Private Industry by Race/Ethnic Group/Sex and by Industry, United States, 2003. Available at http://www.eeoc.gov/stats/jobpat/2003/national.html. Accessed Feb. 1, 2007.
3. "Romney for President Launches First Spanish Radio Ad," *MittRomney.com* press release, Mar. 6. 2007.
4. Doug Muzzio, "The Hispanic Vote; Also, New Charter Commission For Non-Partisan Elections." *Gotham Gazette*, March 2003. Available online at http://www.gothamgazette.com/article//20030328/17/331. Accessed Dec. 20, 2006.
5. Adam J. Segal, "Bikini Politics: The 2004 Presidential Campaigns' Hispanic Media Efforts Cover only the Essential Parts of the Body Politic," *Hispanic Voter Project*, Johns Hopkins University, Sept. 28, 2004.
6. Radio Address by President Ronald Reagan, Dec. 25, 1982. Available at http://www.presidency.ucsb.edu/ws/index.php?pid=42147. Accessed Dec. 25, 2006.

index

Please note that page numbers followed by the letter *f* are located in a Figure or Chart. Page numbers followed by *n* are located in a footnote.

A-Rod, 43
Abernathy, Ralph, 153
abortion, 2, 74, 76, 136–138, 146; Democrats' support of, 47, 63, 110,
Adams Morgan, 42
affirmative action, 124,
African American, 31, 45, 81, 83, 91, 108, 149; Democratic Party and, 5, 29, 32, 145, 150–151, 162, 164; education and, 38, 125–134; community organization of, 50, 154; homeownership and, 119; Civil Rights Movement and, 149, 156; GOP and, 149, 156, 162, 170
Aguirre, Robert, 134
Air Force Academy, 33, 94
Alba, Richard, 213n
Allen, Michael, 212n
American Association of Hispanic Certified Public Accountants, 68
American dream,
American GI Forum, 37f
American Southwest, 25, 44, 155
Amnesty, immigration policy and, 25, 100, 101, 173, 176, 183, 187, 195; Vietnam draft and, 110
Anglo, 4, 35, 52, 61, 114, 175,
ANSWER (Act Now to Stop War and End Racism), 158f
Areu, Cathy, 42
Arizona, 3, 30, 35, 57, 77, 87, 150, 148f, 169f, 176, 177, 182, 185, 205; school choice in, 133–134, 212n
Arizona Proposition 103, 182
Arizona Proposition 300, 182
Arkansas, 77

Asian-Americans, 125, 129, 185
Associated Press (AP), 98, 100, 190; Spanish translators of, 99
Association of Hispanic Advertising Agencies (AHAA), 46; Latino Identity Project and, 47
Association of Latino Professionals in Finance and Accounting (ALPFA), 67
AT&T, 69
Aztecs, 49

Badillo, Herman: *One Nation, One Standard* (2006), 56, 214n
Bailey-Hutchison, Kay, 186
Baltimore, Lord, 29
Bank of America, 69
Baraka, Amiri, 219n
Barnes, Fred, 107,
Barone, Michael, 77, 79, 156, 223n
Bell, Chris, 186
Bendixen, Sergio, 36, 167, 170, 180, 213n
Berman, Howard, 158f
Bermeo, Adolfo A., 220n
Biden, Joe, 141
bilingual education, *see* education
bilingualism, 10, 41, 44, 92, 138; job opportunities afforded by, 58,124; political outreach and, 165
Bishop, Tim, 178
Bonilla, Henry, 19–20, 94, 146, 187–188, 188f
Border Patrol, 183
border security, 4, 25, 98–100, 142, 179, 183–184, 187
Borjas, George, 191

Bredesen, Jim, 178
British Broadcasting Corporation, 179, 222
Bronx, the, 56, 66, 205
Brown, Maria Perez, 51
Brownback, Sam, 205
Brulliard, Karen, 214n
Bryson, Jim, 178
Buchanan, Pat, 5, 43, 82, 101, 155,
    195–196, 222n
Bureau of Engraving and Printing, 24
Bush, Colomba, 165
Bush, George H. W., 35, 37f, 108, 201
Bush, George W., 3, 34, 81, 108, 112, 158f,
    169f, 189, 202, 215n, 218n; 2000
    election and, 38, 151, 165–166, 168;
    2004 election and, 38, 62, 74, 110,
    166–169; CA Proposition 187, views
    on, 94–95, 153; education policy and,
    101, 126, 128–129, 131–132, 135;
    immigration policy and, 100, 175–176,
    185; judicial nominations by, 71, 78;
    Latino voters and, 30, 36, 53, 62,
    78–79, 91–92, 105, 109, 137, 151,
    165, 174, 180, 183, 201; minority
    homeownership and, 112, 118–119,
    122; defense, views on, 140; Social
    Security reform and, 123; tax policy
    of, 114
Bush, George P., 61, 165
Bush, Jeb, 38, 61, 78, 165, 170, 204, 205
business community, 27, 111; see also small
    businesses

Cabral, Anna Escobedo, 23
Cabinet Committee on Opportunities for
    Spanish-Speaking People, 37f
Calderon, Felipe, 57, 64, 70
California, 22, 25, 30, 35–36, 71, 75, 77,
    78, 79, 84, 94, 95, 109, 113, 125, 130,
    137, 138, 141, 148f, 152–153, 163,
    165, 169f, 185–186, 187, 199
California Proposition 187, 36, 95,
    152–153, 187
California Proposition 22, 75, 137
Camarota, Steven A., 215n
Canada, 27
Cannon, Chris, 158f
Capital Life Church, 211n

Capitol Hill, 20, 96, 119, 181
Carlson, Tucker, 224n
Carpenter, Amanda, 219n
Carrillo, Victor G., 203
Carter, Jimmy, 15–16, 37f
Castro, Fidel, 31, 96, 155, 220n
Castro, Tony, 31, 212n
Catalina Magazine, 42
Catholic Church: see Roman Catholic
    Church
Catholics: see Roman Catholics
Census Bureau: see U.S. Census
Center for Immigration Studies, 192, 215n
Chaput, Charles, 76
Cherokee Indians, 80
Chicano Movement, 71, 155–156
Chickasaw Nation, 24
Child Interstate Abortion Notification
    Act, 219n
Chile, 27
Christians, 2, 50, 63, 76, 196
Cisco Systems: Conexion, 69
Cisneros, Henry, 146, 220n
City Journal, 193, 223
Civil Rights Act of 1964, 149
civil rights, 50, 61, 68, 71, 145, 148, 149,
    150, 151, 156, 201, 220n
Clinton, Bill, 37f, 98, 101, 118, 128, 137,
    146, 153, 217n
Clinton, Hillary, 136, 170, 206
Clyburn, James, 83
CNN, 107, 185, 213n
Cohen, Richard, 223n
Cole, Tom, 24, 164
collectivism; in Latino culture, 46, 48f,
    51–53, 102, 102f, 104–105,
    105f, 142
Collins, Mike, 163
Colorado, 3, 30, 77, 148f, 169f, 192
Columbus, Christopher, 2
Communism, 4, 139–140, 155
Council on Faith in Action (CONFIA),
    74, 201
Congress, see U.S. Congress
Congressional Hispanic Leadership Institute
    (CHLI), 71, 124
Continental Airlines, 10
Corpus Christi, Tex., 13, 73

corruption, 4, 28, 50, 57, 58, 174, 191, 194–195, 205

Cortés, Luis, Jr., 75, 179, 222*n*

Cosby, Bill, 5

Council for Reform and Educational Options (CREO), 134, 201, 219*n*

Cox, James, 144

Coy, Peter, 114, 217*n*

Craig, Larry, 158*f*

Credit Suisse First Boston, 202

Crist, Charlie, 186

Cristero movement, 50

Cruz, Celia, 73

Cruz, Ted, 107, 122, 218*n*

Cuba, 9, 31, 79

Cuellar, Henry, 124–125, 136, 146, 220*n*

Cummings, Jeanne, 222*n*

Curi, Ali, 70

Dalton, Ga., 77

Davis, Jim, 186

Day, Jennifer, 214*n*

de Soto, Hernendo, 58

de Quiroga, Vasco, 49

death tax, *see* estate tax

Delay, Tom, 81, 181–182

Dellanos, Myrka, 85

Deloitte, 69

Democratic National Committee (DNC), 103, 146, 219*n*, 220*n*

Democratic Party, 5, 9, 16, 31, 33, 63, 71, 72, 81, 98, 103, 144, 149–151, 163, 170, 200, 207, 221*n*

Department of Education, *see* U.S. Department of Education

Department of Homeland Security, *see* U.S. Department of Homeland Security

Derby, Jill, 189*f*

Detroit, 220*n*

Diaz-Balart, Lincoln, 71, 124

Diego, Juan, 49

Dobbs, Lou, 185, 222*n*

Dodd, Christopher, 132

Dole, Bob, 37*f*, 162, 166, 168

Domenici, Pete, 35–36, 53, 213*n*

Dominican American National Roundtable, 45, 70

Dominicans on Wall Street, 71

Dowd, Matthew, 151, 220

Duckworth, Tammy, 189*f*

Eastwood, Clint, 220*n*

economy, 67, 84; of the U.S., 27, 62, 107, 191, 195–196, 221*n*; of Mexico, 57; of Latin American nations, 57

Edmunston, Barry, 213*n*

education, 1, 4, 6, 12–13, 15, 17, 36, 38, 43, 56, 66, 70, 81, 85, 90*f*, 101, 119, 125–135, 137, 141, 191–192, 198, 201–202; bilingual, 38, 131, 175; school choice in, 7, 133–135

Edwards, John, 87, 206, 215*n*, 217*n*

Eisenhower, Dwight D., 149

El Diario, 224

El Movimiento: *see* Chicano Movement

El Paso, Tex., 143, 187

El Salvador, 75

Election 2006, 95, 167–168, 174–177, 184–189

Elgin, Lord James, 28, 212*n*

Ellsworth, Brad, 184

Emanuel, Rahm, 121–123, 217*n*, 218*n*

employment, 28, 67, 114, 125, 200–201; *see also* unemployment

Engler, John, 36

English language, 10, 13, 41–42, 44, 85, 92, 96, 100, 101, 130–131, 134, 165, 176, 182–183, 193

Ensign, John, 186

enterprise, 24, 48*f*, 55–59, 102*f*, 105*f*, 112, 122, 142, 207

entrepreneurship: Hispanics and, 24, 102, 105, 112, 119, 142, 201

Escobar, Gabriel, 176

Espinoza, Manny, 67–69

estate tax, 42, 111, 115–117

Estevez, Ramon, *see* Sheen, Martin

Estrada, Miguel, 36, 71

Estrada, Robert A., 33–35, 94

Europe, 29, 196

faith: as part of Hispanic culture, 17, 46, 48*f*, 49–51, 72–76, 102, 105, 110, 135, 138, 142, 147, 173, 201, 207; *see also* Council on Faith in Action (CONFIA)

Faith seekers, 72–76
family: importance of in Hispanic culture, 2,
    6, 14–15, 24, 41, 46, 48*f*, 51–52,
    53–54, 73, 76, 83, 89, 90*f*, 102, 102*f*,
    105*f*, 110, 112, 119, 135–137, 142,
    200, 205, 207
Farrell, Diane, 189*f*
FDR, 162, 206
FDR generation, 206
Fears, Darryl, 222*n*
Federation for American Immigration
    Reform (FAIR), 99, 211*n*
Feierstein, Mark, 174–175, 221*n*
Florida International University, 153
Florida, 3, 31, 61, 77, 84, 133, 148*f*, 153,
    169*f*, 170, 186, 188, 203–204; 2000
    election in, 78–79, 166; 2004 election
    in, 166–169
Foley, Mark, 99, 188, 216*n*
Forbes, 45
Fortuño, Luis, 78, 167, 199
Fourquet, Jose, 201
Fourquet, Karen, 44
Fox News, 106
Fox, Marta Sahagún de, 15
France, 196
Freddoso, David, 219*n*
Frederick, Jeff, 203
Friedman, Kinky, 61, 186

Gaete, Marcelo, 161–162, 170
Gallup News Service, 53, 63, 63*f*, 64, 64*f*,
    87, 88, 88*f*, 89, 89*f*, 157, 157*f*, 212*n*,
    213*n*, 214*n*, 215*n*, 217*n*
Gallup, Alec, 213*n*
Gamonal, Ana, 165
gangbanger, 51
Gaouette, Nicole, 222*n*
Garcia, Charles, 202
Garcia, Javier, 80
Garcia, Marilinda, 202
Garza, Dan, 201
George Washington University, 12, 20, 97,
    179
gerrymandering, 5, 148
Gibbons, Jim, 186
Giffords, Gabrielle, 183, 188*f*

Gillespie, Ed, 78, 145
Gingrich, Newt, 111
Giuliani, Rudy, 205
Goldberg, Michelle, 223*n*
Goldman Sachs, 202
Goldwater, Barry, 149, 220*n*
Gonzales, Alberto, 43, 203
González, Henry B., 156
Good Housekeeping, 15
GOP, *see* Republican Party
Gore, Albert, 150, 166, 170
Goya Foods, 43
Graf, Randy, 183–185, 188*f*
Gramm, Phil, 34
Gray, Adrian, 174
Great American Boycott, 158*f*
Great Depression, 38
Greenberg, Stan, 175
Greene, Graham: *The Power and the Glory*, 50
Greenville, South Carolina, 80–84, 100
GDP, 115
Guatemala, 92
Guerra, Frank, 163
guest worker, 96, 98, 100, 183, 185,
    186, 205
Gutierrez, Carlos M., 41, 43
Gutierrez, Luis, 154

H.R. 2014, 217*n*
H.R. 4437, 216*n*
Hafen, Tessa, 189*f*
Hanjour, Hani, 177
Harrison, Patricia, 165
Harkin, Tom, 215
Harvard University, 107, 191
Hayworth, J. D., 96, 182–184, 185, 188*f*
Head Start, 131–132
health care, 62, 81, 142, 175
Hearn, Josephine, 219*n*
Heller, Dean, 189*f*
Henderson, Nell, 223
Heredia, Lourdes, 179, 222*n*
The Hill, 219*n*, 223*n*
Hispanic Alliance for Progress Institute,
    70, 201
Hispanic Association of AT&T Employees
    (HISPA), 69

Hispanic Business Resource Group, 69
Hispanic Business Roundtable, 133, 215*n*
Hispanic Business, 69, 70
Hispanic Council for Reform and
    Educational Options (Hispanic
    CREO), 134, 201, 219*n*
"Hispanic Heart," 48, 48*f*, 105, 105*f*
Hispanic Heritage Month, 72, 215*n*
Hispanic/Latino Association for Leadership
    and Advancement (HOLA), 69
Hispanic Professionals Networking Group
    (HPNG), 70
Hitler, Adolf, 44
Hoffenblum, Allan, 178
Hostettler, John, 183–184
House Judiciary Immigration and Border
    Security Subcommittee, 183
Houston Chronicle, 176, 221*n*, 222*n*
Houston, Texas, 18, 72, 73, 133
HUD, 9, 119

identity politics, 3, 5, 215*n*
illegal immigration, 36, 66, 95, 98,
    178–179, 180, 182, 184, 187, 195
Illinois, 77, 79, 121, 148*f*, 206
Immigrant Workers' Freedom Ride, 158*f*
Immigration Reform and Control Act of
    1986, 37*f*
Immigration and Nationality Act, 158*f*
Immigration and Naturalization Service
    (INS), 158*f*, 220
Immigration Reform Caucus, 95
Impacto Group, 55, 80
incarceration rates, 150
Independent Women's Forum, 138
Inglis, Bob, 81–83, 100, 190
Inter-Agency Committee on Mexican
    American Affairs, 37*f*
Iraq War, 85, 139, 166, 174, 176, 180, 184
Ireland, 28

J-Lo, 43
JCPenney, 15, 17
Jackson, Jesse, 153, 154
Jackson, Leslie, 97, 216*n*
Jackson, Michael, 132
Jackson, Scoop, 139

Jacoby, Tamar, 180, 215*n*, 222*n*
Jayson, Sharon, 211*n*
Johnson, Carla K., 216*n*
Johnson, Lyndon, 33
Johnson, Nancy, 188*f*
Judis, John, 38, 110, 217*n*

Kaiser Family Foundation, 152*f*
Kasich, John, 118
Katz, Lawrence, 191
Kennedy, Edward, 158*f*
Kennedy, John F., 149
Kennedy, Robert F., 99, 149
Kerry, John, 83, 110, 150, 169*f*, 161, 166,
    206, 217*n*
Kiely, Kathy, 222*n*
Kilgore, Jerry, 184–185
Kim Jong Il, 140, 141
King, Coretta Scott, 149
King, Martin Luther Jr., 149, 153, 154
King, Pete, 185
King, Steve, 96
Klein, Ron, 188*f*
Knoedler, Matt, 176
Kolbe, Jim, 183
Korwin, Alan, 214*n*
Korzenny, Felipe, 154, 220*n*
Kovacs, Joe, 216*n*
Kravetz, Carl, 45–46, 48, 52–53, 213*n*;
    see also Association of Hispanic
    Advertising Agencies
Krugman, Paul, 191, 223*n*
Kyl, Jon, 185

La Opinion, 98
labor unions, 58, 110, 124, 127, 129, 134,
    145, 146, 169, 201, 206; *see also*
    teachers' unions
Lakewood Church, 72
Lampson, Nick, 188*f*
Laredo, Texas, 34, 187, 220*n*
Latin America, 27, 28, 50, 53, 81, 92, 115,
    140, 154; culture of, 43, 49, 73, 167,
    194; U.S. trade with, 57–58, 123–124
Latino Coalition, 70, 201, 212*n*
Latino Identity Project, *see* Association of
    Hispanic Advertising Agencies (AHAA)

Latinos in Information Sciences and
    Technology Association (LISTA), 70
League of Nations, 144, 219*n*
League of United Latin American Citizens
    (LULAC), 34, 154
Leahy, Pat, 141
Left, the, 3, 107, 137, 146, 155, 191, 197
Let Freedom Ring, 215
Lincoln, Abraham, 83, 162, 220*n*, 221*n*
Long Island, 177, 185
Lopez, Jennifer, *see* J-Lo
Lord Baltimore, 29
Los Angeles, California, 220*n*
Los Angeles Times, 36, 97–98, 155, 174
Lueck, Sarah, 212*n*, 222*n*, 223*n*
Lujan, Manuel, 37*f*, 201
Luna, Tom, 203
Luntz, Frank, 185, 223

MacDonald, Heather, 193–194, 223*n*, 224*n*
Madrid, Mike, 163
Madrid, Patricia, 189*f*
Mahoney, Tim, 188*f*
Marin, Rosario, 146, 186
Marqeuz, Jose, 70
Martinez, Bob, 37*f*
Martinez, Jose, 34
Martinez, Mel, 9, 37*f*, 78, 119, 166, 167,
    203, 204
Marxism, 50, 155, 191
Maryland, 29
May, Clifford, 163
McCain, John, 35, 165, 205
McDonald's, 69
McGlowan, Angela, 150
McNerney, Jerry, 188*f*
Medicare, 28
Mehlman, Ken, 184, 223*n*
Mejias, David, 185
Mencia, Carlos, 161
Menendez, Robert, 121
Mercedes Benz, 68
mestizo, 49
Mexican American, 1, 10, 13, 19, 24, 30,
    31, 56, 61, 73, 76, 179, 204;
    Democratic Party and, 33, 75, 146;
    education and, 56, 127; Republican
    Party and, 34, 77, 146, 162;

Mexican American Republicans of Texas, 33
Mexican-American War, 155
Mexico City, 28, 44, 49, 194
Mexico, 79, 91, 92, 112, 122, 125,
    143–144, 155, 173, 183, 194–195, 199
Miami, Florida, 4, 42, 45, 48, 52, 79, 86,
    87, 95–96
Micklethwaite, John, 81, 215*n*
Middlesex County, N.J., 217*n*
Millennium Biltmore, 69
Miller, Brad, 177
Miller, George, 132
Millman, Joel, 212*n*, 222*n*
Minuteman Project, 95, 158*f*, 173, 183
missile defense, 140–141
Mitchell, Harry, 188*f*
Mondale, Walter, 3, 35, 37*f*
Montañez, Benito, 92–94
Montelongo, Michael, 202
Moore, Art, 211
Morales, Edgar, 69
Moreno, Celso, 34
Moreno, Daniel, 153
Morgan, John, 77, 78
Morgan Stanley, 202
MS-13, 51, 75
MSNBC, 107
Munsil, Len, 177, 178
Murphy, Chris, 188*f*
Musgrave, Marilyn, 189, 189*f*
Muslims, 73, 196
Muzzio, Doug, 224*n*
Myers, John, 76

NAACP, 154
NAFTA, 199
Napolitano, Janet, 134, 177
NASA, 13
National Association of Latino Elected and
    Appointed Officials (NALEO), 161,
    170, 203, 204*f*
National Center for Education Statistics,
    National Center for Education
    Statistics, 126, 126*f*, 128, 128*f*
national defense, 90, 90*f*, 139; *see also*
    national security
National Hispana Leadership Institute,
    62, 70

National Hispanic Prayer Breakfast, 75
NPR (National Public Radio), 161
National Review Online, 193, 223*n*
NRA (National Rifle Association), 47
national security, 4, 66, 139–141, 157, 195;
  see also national defense
National Society of Hispanic MBAs
  (NSHMBA), 70
Native American, 24
naturalization, 142, 153
Navarette, Ruben Jr., 86
Negron, Joe, 188, 188*f*
Netherlands, 196
Nevada, 3, 77, 169*f*, 186, 203
New Hampshire: state House of
  Representatives of, 203
New Mexico, 3, 30, 35, 37*f*, 77, 80, 147,
  169*f*, 201, 212*n*
New Jersey, 110, 133, 148*f*, 169*f*, 219*n*
New York, 77, 79, 80, 81, 148*f*, 169*f*, 177
New York City, 13, 56, 65, 67, 104, 158*f*,
  170, 202, 205, 220*n*
New York Journal News, 132
New York *Post*, 43
New York Times, 72, 163, 191
Nicholson, Jim, 163–164, 165, 168, 221*n*
Nickelodeon, 51
Nightengale, Chelene, 95; *see also* Save Our
  State
Nixon, Richard, 2, 13, 37*f*, 149, 173;
  "Hispanic strategy" of, 29–33
No Child Left Behind Act, 101, 127, 129
North Korea, 140–141
Novak, Robert, 212*n*, 215*n*
Nueva Esperanza, 75

Obama, Barack, 83, 206
Ochoa Levine, Cecilia, 143
O'Donnell, Rick, 188*f*
Ohlemacher, Stephen, 190, 223*n*
Oklahoma, 24, 164
Ortiz, Solomon, 136
Osteen, Joel, 72–73
Our Lady of Guadalupe, 49, 213*n*

P. F. Collier, 11
Paccione, Angie, 189*f*
Paige, Rod, 131, 218*n*

Paine Webber, 45
Pederson, Jim, 185
Pelosi, Nancy, 218*n*
Pennsylvania, 211
Pentagon, 158*f*
Pepperdine Institute for Public Policy, 153
Perlmutter, Ed, 188*f*
Perot, Ross, 37*f*, 168
Perry, Rick, 186
personal responsibility: Latino attitudes
  toward, 65, 110, 138–139; Republican
  Party and, 18, 110, 138, 139
Peru, 57, 144
Pew Hispanic Center, 152, 152*f*, 176, 214*n*,
  218*n*
Philadelphia, Pennsylvania., 75, 94, 165;
  Federal Reserve Bank of, 223*n*
Phillips, Deborah A., 131
Phoenix, Arizona, 220*n*
Pizza Hut, 77
Pombo, Richard, 188*f*
population; growth among Hispanics 25–29,
  27*f*
Porter, Jon, 189*f*
Prado, Miguel, 57
prejudice, 90–97, 101, 109, 110, 137
President's Cabinet Committee on
  Opportunities for Spanish-Speaking
  People, 31
President's Commission to Strengthen Social
  Security, 120, 217*n*, 218*n*
Prudential Financial, 69
Puerto Ricans, 4, 77, 204; voting trends of,
  78–79, 167, 170, 212*n*
Puerto Rico, 51, 78, 167, 199
Puritans, 29

Quebec, 28

racism, 5, 82, 91, 94, 95, 97, 108, 110, 149
Ramos, Jorge, 43, 100–101, 213*n*, 216*n*
Reagan, Ronald, 2, 10, 20, 34–35, 37*f*,
  221*n*; Hispanics and, 2, 35, 162,
  199–200, 203, 206, 207; missile
  defense and, 140; economic policy
  of, 191
Reed, Bruce, 122, 217*n*, 218*n*
Reed, Jack, 141

Reid, Harry, 121, 217*n*

Renzi, Rick, 189, 189*f*

Republican National Committee, 3, 9, 44, 65, 66, 78, 87, 119, 139, 145, 162–167, 174, 175, 184, 221*n*

Republican National Hispanic Assembly: creation of, 37*f*, 38

Republican Party, 4, 20–21, 38, 63, 145, 162, 215*n*, 220*n*, 221*n*, 222*n*; immigration and, 24, 98, 153, 164, 175; misunderstandings between Hispanics and, 5, 36, 59, 93, 98, 109; outreach to Hispanic voters, 34, 61, 84, 168, 205; successes with Hispanics, 59, 189, 203; values held in common with Hispanics, 7, 42, 61, 81, 89, 119, 205

Rice, Condoleezza, 219*n*

Richards, Ann, 16, 18

Rio Grande, 13, 23, 31, 44, 187

Rio Rancho, New Mexico, 80

Robinson, Vernon, 177, 222*n*

Rockridge Institute, 103, 217*n*

Rocky Mountain News, 146, 220*n*

Rodriguez, Alex, *see* A-Rod

Rodriguez, Ciro, 188*f*

Rodriguez, Gregory, 153, 155, 221*n*

Rogers, Marvin, 81

Roman Catholic Church, 51, 57, 76

Roman Catholics, 14, 19, 29, 49–51, 63, 75, 78, 213*n*, 215*n*, 217*n*

Rome, Italy, 173

Romney, Mitt, 205

Roosevelt, Franklin, *see* FDR

Rosenblum, Keith, 213*n*

Ros-Lehtinen, Ileana, 37*f*

Roskam, Peter, 189*f*

Rove, Karl, 218*n*

Ruhlen, Steve, 20

Saad, Lydia, 213, 214

Salazar, Ken, 76

Salvadorans, 43

San Antonio, Texas, 52, 93, 94, 125, 155, 156, 163, 187

Santiago, Bill, 10

Savage, Michael, 97, 216*n*

Save Our State, 95

Schweikart, Larry, 212

Second Amendment, 47, 76

Secure Fence Act, 158*f*

Segal, Adam, 224

Sekula-Gibbs, Shelley, 180, 188*f*

Sensenbrenner, James, 98–99

Sharpton, Al, 153

Shaw, Clay, 188*f*

Shays, Christopher, 189*f*

Sheen, Martin, 43

Sierra Vista, Arizona, 183

Simon, Ellen, 189*f*

small business owners, 18, 81–82, 114; Hispanic owners, 10, 42, 55, 68, 109, 111, 113, 113*f*, 114, 116, 117, 124; estate tax and, 116

Social Security, 28, 115, 123, 177, 183, 186; reform of, 56, 112, 119–123, 218*n*

Sodexho, Inc., 202

Sosa, Kathy, 163

Sosa, Lionel, 34–35, 163, 179, 187

South America, 76, 77, 78, 204

South Carolina, 77, 80, 83, 190

Southern newbies, 76–84

Southern Strategy, 32, 164

Spanglish, 10, 45, 51, 52, 93

Spanish: conquest of Latin America, 49, 57

Spanish language, 3, 4, 10, 13, 14, 30, 36, 43, 44, 46, 48, 54, 61, 73, 75, 81, 92, 96, 123, 124, 130, 138, 154, 165, 175, 177, 193, 212*n*, 213*n*, 216*n*, 220*n*, 224*n*; political advertising in, 165–166, 205; Spanish-language media, 5, 83, 85, 90, 97–101, 134, 145, 175

Specter, Arlen 158*f*

Spencer, Glenn, 25

spirituality, 48*f*, 102*f*, 104, 105*f*, 154; in Latino culture, 48*f*, 48–51

stereotype, 2, 55, 78, 86, 91, 146, 161, 180, 207

Suffolk County, New York, 178

Sugar Land, Texas, 72, 181

Tacoma, Washington, 55

Taeuber, Conrad, 212*n*

Taina, 51

Taliban, 215

Tancredo, Tom, 4, 44, 82, 95–96, 98, 99, 101, 147, 175, 190, 191, 205

Tanton, John, 194

Tarrance, Lance, 30, 31, 34, 38, 78, 162, 163–164, 221*n*

tax hike, 7, 102, 122, 203

teachers' unions, 129, 134

Teinowitz, Ira, 221*n*

Tejano, 13, 52, 72

Telemundo, 55, 100

Tempe, Arizona, 182

Tennessee, 77, 178

Tepeyac, 49

terrorism, 4, 66; *see also* national security

Texas Republican Party, 34

Texas, 12, 13, 16, 17, 18, 19, 30–36, 46, 51, 52, 74, 77, 78, 79, 84, 92, 107, 113, 122, 124, 146, 148*f*, 153, 156, 165, 168, 169*f*, 182, 186, 187, 194, 203, 212*n*

Texeira, Ruy, 38, 110, 170, 217*n*

Third World, 4, 95, 96, 97, 107

Thomas B. Fordham Institute, 211*n*

Time magazine, 75

Tornoe, Juan Guillermo, 91–92

Tower, John, 33–34, 94; Hispanic strategy of, 34–36

Turkey, 196

Tucson, Arizona, 183

U.S. Census, 2, 25, 26, 27, 27*f*, 30–31, 51, 54, 56, 77, 80, 111, 120, 188, 194, 212*n*, 213*n*, 214*n*

U.S. Congress, 5, 19, 24, 26, 70, 71, 81, 82, 87, 95, 99, 112, 118, 124, 129, 131, 136, 146, 165, 167, 173, 174, 179, 190, 199, 201, 203, 205

U.S. Department of Education, 126*f*, 128*f*, 218*n*

U.S. Department of Homeland Security, 158*f*

U.S. News & World Report, 79

U.S. Peace Corps, 173

U.S. Senate, 24, 33, 34, 35, 76, 121, 166, 186, 219*n*, 220*n*

unemployment, 28, 95, 150; among Hispanics, 56

United Nations Food and Agriculture Organization, 173

United States, 211*n*, 213*n*, 214*n*

University of California Santa Cruz, 24

University of California at Berkeley, 192

Univision, 43, 55, 66, 85, 89, 99, 100, 153, 154, 163, 215*n*, 216*n*, 220*n*, 221*n*

USA Today, 187

Vargas, Arturo, 148, 203

Vasquez, Gaddi Holguin, 173

Virginia, 12, 145, 184, 185, 195, 203

Voices of Citizens Together, 25

Voter News Service, 32, 182, 223*n*

Wall Street Journal, 30, 180, 183

Wallsten, Peter, 213*n*, 221*n*, 222*n*

Walt Disney Company, 68

Washington Post, 19, 179

Washington, D.C., 2, 10, 11, 12, 15, 18, 19, 20, 21, 42, 44, 55, 71, 76, 170, 181, 199, 201

Watanabe, Teresa, 222*n*

Watergate, 33

wealth: building of, 55, 56, 61, 68, 106, 111–112, 115, 117, 118–119, 121–123, 125, 202

Weekly Standard, 107, 151

Weisman, Jacob 218*n*

Western Union, 54

white-collar, 201, 214

White House Initiative on Hispanic Education, 129

Wickham, DeWayne, 220*n*

Williams, Juan, 5, 151, 220*n*

Wilson, Cid, 45, 71

Wilson, Heather, 147, 189*f*

Wilson, Pete, 36, 94, 103, 152–153

Wilson, Woodrow, 144, 219*n*
Winn Dixie, 202
Witt, Marcus, 72, 73–74, 75
Wonderbread, 52
Wooldridge, Adrian, 81, 215*n*
World Trade Center, 158*f*
WorldNetDaily, 96, 211*n*, 216*n*

Young Professionals for W., 202
Youngbloods, 67–72, 201
YouTube, 95, 222*n*

Zanzi, Italo, 178
Zapatistas, 220*n*
Zucchino, David, 219*n*

acknowledgments

Beyond those listed on previous pages, I wish to acknowledge those who contributed their time and insights to this book. Some gave me an hour of their time—others so much more including Ruben Barrales, Hector Barreto, Anna and Victor Cabral, Tom Cole, Rita DiMartino, Ed Gillespie, Jack Kemp, James H. Lake, Sonya Medina and Ileana Ros-Lehtinen.

Behind the scenes, several people do not appear by name but their insights were critical in shaping the content. Michelle Bernard and Carrie Lukas of the Independent Women's Forum, Clifford D. May, Beth Sturgeon, Ronald Blackburn-Moreno of ASPIRA, Octavio Hinojosa-Mier of the Congressional Hispanic Leadership Institute, trade specialists Jorge L. Arrizurieta and Juan Carlos Iturreggi, Alma Morales-Riojas of MANA, Stephen Vermillion of ObjectVideo, Rafael Toro of Goya Foods, Tom Josefiak, David C. Lizarraga of the U.S. Hispanic Chamber of Commerce, Arturo Vargas and the research team at the National Association of Latino Elected and Appointed Officials, Jeff Jones and Albert D. Winesman of the Gallup Organization, author Kathleen Felesina and Stan Greenberg of Greenberg Quinlan Rosner.

I give special thanks to Pedro Celis and Bettina Inclan of the Republican National Hispanic Assembly, as well as the talented Alejandro Burgos, Adam Chavarria, Raul Damas, Danny Diaz, Hessy Fernandez, Jose Fuentes, Alison Ream Griffin, Peggy McCardle, Jose Nino, Javier Ortiz, Thomas E. Patton, Michael J. Petrilli, Jorge Plasencia and Mercedes Viana Schlapp.

I thank Peter Roff, Jeffrey Rudell and Lance Tarrance. From the beginning, Peter and Lance read countless drafts and spent many weekends over the course of six months editing and guiding this process.

Jeffrey's creative genius helped define the personal stories expressed on these pages.

Great thanks to the brothers Freddoso: David, Michael and Stephen. David spent countless hours writing, researching and editing to produce a coherent manuscript. Michael and Stephen kept the ball rolling when we faced tight deadlines, as did Chad Wooton as he labored to create the graphs and charts. Special thanks also to one of the hardest working publicists in Washington, Mike Collins.

I owe a particular debt to my editors at Palgrave Macmillan, Gabriella Georgiades and Jake Klisivitch, for believing so strongly in this project.

Writing a first book can be daunting—but rewarding—work. To my mother, my brother, my husband and my friends—thank you for making this possible. I appreciate the prayers and support from my extended family and from the countless Republican allies who asked me to "make the book compelling!" Finally, to the women of St. Louis Catholic Church in Miami, Emmaus #53, thank you for believing! Keep the faith always.

LESLIE SANCHEZ
Washington, DC
May 2007